APPALACHIA NORTH

Matthew Ferrence

APPALACHIA NORTH

A MEMOIR

WEST VIRGINIA UNIVERSITY PRESS

MORGANTOWN 2019

Copyright © 2019 by West Virginia University Press
All rights reserved
First edition published 2019 by West Virginia University Press

ISBN:
Paper   978-1-946684-70-7
Ebook   978-1-946684-71-4

Library of Congress Cataloging-in-Publication Data
Names: Ferrence, Matthew J., author.
Title: Appalachia north : a memoir / Matthew Ferrence.
Description: Morgantown : West Virginia University Press, 2019.
  | Includes bibliographical references.
Identifiers: LCCN 2018033186| ISBN 9781946684707 (pbk.) | ISBN
  9781946684714 (ebook)
Subjects: LCSH: Ferrence, Matthew J. | Appalachian Region--Description
  and travel. | Appalachian Region--Social life and customs.
Classification: LCC F106 .F47 2019 | DDC 917.404--dc23
LC record available at https://lccn.loc.gov/2018033186

Book and cover design: Than Saffel / WVU Press

Essays in this collection previously appeared in the following
  publications:
"Depredation." *Creative Nonfiction* (Spring 2014).
"Exoskeleton." *Gettysburg Review* (Spring 2014).
"The Foxes of Prince Edward Island." *Gettysburg Review* (Spring 2017).
  Reprinted in *The Fiddlehead* (Summer 2017).
"Highways and Fairways." *Crab Orchard Review* (Winter/Spring 2009).
"Mos Teutonicus." *Colorado Review* (Fall/Winter 2014). Reprinted in
  Beautiful Flesh: A Body of Essays (U Colorado Press 2017).
"Moving Water." *Cimarron Review* (Fall 2017).

To Jennifer, my cartographer.

Contents

A PREFACE (OF SORTS) / ix
ACKNOWLEDGMENTS / xix

1. FLOODS / 1
2. THIS IS NOT A MOUNTAIN / 39
3. MARGINAL APPALACHIA / 67
4. APPALACHIAN FLESH, APPALACHIAN BONE / 87
5. LEARNING TO SAY APPALACHIA / 109
6. THE MOLT / 137
7. CONDUITS / 159
8. READING LIKE AN APPALACHIAN / 175
9. JOURNEY TO CANAPPALACHIA / 213
10. COORDINATES / 243

BIBLIOGRAPHY / 271

A Preface (of Sorts)

Memories lie slumbering within us for months and years, quietly proliferating, until they are woken by some trifle and in some strange way blind us to life. How often this has caused me to feel that my memories, and the labours expended in writing them down are all part of the same humiliating and, at bottom, contemptible business! And yet, what would we be without memory? We would not be capable of ordering even the simplest thoughts, the most sensitive heart would lose the ability to show affection, our existence would be a mere neverending chain of meaningless moments, and there would not be the faintest trace of a past.

—W. G. Sebald, *The Rings of Saturn*

I began this book with an idea, based on casual observation, that the functional realities of rural communities located along the entire chain of the ancient Appalachian Mountains carry certain similarities. In West Virginia, Pennsylvania, rural New England, and Atlantic Canada—places connected by the geology of the Appalachians—the people are thought of as poor and backward, as rural curiosities, and always as troubled. All along this ancient mountain chain, people have also struggled from a material lack of work: waning coal industries, timber industries, fisheries, and mills. Yet from Pennsylvania northward, very few people actually see themselves as *Appalachian*, despite the mountains and despite the reality that parts of Pennsylvania and New York do, in fact, lie within zones officially designated as such.

I grew up in Pennsylvania, where I was stricken by the tensions of being Appalachian even though I didn't know I was. Though I now proudly identify as such, it was a long time coming. That identity feels partly like an imposition placed upon me from the outside and partly a welcome affirmation of my home. The writing of this project is at once the continuation of my own self-discovery as Appalachian, a reassertion of the validity of western Pennsylvanian experience as more than Pittsburgh steelwork, and a further investigation into how the labels of Appalachia have been drawn and written.

I started this book with an impulse to read, perhaps not surprising for someone whose life is dictated by the consumption and creation of books. At the same time, that impulse meant I began by immersing myself in books about my region, by looking at what others have said and how others have defined my home. I realized, not soon enough, that I was afraid to offer my own definitions as a peculiar kind of Appalachian, a *Northern* Appalachian. I was afraid to confront and declare my experiences and allow them to stand in for a particular claim of being Northern Appalachian, which is very different from declaring what Northern Appalachia is.

One of the problems of regional definitions is that they make use of generalizations that, for good or usually not, erase the validity of the particular. That makes a certain academic sense, as particulars are messy and difficult to line up. Particulars refuse the comforting stability of a graph, demand attention to every outlying dot on a field. Trends, in that sense, or definitions or types, can only be recognized if we willingly go partly blind and fail or refuse to see each dot for itself. Arguments often rely on that sense of generality, built, as they must be, on the distant view.

This is a book without an argument at its core. Argument has been a problem with Appalachian books, in my view, and perhaps with all regional studies. So many writers and so many books seek to make a declaration: *this* is what a place *is*. Perhaps my discomfort with such certainty is borne of my own roots in a place where regional identity exists as a blank. My home is sometimes called Appalachia, sometimes Rust Belt, other times the Midwest, even though very few who live there would accept any of those labels as correct.

Thus I write from my own position as Northern Appalachian and, crucially, as an essayist. Scott Russell Sanders addresses the stance I reference, using the language of astronomy and physics in "The Singular First Person" to defend the valence of the individual:

> The boldest and most poetic theories suggest that anything sucked into a singularity might be flung back out again, utterly changed, somewhere else in the universe. The lonely first person, the essayist's microcosmic *I*, may be thought of as a verbal singularity at the center of the mind's black hole. The raw matter of experience, torn away from the axes of time and space, falls in constantly from all sides, undergoes the mind's inscrutable alchemy, and re-emerges in the quirky, unprecedented shape of an essay.

That's my stance too, a first-person perspective that on the page might appear particularly lonely, moving through the world as an observer and a thinker, trying to toss my own experiences back as transformed matter. In so doing, I seek in the project to build layers of my own observation in a way not unlike the layers of sediment that form the substrate of this region. Appalachia is bigger than its perceived borders, and my desire to write about my Appalachian rootedness is built from the impulse to find out instead of define. I write in layers, both geological and metaphorical, to foreground complication, to bring strange matter into the gravitational field of my own singularity.

A metaphorical gesture of my project: most inland bodies of water experience cyclical turnover. In temperate climates, lakes and ponds are usually dimictic, which means the body of water mixes completely, from top to bottom, once in the fall and again in the spring. In this process, warm, biotically crammed water from the top layer exchanges with cold water from the deep parts, where temperature and lack of light make for an oxygen- and organism-light fluid. Through this cycling, the water of a lake mixes thoroughly, freshening the stagnation of the depths and diluting the thick growth of the shallows. For a couple of brief periods of each year, right after the ice thaws in the spring and right before the ice forms in the winter, the entire column of water exists in balanced uniformity: temperature from the top to the bottom of the lake will be the same. Depending on the size of the body of water, and depending on the conditions of geology and climate, this isothermal condition might exist for a few weeks or even a few months. It is only during these moments of stasis, when uniform temperature also means uniform density, that winds set off the mixing of the water.

I used to swim often in the farm pond of my childhood, enjoying the collected heat in the black inner tubes of old tractors that I floated across the warmed surface. Most often, I kicked and paddled through the epilimnion, a relatively thin top layer warmed by the sun to sometimes surprising temperatures. Below that is the thermocline, called the metalimnion, which for me marks one of the great pleasures of open-water swimming: while my body floated in the warmth of the top water, I could plunge a foot into the marked chill of the pond's thermocline, that thin boundary where the temperature radically dropped. Maybe it's some kind of dance with mortality from which I derived pleasure, that sudden jolt of frigid water, a sign that below the surface water isn't nearly as inviting. Or maybe the cold water reminded me of the seasons, so that even while summer lay atop the lake, autumn and winter were barely contained beneath. Summer is stifling, after all, and I jumped in ponds and lakes usually as relief. Mostly, I imagine the jolt is welcome simply because it is a jolt. The thermocline is a reminder of life, a reveille against complacency, encouragement to kick and move.

So, too, is the thermocline the cap that lies above the hypolimnion, that largest area in most lakes and ponds where dense, cold water sinks to the bottom and where thin light snuffs out most aquatic life, including the microorganisms that break down organic matter. There in the cold dark, wood can be sequestered away, forgotten, maintained outside of time. It does not decompose, because the deep water holds at bay the microorganisms that feed on wood fiber and because light can't reach through to weaken cellulose bonds.

The depths hold many secrets, as we know, and among them are collections of treasured old wood, dead falls in some cases, and often water-logged timber that sunk during transport. Now, enterprising lumberjacks troll lakes with sonar probes, searching the bottom for these sunken logs. While raising them to the surface is often time consuming and more expensive than the chainsaw and heavy leather chaps that can fell a forest tree, the payoff can be dramatic. Most of these sunken logs are old growth, virgin timber cut during the first efforts of clear cutting, before anyone worried about the sustainability of our forests or even considered the difference between the dense grain of old wood and the lesser character of replanted, short-cycle, managed timber.

And what of layers? I don't know how to separate my internal hypolimnion from meta from epi, how to recognize when my layers were formed, where they deviate, and when the winds will blow me to mixture. I don't know when I will settle once again into a structure I recognize. My layers have been unsettled by region and health, each its own kind of existential crisis.

In writing through my relationship to the understructure of myself and my region, I long to find the light of the last morning I visited a mountain lake in a part of the Appalachians far away from my home. I had slipped out of my cabin before sunrise, parked at the trailhead leading to the lake and followed the thin beam of my flashlight up the trail. Halfway there, I stopped at the lift house atop a ski run and waited while the sky brightened from purple dawn to hazy morning. I listened to the whine of cars climbing the mountain, unseen except for occasional flashes of headlights. Transmissions labored, downshifting for power on the climb. Below me, an SUV crunched along the gravel of the ski area parking lot, then disappeared behind a building.

I walked on toward the solitude of the morning lake, tucked into a bowl a half mile farther down the trail, perhaps fifty feet lower than the lift. On the descent, I clutched the rough bark of nearby hemlocks to keep my footing, stumbling over half-buried boulders and decaying dead falls. By the time I'd hiked to the lake, the morning light held the angle favored by photographers, low and intense, backlighting the rocks and trees around the water with proper artistry. There was no wind, and the lake's surface offered a perfect reflection of the mountains, ground, and sky merging together. I lingered for a while, taking pictures of mossy rocks. I considered the merits of a cold morning swim but finally decided to walk back for morning coffee.

On the return climb, my thighs burned. I paused to massage the lactic acid free and scanned the forest nearby. Along the trail, an early morning yoga group had fastened prayer ribbons to tree limbs. Some had fallen to the ground. Most remained pierced by branches, waiting for the wind to build and then blow prayers across the mountain. I crossed a clearing, then flushed a grouse as I entered the last stretch of woods before reaching my car. I never saw the bird. I only heard the thumping of the wings, the rumble of feathers disappearing into the woods while my pulse quickened.

M. J. F., Northern Appalachia, 2018

Acknowledgments

Thanks are immeasurable and risky. People have been left out, for which I apologize. I'll try to offer a blanket antidote: thanks to everyone I have ever known who makes up part of the complicated Appalachian map I have tried to build.

Special thanks to the following:

The Appalachian Radiation Road Crew: Ian Binnington, Zac Callen, Jen Dearden, Brian Harward, Briana Lewis, Ryan Pickering, Ben Slote, Lisa Whitenack.

Writers and friends who helped me figure out this project, and how to balance a writing life with a life, and particularly for patient readings of early drafts, and kind ears in listening to ill-formed ideas, and food when I was down, and for doing what friends do: there are a lot of you, and I am eternally grateful to each and every one. Kevin Oderman, for bringing me back into creative nonfiction when dormancy and literary theory threatened to consume that voice. Aaron Calhoun, John Christodouleas, and Ben Ott, for deciding to be doctors willing to explain stuff to me and, most of all, for remaining dear friends since we were all so young. Christopher Bakken, John Copenhaver, Kafah Haggerty, Jennifer Hellwarth,

Brad Hersh, Doug Jurs, John Miller, Jessica Nelson, Adam Olenn, Susan Slote, Noah Stetzer (whose conversation about not-mountains led to the idea that unlocked this project). The golfers of Andersons Creek who welcomed me into a new home: Peter Bernard, Gary Crosby, Jimmy Daw, Pierre Gaudet, Dave Herring, Steve McFeeters, Trent Olney, Gregg Stewart. The Pittsburgh Penguins for winning the Stanley Cup when I was recovering, then winning again the next year. Fellow travelers in this hard road to not-reclamation: Soledad Caballero and Mark Simmons. Allegheny College, particularly Provost Ron Cole and President Jim Mullen, who needed less than a second to offer institutional support after my diagnosis. The students who have been a part of my life for so many years. Special shouts to Vyasar Ganesan and Tianli Kilpatrick. The Department of English in its entirety. Allegheny Health Network, particularly doctors Aziz, Happ, and Fuhrer. To the legions of good-spirited frontline nurses and staff who helped along the way. To that hospital dietician, whoever you are, who took my order for Jell-O every day and never complained when I didn't eat it: thanks again. Cathy Rowell Bowers, for all of the *how are you today* texts. The Bread Loaf Writers Conference, for support and inspiration. The Lia Purpura workshop: remarkable! All of the editors of the literary journals that have taken my work and helped me build a career. All of the editors of all of the literary journals everywhere, for serving at the frontline of the defense of the written arts. Teachers. Golf course superintendents. Canada.

Andrew Berzanskis, for astonishing patience and guidance as this book developed from a refusal, to an idea, to a rather different idea, to what it is now. A lesser editor would have given up many, many times. And to West Virginia University Press, Derek and Abby and Sara and Than and the whole crew there, showing how it's done. Plus copyeditors. Wow, do I love copyeditors, particularly Rebekah Cotton, whose work on this project made me sound much better.

To my family, Mom and Dad, Greg and Jeanine. Youngest children and little brothers are annoying. But that's our charm.

And, first rank always, in craziness and joy and love: Jozef and Sébastien.

Beyond everyone, for listening, loving, caring, reading, thinking, TVing, tending to my down days, sharing the great ones: Jennifer.

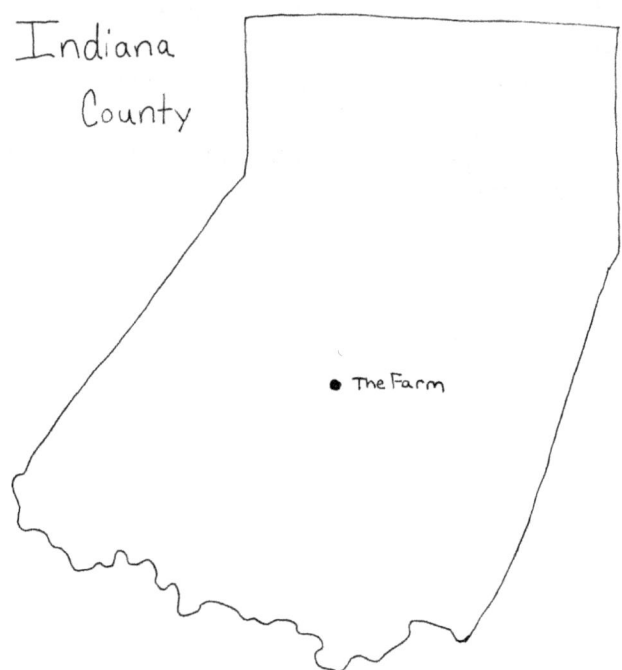

CHAPTER 1

—

Floods

—

My father and I had just finished pulling the last bits out of the rental truck when the heavy clouds released. Fat drops first, cold ones signaling the sheets that would soon follow. We took shelter in the old garage, leaning against the fieldstone walls while the shower gathered force. Soon the hillside of the lower pasture had become invisible, and we heard the growing rush of water in the stream that lay at the bottom of that valley. This rain was more than a usual summer deluge. We soon noticed water flooding across the road, a thick brown sluice gathering around the wheels of the truck.

A flow of water thickened by mud from the uphill fields formed a ribbon of standing waves through the middle of the lawn, cascading over my parents' flagstone walkway, breaking against the trunks of the hemlocks near the garage. The upper fields had recently been laid open for replanting, the earth stripped of old corn and hay to make room for wild grasses. The brown of the water gathering force on the slopes of the farm came from the topsoil, now washed away, and it hurtled along the gas-well access road toward the stream at the bottom of the farm. The rush overwhelmed the drainage ditches beside the gas-well road, cut channels through the diversion humps my father maintained on that road in hopes of stemming such water, split in two near the burn barrel; one rush of water headed toward the garage, the other straight toward the back of the house, where a waterfall splashed over the stacked stone wall straight into the sliding glass door of the side porch.

The rain slowed, and we climbed into the truck. We drove among trees glistening and green, the road following the bends of the stream that now ran heavy. At the fork in the road, where the stream normally trickled beneath the surface, it had gathered and flooded. The current was clear, large ripples of muddy water twenty feet wide, the collection of that thunderstorm too much to be handled by the culverts.

I paused at the edge of that flood, thinking about what it would mean in the desert from which my wife and I had just moved, how deep that water might have been if the flood had happened near our former Arizona home. I thought about the abandoned car found in the wash not far from our desert house, how it had been caked in mud knocked loose by rushing water; about the camps built in those washes by terrified people racing north under the cover of darkness; about Arizona's Stupid Motorists Law, fools liable for the cost of their own rescue if they knowingly drive into flooded danger; about where water goes and what it takes; about the muddy churn in front of me, the size of the tires on the yellow rental truck, and how strong currents might lift the tires of the trailer latched behind; about the force of moving water. My father said nothing, urged my direction neither forward nor back. He merely sat beside me, ready. And I turned into that stream, raising a rooster tail as I pushed through, this water yielding and not so deep and somehow familiar.

I am writing about a farm here and about two Southwests: one, the broad region my wife and I had moved to a few years earlier, and the other, a corner in Pennsylvania where I was born and to which I'm rooted. And I am writing about floods, currents, exile, and all sorts of unseen, powerful forces that move a life. I am also writing about Appalachia, a region that stretches officially from the northern parts of Mississippi, Alabama, and Georgia, up through portions of Tennessee, the Carolinas, the eastern third of Kentucky, the western quarter of Virginia, the Maryland panhandle, all of West Virginia, the eastern edge of Ohio, nearly all of Pennsylvania, and the Southern Tier of New York.

I am from a subsection of the region, designated as Northern Appalachia to confirm both where it is and that it is not exactly what you think of when you think of *Appalachia*. This isn't necessarily a comfort, as bearing the identity of a subset of a subset of America offers little clarity in thinking about who you might be. And, indeed, officially: Appalachia is defined and outlined by the Appalachian Regional Commission (ARC), designated through an act of Congress in 1965 as part of Lyndon Johnson's War on Poverty.

The prototyping of the ARC began years earlier, when the Conference of Appalachian Governors pitched their case to John F. Kennedy, who in 1963 responded by establishing the President's Appalachian Regional Commission (PARC). This group convened an extensive and impressive array of government and private sector individuals to perform and collate various studies, with representation from federal and state agencies, including Rural Electrification, the Forest Service, the Bureau of Land Management, agriculture extension units, the US Department of Agriculture, the Geological Survey, educational policy experts, and public health officials. All of this was spearheaded by the Center for Regional

Economic Studies at the University of Pittsburgh. The results of these studies were turned into a comprehensive, weighty, and bureaucratically titled document produced by the PARC: "Appalachia: A Report by the President's Appalachian Regional Commission, 1964."

The front matter to this report includes signed letters of support from Lyndon Johnson's cabinet, Kennedy having been assassinated before the work was completed, as well as from the Conference of Appalachian Governors, which included governors of West Virginia, Maryland, Alabama, North Carolina, Georgia, Tennessee, Kentucky, and Virginia. A separate letter of support appears from Governor William Scranton of the Commonwealth of Pennsylvania, since my home state was not then considered in the notional limits of Appalachia. Indeed, the 1964 report appears to be the first moment that Pennsylvania *officially* began to be recognized as part of Appalachia. Pennsylvania's Appalachian origins appear as a literal and conceptual outlier.

My home state's exclusion is consistent with how most people know the broader region unofficially, the word *Appalachia* calling up a long history of stereotyping and struggle in places farther south than a state known for Benjamin Franklin and the Liberty Bell. Nonetheless, Appalachia is recognizable by the frequent gunshots that echo in the hills around our family farm, the sound of hunters when I was a boy but now, more and more often, men shooting semiautomatic black rifles at targets, preparing for some imagined totalitarian threat. My county is named Indiana, which on a map is shaped nearly identically to the state of the same name. The town, county, and farm are seated among steep hills and impressive ridges, many dotted with blackened piles of abandoned coal slag. The same ancient seas that made West Virginia and Kentucky famous for coal also made southwestern Pennsylvanian fortunes, and the steel that built Pittsburgh was forged in furnaces fueled by the coal dug from the hills of my hometown, quite likely from the miles of tunnels that lie directly beneath the family farm. Those mines closed long ago, leaving behind only the residue piles and a suffering economy.

This is a common story, of course. You can't go far in thinking or reading about Appalachia without running aground on the shoals of industrial collapse and, of course, coal. It's inescapable, part of the history of the place and people, but it's also an exiling history, since so much of my hometown has nothing to do with energy production these days. That's true of large swaths of this corner of the state, our flagship city of Pittsburgh thought of still as the Steel City, even though it long ago reinvented itself as a health-industry center, a high-tech hub, and an arts haven of cheap houses and lively neighborhoods and museums.

Sure, the relics remain, one notably being the name *Carnegie*, as good a shorthand for extractive industrial domination as any. The name sits upon so much—libraries, a science center, and museums of art and natural history and Andy Warhol, and a university known for its computer science—and reflects how contemporary, progressive Pittsburgh is built on the layers of former industrial exploitation. In my home county, the chief relic of our industrial past is the color red. Many of our creeks and streams carry the stains of iron sulfate, a byproduct of naturally occurring chemosynthetic bacteria that bloom when coal mines are first opened, fueled by the influx of oxygen introduced by the cutting of portals and tunnels. Water flows in and out, taking those bacteria to the surface along with acid and whatever else we have left behind. The gash itself introduces the conditions that alter the landscape, the mixture of external and internal colliding, more or less, as rusted iron.

Waterways like Two Lick Creek, which shaped the valley within which our family farm rests, ran red throughout my childhood. It's much better now, and this is important to consider. As with many other places in western Pennsylvania, restoration wetlands have been built to filter the contaminated water flowing perpetually from boreholes and seeps, the legacy of mining and bacteria flowing ever downstream. These wetlands drip tainted water through a series of ponds planted with native grasses and reeds, cattails and bulrushes, where red-winged blackbirds chatter. In the slow drip from pond to pond, contaminants fall to the mud beneath, cleaner water left behind in each subsequent basin. In this way, time is accelerated, natural processes are fast-forwarded to strip away what mining had damaged. In a sense, these projects reengineer nature as a time-lapse film, using the geology and the landscape on fast-forward to rid the earth from the violence we applied.

Yet I imagine that even if most residents of Pennsylvania know the legacy of coal that brought this destruction, or even if they recognize the success of restoration projects, they are likely to be unaware of, even uncomfortable with, their inclusion in Appalachia. Many probably don't know what the ARC is, and they wouldn't want to consider themselves as part of that pejoratively characterized place. Regional identities are thorny things, particularly when an identity carries historical baggage.

To more accurately define Appalachia, you must first think differently about words, which are themselves a different sort of cartography, certainly no less powerful in establishing perspectives. I would begin in thinking about how economy and value have defined the region and why. I would suggest an antidote, thinking about how the sense of the region's past and future must always contend with rivers and water and how the geological origin of my part of Appalachia is different than we think, not as a landscape of ancient mountains but, instead, an eroded plateau made to look mountainous by eons of carving water. The dominant landscape relies on the flow of streams and rivers, on the acts of erosion and the long application of water. Northern Appalachia, carved by the way water moves, is very much made by the gathering forces that lead streams into creeks, small rivers, and the Ohio River. Water made us, just as it now can save us when allowed to filter through restoration wetlands before heading away.

When I think about ways to define Pennsylvania and Northern Appalachia, I find tracing water is the best way to conceptualize locality. Maybe this is even the key to defining ourselves. Where our water goes matters at least as much as where it came from. Yet even this simple recalibration runs counter to the dominant economic mind-set, which would suggest that downstream isn't a problem—it's instead where you send your problems. But we are what we are, cut, worn, old, tired, but not finished becoming who we want to be.

Before I returned to the farm, I had to move away. That's an obvious statement, but also one that carries the heavy weight of meaning, at least to me. The truth is, when I describe southwestern Pennsylvanians who wouldn't know they were in Appalachia, I am describing myself. I never thought of myself as Appalachian, not when I was young. We never talked about it. My friends didn't play mountain music; they learned classical violin instead of fiddle. We didn't speak with twanging accents, drive pickup trucks (other than me), clog dance, or do anything that marked us as Appalachian. We didn't harbor feuds, make moonshine, or smoke corncob pipes. Another truth is that so many people throughout Appalachia don't do these things, even if those are still the caricatures that come to mind. Certainly my friends and I would have imagined those stereotypes when thinking of Appalachia, not realizing this was also us. But south of the Mason-Dixon line in *real* Appalachia, at least things carried a more easily recognized inflection. Up north, we lacked even a clear marker of who we were, so we said we were *from Pittsburgh*, even as the city lay more than an hour away and, really, wouldn't have claimed us anyway.

Still, moving away might also be the biggest marker of my Appalachian identity. What Appalachian kid doesn't do it, dream of it, think of it as the only thing to do and the worst thing to do? There's a romantic way to think of this push and pull. On one hand, the landscape is so pure, with mountain laurel abloom, summer thunderstorms, and all of the mountain clichés you can think of. And, on the other, you have the mines, both as sites of waning work opportunity and relics of destruction and exploitation. Hell, wanting to move away is precisely the thing you're supposed to want to do as an Appalachian—because how could you ever want to be stuck in the place forever, what with the presumed lack of opportunity and backward ways? But just as you can't ever leave because of the presumed fallout, you become a denier of all that you really are.

Just the same, my own nativity to Appalachia is troublesome, at least in the broad strokes we tend to think define the region. I was born here, but I was born in that swath of the ARC north of the Mason-Dixon line, which makes me a marginal Appalachian at best. I grew up without many of the expected markers, meaning little moonshine and fiddle and no mountain accent in a part of the state with a heavy industrial past to go along with our coal. Weird, also, that mine is a lack that I define through an absence of stereotype. Part of the longing I feel as a Northern Appalachian is a longing for a shorthand, even a limiting shorthand, that offers a quick definition. And, the truth is, certain parts of Pennsylvania do carry accents similar in tone to what might be called *mountain*, gradations of Appalachian speech that are as difficult to delimit as anything else existing on a spectrum. The Whiskey Rebellion happened in western Pennsylvania, so rogue alcohol matters to our history even if we lack the folklore of backwoods distilleries. Still, somehow everything feels different to me in Northern Appalachia, more hollow and undefined, liminal.

Worse than even these absences, my personal ancestry can't be traced back in generations, another supposed qualifier for Appalachian identity. My father may technically be from Appalachia, as far as the ARC is concerned, but his home turf is eastern Pennsylvania, on the other side of the state in a place that aligns more with the Amish and Philadelphia than with hillbillies. He grew up in a Pennsylvania Dutch community (not the Amish; that's a different thing) and had to shed that accent when he went to school because of linguistic bullying. He was poor: that's Appalachian, at least. And his father dug coal, but he did it with a giant dragline shovel in open-pit anthracite mines, a far different cultural marker than subterranean soft coal bituminous tunnel mining.

My mother is from Gary, Indiana, with grandparents who emigrated from Poland. Her father was a postman, and her mother a school secretary with a savvy mind for investments. My mother, who went to a Catholic boarding school in South Bend and then a Catholic women's college in Chicago, remembers wearing long white gloves to go to town. This is a prim, proper, urbane sort of childhood that doesn't fit the idea of the Appalachian at all and, in fact, is not. My mother is from the plains and prefers the flatlands of the Midwest to the hills of our Pennsylvania farm. She used to complain about how fast the sun disappeared at night, how sunsets were less of a production than they were on the golden fields of the country's agricultural center. In Appalachia, the sun seems to just disappear, like the extinguishing of a candle.

Then there's me, the faux Appalachian: a northerner, in fact, with parents born elsewhere, and no mountain accent, on which I'm often complimented. *You don't talk like you're from Appalachia*, more than a few people have told me. I have a PhD. I teach at a private college. I play lots of golf. These things disqualify me as hillbilly, if not as Appalachian altogether.

Ultimately, this is one of the chief problems of being Appalachian, that we're not afforded the capacity of multitudes. We aren't permitted to be Whitmanesque, and, if we want to *count*, we have to take on the markers of the Rustic Ideal. Yet the rocks from which we take our name keep rolling from Georgia to Newfoundland, and the borders are drawn, not real, so there must be space for, well, something. New definitions or, at least, new directions.

When I left Pennsylvania, I did so for no particular reason, fleeing nothing other than my own childhood. I never thought of it as an escape from Appalachia or as part of the long tradition of youth leaving the region for opportunity elsewhere. Instead, the facts were just that I had married young—at twenty-four, my wife then twenty-one—and a year or so later the two of us headed to Arizona where I sought a PhD in Tucson. I quit that program after a semester, hating it, and lingered as a freelance writer for a couple of years before we moved to Paris, where my wife earned her master's degree in French and I became a professional golfer, each of my would-be careers mere paper designations that led to extraordinarily low earnings and unsustainability. I lacked the hustle to make either profession work.

Moving away did bring interesting discoveries of place, however. Never before had I thought of myself as *from* or *of* somewhere, but the stark contrasts of landscape in Arizona and culture in France got me thinking, particularly about my own embeddedness in western Pennsylvania, which I had yet to recognize in any serious way as Appalachia. I started penning essays that took place in Pennsylvania, often using the family farm as the counterpoint to the examination of self and reconnoitering of new locales. In the desert, I missed water. In Paris, I missed wild animals. Appalachia has these things in abundance.

When we returned home to Pennsylvania, both jobless, my wife got lucky and wound up working at a private elementary and middle school—funded and populated by the legacies of money and remaining family of the Carnegies and Mellons—in the Laurel Highlands. We lived then in a gorgeous mountain town twenty minutes from her home turf of Johnstown and forty-five from my parents' farm. It fit us, and we settled in. After a year, I returned to graduate school in West Virginia, traveling often through the heavy rolls of the southwestern corner of my home state, on into the beauty of a state I'd grown up disdaining but now consider essential to who I am. At WVU, I learned about Appalachia, recognized myself as part of it, and began thinking about what that all could mean.

First came the exile, though, a state of being that I don't think I have yet escaped, and so I write. And if exile might be described as a contrast of a home condition versus a new one, it was exile from water that first made me feel from a place. When Jen and I pulled up stakes in western Pennsylvania, we first crossed the border into our new home of Arizona as a departing summer monsoon turned the desert air into perfume. Monsoons are the manner of summer rain in the Southwest, hot mornings that lead to violent afternoon storms. I knew nothing of this phenomenon until we were part of it, and our first few weeks in the southeastern corner of Arizona were punctuated by afternoon thunderstorms and the seasonal appearance of moving water in the streams and rivers that normally lay dry.

I was spooked, in certain ways, by this new pattern of water but also thrilled. I couldn't get enough of the moments that arrive just after desert thunderstorms slip away. Always, it is late afternoon. The relentless morning sun has been muted, first dimmed by the appearance of the storms, then reappearing through curtains of thinning clouds. The angle of light is low then, and the desert plants are coated in a sheen of moisture that ignites as the sun reappears. The air is filled with the smell of fresh rain, the musty fertility of moistened dirt and emerging creosote bush. I carry that smell as my fondest memory of our desert life, longing for rain satisfied.

Yet during the monsoon season, the TV news always seemed to carry footage of thick water flowing across roads, a car trapped in the rush created by these rains. We were warned nightly about flash floods, how what appears to be a dip in the road during dry weather is, in fact, the path of a stream. The water will claim its course, and anything caught in the wash will be swept away. *Do not drive through standing water,* TV reporters always reminded. *You can't tell how deep water is,* other transplants to the desert told us, often citing Arizona's Stupid Motorist Law. Water seems so foreign to the land that, when it gathers, it conceals the dips and holes, particular human-built ones beneath roads, where puddled water finds the level of the flattened landscape and hides its own depth.

In Arizona, geology is laid bare. Most landscapes are devoid of trees and heavy vegetation, so the stacking of rocks and forces of erosion are clear. One of my favorite spots in the state, the Chiricahua National Monument, was a couple hours away. There, ancient flowing water long ago shaped pillars and canyons and formations of eroded rock. I drove there often when Easterners visited, usually along the safe corridor of I-10 to Wilcox, where a massive playa lies as a signal of the waters that used to cover the area. Each year, sandhill cranes stop by the playa on their migration, arriving for the shelter of collected water, guided perhaps by prehistoric memory of the lake that used to be there. They are driven to return, cannot resist the pull of ancient waters, the pull of instinct to travel where they always have, to follow ancestral thirst toward home.

Once, the cranes flew over our heads while my father and I walked the canyons of Chiricahua. He heard the honks in the distance first, as he paused and cocked an ear toward the sky. *Sandhills*, he said, and we watched as a small V flew by, part of their annual migration between Iowa and Arizona. My father loves these birds more than any other; they are living affirmations of the vision of Aldo Leopold, signals of the innate desire to return, always, home. The cranes understood themselves better than I understood myself. Their primal attraction to water reflected my own as yet unformed desires. They knew what they needed and, more importantly, where they needed to be.

I wonder now about the appearance of those sandhill cranes, particularly as I live near one of the few eastern nesting groups, the mighty threatened birds having mysteriously begun moving into the Pymatuning Reservoir of northwestern Pennsylvania over the past few decades. I have seen them in recent years, calling from high above, the same unmistakable croon that alerted my father in Arizona. They flew then in a place marked by the relic of erosion, clear and evident because of the desert climate, very little vegetation to conceal the rock. Layers are easy to see in the desert, while they are hidden in Pennsylvania. You have to know what you're looking for and where to look. And though the rocks are from different origins in each place, Chiricahua and the desert around it are as much shaped by the presence of water as the lush hills of my home.

When my brother visited Arizona, my wife and I drove him to Chiricahua too. This time, we ignored the main highway and instead took the back way through Bisbee and into wilderness dirt roads that wound past gold-mine ghost towns. Jen sat in the back seat and nervously handed us chocolate chip cookies as I showed off for my big brother, gunning my Bronco over washboarded dirt. We bounced on the worn-out springs of the Bronco, which later would catch fire in a bookstore parking lot and, after expensive repairs, the smoke from burning transmission fluid would billow through its tailpipe on a long drive home through the Utah Badlands. This was an unreliable vehicle, driven by a younger brother who made it even more unreliable by the desire to impress. A low spot appeared in the road before us, water flowing along a small stream. I gunned it again, spraying muddy water along the rocker panels while my wife gritted her teeth, reminded me about the Stupid Motorist Law, and passed out more cookies.

After Arizona came France, certainly not an arid climate but one more temperate and less humid than Pennsylvania. I remember it as a welcome change, though—green trees, blooming spring chestnuts, and golf courses devoid of cacti. Our belongings remained in the desert while we lived there, stacked in a storage garage. When it came time to move back to the United States, we went to Arizona first, cramming a rental truck full and finally heading home. I was shocked to find that my body had, in just a year, lost its capacity to enjoy Arizona summer heat. The sun was relentless, the landscape wrung out and olive drab. I remember this as disappointment but also as another recognition of how deeply ingrained are our home geographies. Landscape matters, as does humidity and weather and, maybe more than anything, the way water works within a given space. Arizona could never be our home. It was too hot and dry, an affront to our native humidities.

Still, at the end of our first day driving home, when we pulled our rental truck to its first lengthy stop in Kansas, I remember not being able to breathe: the world outside of the air-conditioned cab carried the summer humidity we had not experienced in three years, certainly never in Arizona or even in France. I drew it in with some difficulty. The first blast of moisture felt like being held underwater. And though it was only seventy degrees, long after dark in the cool of a summer evening, sweat immediately popped through my skin. I remember wondering if I could ever live in such places again, where humidity joins heat and the air is never free of water. I remember wondering if Arizona had ruined me somehow, if I'd become far too acclimated to high-pressure air and blue skies and dryness.

Four days later, we unloaded the truck at the farm, stashing our furniture wherever it would fit, in the dining room, under tarps in the barn. Then my father and I stood in the garage near the empty truck while the summer rainstorm gathered into a rolling wave down the Two Lick Valley.

My parents bought the farm property when the man seeking to develop it into a suburban subdivision spiraled toward bankruptcy. Eventually, my father repurposed the painted wooden sign declaring its hundred acres as the future

"Hidden Valley Estates" as part of the new goat barn roof. Before that, he bought a goat to eat away the poison ivy choking the lawn. And before that, he bulldozed a new farm pond to replace the swamp that had formed as the old pond filled in. And before that, he arranged to have a local dairy farmer reopen the fields in a rotation of oats, corn, hay, and eventually sorghum. My parents are both lovers of Wendell Berry, and the farm presents their own kind of homage to his work, their own experiences with resistance to minds oriented toward the restoration of land. For years, the dairy farmer who rented the fields rolled his eyes and complained about this conservation plan, that crop rotations, liming, and the limitation of chemical fertilizer was no way to farm. And each year, when the farm pond bloomed in neon algae, my father knew the farmer had ignored him again.

Eventually, when my brother, sister, and I grew up and left the farm, my parents decided to sell off the remaining animals, and my father decided his patience with modern chemical farming had ended. With the animals gone, he no longer needed the share of feed he received as partial rent for the land. Most of all, he wanted to finish the long process of land restoration he'd begun thirty years before. He enrolled the farm in a state-sponsored soil conservation program. State tractors came in, ripped out the leftover cover, tilled the soil fresh and deep for the last time, and then planted a mix of wildflowers and prairie grasses. My father worried about the exposed dirt until the day of that heavy rain, when the soil and water came washing down the hill in a torrent, some of it caking to the flagstones in the patio, other parts seeping underneath the door into the sunporch.

Certainly, there is heavy irony in the effects of that flood. The land had been stripped as a measure of recovery, and fertilizer-dependent crops had been removed to make way for hardy perennial natives, which had not yet been planted. The state program was designed for soil conservation, intended to prevent topsoil from washing away from exposed hilltops—erosion always a threat in a landscape shaped by that dynamic. Yet the program worked badly in its short-term implementation, as do most bureaucratic impulses: official delays meant open dirt and exposure to precisely the condition that my father had hoped to avoid. Yet when I consider the flooding, the lost soil, and the hope for the future, I also see the force of meaning at work. Sometimes the only way to move past a problematic, if quiet, past is to take a risky step. Things must be laid bare and, yes, the floods may wash across the surface. On the farm and elsewhere, we must also trust that a break is also an opportunity for further healing and, dare I say, recognition of identity. Planted in corn and oats, our farm was not itself. It had been shaped into a market-driven version of itself. I veer toward the biblical when I think of the water coming down the hill, carrying away the residue of the past to open fields for the future. I veer further when I think about myself and the many slow floods that have ushered me toward something greater than the inertia of the past.

I am not yet ready to tell you about my brain tumor, that flood and recovery and hopeful renewal.

Now, I write only of the farm: some of the washed-out soil collected in the stream at the bottom of the valley, a small, unnamed waterway that always floods during heavy rains. Eventually, that soil flowed on to the Two Lick Creek, source of the nearby town's drinking water and one of many waterways in western Pennsylvania that had been stained red-orange by leakage from abandoned coal mines. Our stream was relatively clean, however, and when we were kids, my sister and I often played in the pools that formed below the culverts beneath that part of the gas-well road. My brother, the oldest of the three, flipped rocks and snagged crayfish.

After rainstorms, the stream took on a different personality, gathering water and mixing silt and soil into a heavy rush. I remember the force of that water during spring and summer rains, the sudden vocalization of a normally quiet stream. I could hear it from the house, where I could also see the brown water stretch beyond the banks, spreading out among the flat bottom of the valley, a heavy current pressing through the concrete portal beneath the earthen bank of the Route 119 bypass that marked the northern edge of the farm, bringing with it whatever happened to get caught up. Even then, I understood the potential of floods properly noticed. I also understood why the gathered force of water should be feared, its strength uncontainable and inevitable.

As a child, I often collected the prizes that washed into the farm, thrilled most when spring rains lifted plastic toboggans from the yards that lay on the other side of the bypass, floated them through the tunnel, and finally left the colorful sleds caught up in the barbed-wire fence that crossed the stream at the southern edge of our property. We used those sleds to ride the steepest hill on the farm, Suicide Hill. A cow path across the lower third of the slope made a perfect jump, and a properly executed ride on well-packed snow meant a brief flight through the air, a numbing landing on frozen horse manure piles, and an out-of-control finish in the ice-covered water of the stream.

As a teenager, my brother sometimes waded through the bypass tunnel, so I wanted to also. I carried a small flashlight, red plastic with a white top, given to me by my sister one Christmas. I knew the flashlight had been coming because I had torn a small hole in the wrapping of the presents hidden beneath the vanity in her room, had seen the flashlight set—one big, one small—and then later denied the snooping. The next summer, I turned the beam from the smaller flashlight into the mouth of the tunnel. The weak light seemed only to be swallowed by the darkness inside. I could see the other portal, maybe a hundred yards away, the arch of sunlight that marked the end of the darkness. I waded in a few steps. The water was low, barely sloshing over the tops of my sneakers. I placed my weight carefully on the wet rock of the stream bed and imagined snakes and spiders and a sudden wall of water until I was about halfway through. The panic rose too far to be ignored, and I turned back toward the safety of the farm.

On topographic maps, the farm stream appears as a nameless thin line that starts somewhere north of the highway bypass and terminates in Two Lick Creek. Mostly, it is a drainage stream, one of countless permanent waterways that collect runoff from high points and then usher it toward a larger body of water. In fact, on the side of the bypass opposite the farm, the stream looks like little more than a ditch, indeed appears to be a hand-dug trench no more than a foot wide, often obscured by tall grasses. A trickle of water runs through suburban yards and through small culverts under driveways. Other ditches intersect with it, feeding the stream with runoff from various high places. There is no clear source to the stream, just as there rarely are dramatic beginnings to even the mightiest of waterways. Still, as a kid I longed to know where it started and, more broadly, just what lay on the other side of the massive berm of the elevated highway bypass. Even now, I long to know these things, albeit in a more conceptual way.

In *Chesapeake*, James Michener writes of an imagined search for the source of the Susquehanna River. His character,

Thomas Applegarth, locates a New York field as the surprising and quiet start of it all:

> I stood in that meadow with sun reflecting back from the isolated drops of water and realized that for a river like the Susquehanna there could be no beginning. It was simply there, the indefinable river, now broad, now narrow, in this age turbulent, in that asleep, becoming a formidable stream, a spacious bay and then the ocean itself, an unbroken chain with all parts so interrelated that it will exist forever.

Seepage: even if lacking in drama, I like the notion. Great power begins with quietness and collection, and I imagine I care today about the origins of the farm stream simply because of the force it holds in my memory. I do not yet understand the origins of its power, literal or otherwise, and I want to.

As a child, I often rode in the family car across the broadness of Michener's Susquehanna, looking through the windows at the wide water dotted by rocks and fisherman and wading herons. The Susquehanna splits the state in two, if not precisely geographically then conceptually. Two of my father's three brothers have lived always near their hometown in the eastern half of the state, and when we traveled to visit them, we traveled also into the birth region of Michener. The Susquehanna always felt like one of the clear dividing lines between our home and theirs. Our lives were separated by five hours, by Steelers versus Eagles, by the Allegheny Front, by a change in geology from the steep rolling landscape of southwestern Pennsylvania to the broad farm valleys tucked between ridges in central and eastern Pennsylvania, by moving into the Chesapeake Bay watershed away from the Ohio River watershed. A person should know where local water comes from and where it goes. The dynamics of what's upstream and what's down matters, affecting us mightily even if invisibly.

In my childhood imagination, the stream at the bottom of the farm was no less impressive than the Susquehanna, and its source seems to me, even now, no less mysterious. It begins as the same gathering of moisture that Michener writes about, an accumulation of the various ditches on the other side of the bypass, that artificial mountain that separates the farm from everything else. The stream begins somewhere in a stand of pines behind the Full Gospel Assembly of God, not far from the Unitarian Universalist Church, around the bend from the East Pike Electric Substation, a half mile or so from East Pike Elementary School, where I once scored four points, my entire season's output, in one game of sixth-grade basketball.

There, my father said to me on a recent drive, pointing through the window of his pickup truck, *that has to be the highest point*. The stream begins *there*, a trickle from an underground seep, perhaps, gathering more water into itself as it rolls through this part of town, disappears into the highway tunnel, and then winds through the bottom of the farm. *There* began at the tip of his finger, pointing toward a landscape that dictated my childhood, and I understand now that his finger is itself a different kind of source. What more powerful river is there than the guiding hand of a parent? This, too, is a dynamic I need to understand.

My father's finger pointed at the stand of pines for a reason. I had recruited him as guide to my own tracing of source. I wanted to see the connections of the farm. I wanted to trace the actual ground to see where the water came from, where it gathered into the little stream, and also where the other flows joined it to become the Two Lick Creek that formed the farm valley.

We began with the farm stream, then drove farther north to the old coal patch town of Commodore, searching for the headwaters of Two Lick Creek. My father, a retired biology professor, had driven this path often, bringing his college students to these waters in the 1970s and '80s to test and observe. We retraced that path, climbing from his truck near an old concrete bridge that crosses the North Branch of Two Lick to just below its own origin in the woods above the village.

From the bridge, we looked at a small collection of trash gathered on the edge of the creek that was no wider than the stream on the farm. We saw the usual stuff: a soda bottle, a fast-food coffee cup, sheet plastic. *Years ago,* my father told me, *a pipe from the old elementary school in town, now gone, used to churn trash from its cafeteria grinder into this spot.* He used to point to that trash, explain to his students how Indiana's water, downstream, started here. *You're drinking that,* he had told them. Next, they tested the water and found pH levels between 2 and 4.5, roughly an acidity between that of lemon juice and tomato juice, the creek turned caustic by outflows from underground mines.

From the bridge, he was impressed to see a small cluster of minnows and strands of algae fluttering in the soft current. We turned downstream, where a thin line of white precipitate painted the course of the current on the rocks. *Mine runoff, probably aluminum sulfate,* he told me. Three boys drove by fast on four-wheelers, kicking up a plume of dust as they raced through a vacant lot near the two-building downtown, rumbled across the bridge, then paused briefly at the stop sign at the intersection with the main road.

The mines are closed, and the fading siding of the homes in Commodore are a clear enough sign of that. But the mine chambers have long since flooded, and what flows out from underground remains toxic many years later. Routes do not change for water, at least not often or quickly. It follows gravity, doesn't seek to avoid the pollution we introduce to streams, aquifers, or mines.

We climbed back into my father's truck and drove through town, past yards filled with burn barrels, broken trampolines, beagle kennels, abandoned lawn tractors, faded Power Wheels cars, and then past a rusty ball field that used to be a boney pile. Near Wandin Crossing, an outcrop of a few homes and a questionable bar, we passed a house that looked vacant: unpainted wood siding deeply grayed, tall weeds around the foundation, the faded ghost lines of a front porch that had fallen away. Children's toys and bikes were scattered across the yard, some bleached by the sun, others brand-new, revealing that someone still lived in the house, despite the heavy layers of decay. I've driven by many homes like this in the remotest parts of the county, structures that would seem worth giving up on. But either because they can't or because they refuse to leave, people tack new layers of tarpaper to the siding, or they duct-tape the broken windows, or slide concrete block under the worst sags, and stay.

Just beyond this decaying house, my father and I stopped the truck again on a concrete bridge, this one crossing the South Branch of Two Lick Creek. Years of acid rain had washed away chunks of concrete along the bridge rails, exposing twisted rebar and aggregate. Beneath us, more minnows darted through water that looked clear of contamination. A great blue heron launched itself from a slow pool of water downstream, close to a nearly invisible nest of monofilament line hanging in the air, caught by overhead branches when a fisherman made a heedless cast. A fish jumped. A deer splashed across the stream. The whole scene appeared like a ridiculous bucolic calendar fantasy, cornfields rustling in the wind, clear sun, the quiet of a country lane. *The South Branch has always been a good trout stream,* my father said, explaining that the mines hadn't seeped here. In fact, according to state maps of underground mines, there are none in the immediate vicinity of the South Branch. On those maps, the county appears as a patchwork of gray and white, the gray indicating known locations of coal mines. After we climbed back into the truck, my father explained how he used to take students to the junction where the North and South Branches merge to form Two Lick Creek in a cloudy churn, the collision of pure water with the tainted. There, the state maps are solidly gray.

In tracing the origins of the farm stream and seeking to identify the interplay of waterways that define my home watershed, I seek a conscious echo of John Lane's project in *Circling Home*. In that book, Lane describes how he placed a dinner plate on a topographic map and traced around it, his house at the center. In exploring a focused circle of land, he seeks to examine the unseen interplay of life and geography, all of it the watershed of his tiny beloved stream. Lane writes:

> How do we decide where to dream a life into existence? On what scrap of this vast planet should we hammer in our stakes and say "home"? How do we live there with our neighbors? What level of commitment to landscape is acceptable? What lack of awareness is unacceptable? These are some of the questions I began this book with. I decided to answer them as best I could through what my geologist-archaeologist friend Terry Ferguson calls "ground-truthing."
>
> Ground-truthing is verification by direct evidence obtained when you visit a place after having seen it in

the abstract on a map or an aerial photograph. It is the truth you can find by interacting with the real world and examining a place and recording the data about it.

Riding around Indiana County with my father in search of the headwaters of the Two Lick Creek was my act of ground-truthing, but I also add to it an abstraction since the whole concept of Appalachia is conceptual. Words are written across the landscape, with so many books defining so many people in so many ways, few of them complete or accurate. All of them are defined by what America wants Appalachia to be, yet America rarely travels the ground of Appalachia and instead believes the falsity of the stories. My own story is my own ground-truth of Appalachia, something we all need to seek if we want to resist falseness.

I worry about this being true for myself, as a resident of both a region and a subset of a region that deserves to have its own sense of self. I drive now, and walk and ride and roam and write, as acts of recovery. I look for the edges of Northern Appalachia and the truth of that ground, seeking to loosen artificial boundaries and create for myself a new map, recognizing water and rocks and all that makes a place my place.

Thirty years after my last failed attempt, I stood at the stream portal again, determined to wade through against the current, under the highway to the other side. My legs itched from walking through what the lower pasture had become, now a bramble of tall grass and briar. The animals that used to graze the turf down to shin-high tufts have been gone for ten years or more; the old pigsty, which often lay at the center of my farm play as a castle or fort or bunker, has been burned away for twenty. Half of the pasture now lay under a two-year-old pond, built by the county as part of an environmental wetlands deal. The airport had expanded its runway, ostensibly to increase the business potential of town but, likely, to satisfy gas exploration honchos flying in on private jets to consider the county's growing Marcellus potential. To do so, the airport bulldozed some wetlands and, to satisfy environmental standards, had to build new ones. This is defined as an act of conservation, even when the act itself moves a tremendous volume of earth.

I think my father understood this dynamic when the county commissioners approached him and brokered the deal. He has since come to regret the implications of that comprehension, perhaps his own failure to see how economic development projects that use the word *conservation* are always talking about money and rarely care much about the lands they use. The deal meant new wetlands and a pond would be built, an act of reclamation on paper. But the engineering firm hired to complete the construction botched the job, building "seasonal wetlands" that hardly survived the first spring flood of our little farm stream. They understood water in the way an engineer does, which is to say they didn't understand it beyond a need for containment, which is also to say they didn't understand it at all.

Botched is probably the wrong word here too. I imagine the engineering firm knew exactly what it was doing. *Botch* would imply that true conservation had ever been part of the intention behind the blueprints. Earthmoving equipment dug soil directly from the streambed, violating environmental law for a project designed to follow it. The pond ended up being an industrial catch basin, twelve feet deep at the bottom of a steep hill, sheer sides that fueled my father's nightmares. He imagined one of his six grandchildren tumbling into the water, trapped, unable to climb out because of the steepness of the sides. Eventually, after repeated requests and legal interventions failed to inspire the county to fix the problems, my father paid a bulldozer driver named Porkchop to regrade the pond and make it safe.

A few years before that, I discovered on my walk that some combination of new wetlands and new basin had changed the stream. At the tunnel's edge, the water had slowed and pooled. I waded in, up to my hips, looked at the concrete arch in front of me, cobwebs hanging low. I calculated three feet of clearance at most between the water and the top of the tunnel. My feet sunk in mud up to my ankles. I considered the tunnel, the water, and the mud, and I felt myself young and terrified, seeing again the torrents and unknown fear that lay between me and the bright arch on the other side of the tunnel. I turned back again, still unable to shake what had frightened me as a child.

Instead, I headed downstream. Immediately, I found myself carefully pushing aside barbed crab apple branches, stepping through small holes in the overgrowth as greenbrier raked across my calves. Blood soon seeped from scratches on my legs. Along the banks of the stream, orange iron sulfate seeped from countless trickles of mine water. Changes in this terrain had wounded us both, and I wondered at the pollution of the water soaking into my bleeding legs.

The stream never used to be like this. Passage had been easy when I was a boy. And there had only ever been one active flow of iridescent mine acid; it came from a small drainage flow next to the tunnel. Now, orange bubbled through fresh half-dollar sized holes in the muddy banks. The stream has changed course, however, and that likely makes all the difference. When the earthmoving equipment scraped out the bottom of this valley to make artificial wetlands, it also scraped away the natural dynamics of water. In flood, the stream ignores old paths and now carves new courses, exposing fresh mud and fresh openings for the mine that lies somewhere deep beneath the farm.

I walked downstream around unfamiliar bends, disoriented from my memory of days spent exploring, flipping rocks to find crayfish or simply to hear the satisfying plunk of a large stone dropped in water. Nothing looked quite right. Even the place where I had spent the most time, the deep pool on the downstream side of the culverts beneath the gas-well access road, was inaccessible. I had successfully waded through that tunnel many times. Now the upstream openings were clogged with mats of sticks and uprooted grass. Overgrowth also blocked my path to the pool, so I had to leave the water of the stream and bushwhack through waist-deep grass until I found a place where I could return to the stream. I did not immediately recognize the spot where I emerged, then suddenly realized that I stood beside the old fallen tree where, some thirty years ago, I had broken my arm. The tree was half rotted, no longer the inviting balance beam that lured me as a boy, and the grasses and shrubs that have returned to the pasture in the years since animals last grazed surrounded its trunk. When I placed my hand on the bark of the old tree, the whole thing crumbled easily, nearly gone already.

I paused when I reached the edge of the farm, where only a single strand of the old barbed-wire fence remained. When the farm had been active, my father walked the fence line every year, mending breaks, replacing rotted posts. The fence kept the animals on the farm, or was meant to, and across the stream it had always seemed an impenetrable border. Our horses broke through once when I was a child and found their way onto one of the nearby highways. A state trooper tried to lasso our big half Arabian and half quarter horse, and my father took pride in that failure of movie-inspired machismo.

My father then directed the collected police and neighbors to corral the horses through calm movements and the careful application of a bridle.

The fence once held me too, a dividing line more felt than physical. It was easy enough to slide through. Not long after first moving to the farm, my brother, sister, and I quickly mastered the trick of sliding between barbed wires without catching clothing or flesh on sharp spikes. Often, those barbs held tufts of wool torn from sheep when they craned necks through to chew grass beyond the pasture. The few cows we raised leaned into the fence, using the barbs to scratch itches in their rough hides. Maybe this is the best use for a fence, a philosophy that cows understand. A fence yields, not fully, but just enough to satisfy. Yet it also offers enough containment to allow comfort. On the farm, I was home. Crossing the fence meant something else, a transgression, a violation, at least a move into the unknown a child fears as he moves away from the center of his life.

Through the years, the pasture fence has become only a reminder of itself. My father has removed most of it, and where it crosses the stream, there's just a single strand now, four feet above the water. No threat from the barbs. The stream is easier there too, wider and flat, the thickness of the forest here blocking out the undergrowth that challenged my walk to this point. I poured a collection of pebbles from my sandals, then quickly ducked underneath the wire.

Physically, the moment should have been harder, considering the quick wave of old prohibition that washed over me, the sense that I was leaving *ours* and entering *theirs*. I thought about state law, particularly about how the water was public property while the ground beneath was not. Crossing under the fence marked the moment I moved, technically, into a state of trespass.

Soon I came to the spot my parents called the party road, a place where college kids used to gather to drink beer and smoke dope. The old road had gone through the stream, no bridge. Discarded beer cans used to gather like fallen leaves in the weeds beside the road, sometimes floating down the stream. A few years ago, a urologist bought the property and turned the old road into a driveway for his new hilltop mansion. The urologist hired someone to build an earthen bridge, culverts directing the flow of the water, and an electronic gate and keypad directing the flow of traffic to his house.

I suppose his improvements mark a different sort of reclamation. There's less trash here now, the gate and his new road dissuading casual use. But his reclamation also cannot be separated from possession and ownership. This space belongs to him and no one else, and the improved cleanliness of the stream belongs to that possession too: once someone cares enough to buy land, it matters. Landscape counts only when dollars flow.

There was no way for me to avoid trespass though. The culverts were too small to wade through. I had to climb out of the stream, up the steep hillside of the bridge, and through joe-pye weed and briar that tore into my feet and legs. Atop the driveway, I considered my path back into the stream. My legs stung from the fresh scratches, and I could see that the slope on the other side was filled with a similar collection of briar. The tight rows of corn on the field beyond the party road looked like a better option, some combination of fertilizer, pesticides, weed killer, and, likely, GMO strains of corn made for an easy, bramble-free route. This field used to be Christmas trees and was once lit on fire by the neighbor's wild oldest child, but for the last couple of years it's been rented to a local agribusiness corn farmer, along with most of the other tillable acres in the valley.

Past the corn, I entered a peaceful section of the stream at the bottom of a steep hillside that feels protected. Large trees line the stream, oak and maple, even an ancient chestnut. Along the water's edge, I walked past part of a lightbulb, an empty cup of ramen, a knot of polyethylene house wrap, a few minnows and stream chub, a stack of thick fiber-optic cables running along the stream underneath the powerline cut. I waded through heavy pools that gathered behind deadfalls, occasionally leaving the streambed to wade through knee-high grass.

The incline of the stream is gentle in this section, so the water is slow. It is the widest portion of the stream, ten feet across in places, sometimes as shallow rocky flats and other times as murky pools that conceal whatever larger fish linger here. Past this flat section, the stream narrows a bit. The high slope to the west side diminishes, the hill shallowing to a spot my parents have always called the squatter's cabin. This is a neighbor of some legend, a series of different neighbors, I think. When we first moved to the valley, an old man lived there who was prone to violent rages when he was off his medication. He used to spend much of his free time holed up in the loft of the garage on our farm, reading nudie mags and drinking Genesee Light. I know this from my brother's old collection of beer cans and from the stories my father used to tell about finding the stash of magazines, of having to confront and run the old man out of the garage for good. Someone else lives in the squatter's cabin now, a woman with whom our next-door neighbor's second husband recently began having an affair. He lives there now too, beyond the rows of rusty fifty-gallon drums that line the top of the stream bank, behind piles of trash covered with tattered blue plastic tarps.

While wading downstream, I had just come even with the squatter's cabin when a yellow dog stretched its chain and starting barking, wild-eyed, flushing me from the creek bed back to dry land. Soon a man's voice barked, low and loud, an aggressive *hey* that I knew was aimed at me. I then remembered my father telling me about a recent visit from a state trooper who asked my father if he'd seen anything strange going on at the neighbors'. There'd been trouble, odd things, nothing specified. I headed out across the field, exposed, then stepped onto the road and considered my options. An engine rasped back by the cabin. I gripped tighter on the hickory walking stick my father had lent me. I had planned to duck back into the stream at the fork in the road, right beside the driveway to the squatter's cabin. Instead, I turned left at the intersection just as I heard gravel spit under truck tires. A GMC Jimmy with rusted-out rocker panels churned down the driveway from the cabin, veered onto the hard road, and gunned up the valley. I imagined ill intent and rage, so I headed home overland, cutting through corn, greenbrier, and a long patch of blackberry bramble until, finally, I breathed freely again on the upper fields of the farm.

I haven't been able to shake the terror of that walk, now four years in the past. More than anything, it hurt to think of the valley as a place where I could no longer freely roam. No doubt, the same forces of anger resided in the same places when I was a kid, but no one shouted at a child in the stream, or at least not in the way the man in the Jimmy shouted at me, angry and intent on violence. Still, I want the valley to be the one I grew up in. I want to be able to restore its quietude, calm, succor. I want it to be a place where I feel settled and safe, and I long, in the end, for any such place. This is the duality of Appalachia, its comfort and terror, a place where I walk streams and risk angry neighbors, where I am proud to be home and risk being taken less seriously since it is my home. Maybe it's the fact of being new to my forties, but I feel everywhere the shouts of anger and fear. I am unsettled and at risk. I feel exiled from places and ideas that I think should be reserved in perpetuity as refuge.

At a point a mile or so below the merger of its branches, Two Lick Creek broadens into the wide flat that it carries for the rest of its course. Spots of rusty orange iron sulfate dot the shore in places, but there is algae too, something that forty years ago could not live in the water. From twenty feet above the creek, my father looks into the water and sees a crayfish swimming around a flat rock. He points to it, and for a good minute I see nothing but water and rock. Even at seventy-two, he has the eyes of a naturalist, trained to see and understand things that I often fail to notice. Eventually, I find the crayfish, a good-sized one.

The pH is at least 5, my father says, *animals with calcium-based shells disappear below 5.*

I think of that fact with the wrong image, tiny crayfish fizzing and dissolving as the acid in the water reacts with the calcium. The truth is no less dramatic: the simple absence of a basic aquatic predator as stark and violent as the active dissolution of them. My father never saw crayfish on those old field trips with his students. He never saw algae. He used to explain to students how our town's water treatment plant sucked water from the creek and hardly had to treat it, just added lime to precipitate out the solids. The pH killed the nasty microbes and purified the water for human consumption even as it made it inhospitable to the things that normally live in creeks.

That crayfish is kind of a reverse canary in the coal mine, I say.

Exactly, my father says.

Down the road in Clymer, we will soon drive past a truck depot full of tankers that mark the next wave of underground industry, the Marcellus gas boom stepping into the forty-year void left by the coal mining collapse. The crayfish in the creek slides under a rock, disappears.

Here, I intercede with a memory of other water, fused with the memory of my father. When I was in grade school at the university lab school, my academic calendar synched with his; I was an elementary student at the same university where he taught college students. With my brother and sister still at the public junior and senior high schools, my father and I each year took a few days in late May to fish and bike along the Tionesta Creek in the Allegheny National Forest.

We spent our days throwing lures into the water, reeling back occasional clumps of creek weed and, rarely, tiny fish. We floated the low creek on black inner tubes. And we biked along the back roads beside the stream. On one afternoon my father led me to an old swinging bridge that spanned the creek. We planned to walk across, for the adventure.

I remember that bridge falsely, I'm sure, as a collection of rusted metal wires and rotten boards. In this memory, I remember placing a foot on a plank, having it crash through and tumble into the Tionesta. I'm sure this is a false vision, one built more by the clichés of action movies than by experience, but I am confident, at least, in the emotion that such an image suggests. I was scared on this bridge, could not stop watching the flashing reflections of the water below, could not help but imagine my body cartwheeling onto the exposed rocks of the shallow creek. My father had me grab his belt, and this I do remember clearly, the touch of leather, the reassuring heft of his waistline, my fingers tucked there between his belt and T-shirt. Even now, I'm hard-pressed to conjure a moment that better describes how I see my father. At risk, worried about the path I walk, I reach always instinctively toward him.

We took a few steps on this bridge spanning the Tionesta, and I felt panic. I don't know what my father felt, if he regretted his decision to bring his youngest child across such a decaying span, if he remained committed to the task of the crossing, or if he was secretly grateful when I begged to turn back. I don't know if he was disappointed. All I know is that we turned around, either in prudence or in acceptance of my fear. Regardless, my father acted as the guide across this creek, followed the lead of my desire but calling the shots, because I needed him to. I'm sure he would have risked that crossing if I'd been determined to do so, and I'm also sure that the bridge would have held. But to my ten-year-old mind, no cabling could have been secure enough to ensure a successful transit over the water trickling below.

A day or so later, I cried on the porch swing of his friend's cabin, wanting to stay always there, in that place, a shabby cabin overrun with mice, listening to the creek. Even then I understood the numbering of days. Soon enough I would head to junior high, and we wouldn't be able to take these trips anymore. He consoled me, understood my tears, and to this day he occasionally remarks on how much those trips meant to him. After my brain surgery, we returned to that creek together, driving the banks and recollecting on those trips from three decades ago. We snuck onto the porch of the old cabin and watched the creek flow by on a summer afternoon. I feared the discovery of our technical trespassing, as unlikely as it would be, and relished the quiet time beside my father, each of us next to a creek that mattered so much to us.

I want to grasp my father's belt for safety, but now I'm a father of two young boys, and I know the fear of watching them grow up in a world that won't respect their innocence for much longer. Planks break beneath my feet constantly, and heavy rains wash away the topsoil, and violent dogs strain at their tethers, and hidden dangers lurk and grow, and I do not know how to be the man who can be at home with all of this, let alone guide others into their adulthood. I fear they will find no home, no place to seep into their souls and settle their minds. Worse, I fear they've been born into a world without places worthy of love or, worst of all, they'll grow up loving the wrong places.

I am left with this: my father knows how to read water, and reading water is everything we have, all of us. Yet we so rarely do because reading requires stillness, and closeness, and the recognition of seeps and flows. Water takes its course, pathways obvious once you know what you're looking for. Still, we build our dams, imagining how we've changed the tides, the floods, or history. Gravity remains, and so too the memory of water.

That's sort of the issue of the old family farm, and that rusty barbed wire over the stream, and the great blind eye of the highway tunnel, through which I have never gathered the courage to wade. There's a powerful visual metaphor at play in these images. In the tunnel are darkness and the unknown, an open cut in a mass of dirt, a portal into either permanent darkness or, I'd like to think, something beautiful on the other side. At the other edge of the farm, beneath the wire, water flows where it will. It understands no border other than its always-changing course. It carves new borders all the time, goes constantly downhill, toward bigger water, recycles in the never-ending evaporative magic of the earth.

And thank goodness, because it's what water does that lets us live, being constantly both itself and something else. I'll be crass: water spends some of its life as piss, some as blood, sometimes as pure H_2O, and other times as a mighty solvent that can transform itself into, say, coffee or acid, or a fox or bear, or a human, or a suspension of life-giving medicine, or nearly anything. Yet above that infinite cycling, water is the wire, that stable marker of here versus there. And I feel it. I feel that border when I see it on the farm, get a little uncomfortable when I duck under barbed wire and go elsewhere. That's an affront to the border so established and, as natural as it might be, it's hard to shake the idea of safety a border implies. Wires wrap around so much, separating here from there.

On our quest to trace the interlocking waterways that feed and are fed by the farm stream, my father and I made one final stop, climbing from his truck on a high ridge overlooking the Two Lick Valley. Just below us, cars rushed by on a divided highway. Farther down the valley, past the highway, the water of the Two Lick Reservoir stretched out in the narrow fashion of dammed creeks and rivers. The creek resumes its course below the reservoir, winds downward through another couple of towns before merging with the Blacklick Creek, which joins the Conemaugh River, which joins the Kiskiminetas River, which flows into the Allegheny River, which contributes to the flow of the Ohio River, which is the largest tributary to the Mississippi, which is the river that flows most through the memory and literature of the United States. Our little farm stream adds to that flow. So does much of Northern Appalachia, in fact, including many other farm streams, each, I hope, meaningful to other small children and grown adults, water gathering together to shape landscape and identity.

The Two Lick Reservoir interrupts the creek about midway along its path, the damming paid for and maintained by the Homer City Generating Station to guarantee a source of water for its cooling towers. Yet when viewed from the promontory above it, the reservoir appears like an end point of the water we'd been tracing that day. The reservoir had the aspect of a lake, a destination. I watched a band of ripples spread and run across the surface, the shadow of wind. I saw it differently, as the signal of a still-flowing channel beneath the backed-up waters. Underneath the reservoir lies a ghost of the creek, still flowing, a current of motion ever forward, ever pressing, water heading always where it needs to be. Two Lick Creek will never be what it once was, but it remains different and powerful, forever ready to be found if I look.

CHAPTER 2

This Is Not a Mountain

Nine months before I knew anything at all about the brain tumor, I drove through the slowly arriving spring of Prince Edward Island National Park. Winter had been rough that year in Atlantic Canada, socked hard by late heavy snows. Even in early May, the shady banks of the coast road still held massive snowbanks, cold and deep with surfaces crusted over and pocked with dirt and twigs. To my right, the Gulf of Saint Lawrence spread across the horizon, gray-blue and nearly as cold as the snowbanks. Lobster buoys dotted the surface, the fleet having finally been able to set traps after several delays to the season, the harbor ice melted and hacked out enough to get going. The ferry had just resumed running from Nova Scotia across the warmer Strait of Northumberland, which was also beset by ice. Coastal shrubs still waited to bloom, their limbs dulled and winterized. Everything about the landscape seemed to be in suspension, everything on pause. New growth came slowly, and though spring carried its usual insinuation of relief and hope, this too seemed measured, cautious.

I steered around a bend, and there in the middle of the road was a fox, one of the many that call the Island home.

He was a typical red, but even from a distance, I could tell his pelt was mottled and frayed. This could have been a sign of spring, the molting of a heavy winter coat in anticipation of summer. But I also knew enough about the foxes of my western Pennsylvania childhood to think about disease, about the slow death of mange, relentless mites causing an animal to turn its teeth on itself. Invisible pain drives afflicted animals mad, resulting in the tearing of fur and opening of flesh, false relief that leads often to infection and demise.

The mottled fox waited, curious. I slowed my car, then stopped, and we watched each other. I then noticed his eye, the glaucous, blind, all-seeing, whitened, magical dead eye, his right. Eventually, he moved out of the road, and I crawled forward. He watched from his good eye as I drove past him along the coast road, and I watched in the rearview mirror until he disappeared from my view.

My wife, two sons, and I came to the Island that spring for a half-year respite. We didn't know then whether this was a more permanent going away or just a brief departure. I had taken a sabbatical from my teaching job, and it seemed the escape could not have come at a better moment. I was off kilter and had been for a long time, feeling displaced by turmoil. I blamed uncommon workplace stress. The easiest and most understandable issue: the previous October, a colleague had been arrested by the FBI, and I'd had to negotiate both the burdens of his teaching load and the psychological crises his betrayal ignited in our students.

At the same time, I had to weigh the various responses among the grown-ups. My former colleague's crimes had been against children, and the shortness of his eventual prison sentence seemed to me an outrage, as did the support some of my other colleagues offered him with visits, hot food, and a compassion that I couldn't understand. I saw, felt, and still feel only anger, coupled with the guilt of wondering if I lack enough humanity to care for the afflicted, topped off with the righteousness of thinking that I do care for the afflicted, and he's not it. Maybe this was because I knew him less well, or because I had young children. Perhaps I carry less capacity for forgiveness, or maybe forgiveness is undeserved when a person collects and shares half a million images of children on a well-cataloged external hard drive.

Perhaps inevitably, this arrest got me to thinking about the place where my family had settled, not by choice but in the fashion of academics, because there'd been a job there, a good one. My wife and I had no particular affections for the northwestern Pennsylvania town where we moved. It appeared like standard Rust Belt despair: industry gone for several decades and the downtown hanging on but struggling, even if certain pockets of surprising devotion to local foods and organics seemed hopeful.

The main drag up to the college, though, is a drive through the familiar decline of the northeastern United States. Once-grand homes sag. Peeled paint hangs like dead skin. Drooping porches reveal ruptured structures. Many houses appear abandoned, a few boarded up by the city in an effort to fight growing blight and a surging homegrown meth industry. There are the usual vacancies in the downtown shopping district, and roughened young men hang out in the downtown park nearby preschool classes that play ring around the rosy. When the temperature tops sixty degrees, those young men take off their shirts and walk around town bare chested and skinny, their threadbare tees or tanks tucked into their waistbands.

Even so, my wife and I originally felt a certain gratitude for the location. I still remember the excitement of a late-night phone call, when I entombed myself in a lovely B&B while on my interview visit. I had spent the day with members of the English Department, convincing them I'd be right for their open position. Things had seemed to go very well. It had snowed hard overnight, as it often does during northwestern Pennsylvania winters, but I was aglow. *This is it*, I told my wife on the phone. *I hope they love me as much as I love them.* In the end, they did, and I got the job, and a city, which let us settle only two and a half hours from our hometowns.

Migrating west to Arizona and then to Paris had felt good. It was exotic and thrilling to live first among the high mountains of Cochise County, hard against the Mexican border, and then in a decaying modern high-rise apartment building in the 15th arrondissement of Paris. We made friends. I roamed the mountains and the city. We argued passionately, laughed often, made love in the smaller-than-double bed in our tiny, thin-walled Paris apartment. I blushed not quite enough when the neighbor winked at us and remarked on the noises he'd heard, saying something in French that I didn't quite understand as much as I did his leering grin.

Still, we missed home, which at first seemed a marker of people. Christmas always seemed like the moment to think about it, persisting in my memory as a snapshot of my melancholy in Paris after receiving packages from family which had been torn into, rifled through, and thieved, just as the packages we sent to them arrived absent the swanky Lacoste hat we'd picked out for Jen's father. Later, I realized that in both places I missed something more elemental and solid. Arizona lacked the proper shade of green and, in some way, the mountains south of our town were too tall, the geology too exposed and brown. In Paris, I missed the roving animals of my childhood, France in general carrying the empty sterility of a landscape hunted out and groomed, old and refined.

After moving back to Pennsylvania, into the mountains of the Laurel Highlands, where we were close to our families and among the familiar and beloved landscape of valleys and steep hillsides, our first child was born. He was delivered in the same hospital where Jen had been born, early on a March morning that broke into clichéd streamers of dawning pink across a blue sky. Even as we moved farther north in Pennsylvania, finding a permanent tether to family proximity struck us as important. Once we birthed our second son a few years into our northwestern Pennsylvania life, the struggles of that city seemed almost worth it. We were close enough to our childhood homes, even if this town never felt like it could fully be home. Things could be worse, certainly. I missed mountains and was bored and uninspired by the glaciated flatness of this corner of the state, annoyed by the tones of Ohio that seemed to dominate in this place. Still, it was fine. It had to be fine.

Then came the arrest of my colleague, after which I googled the state registry of sex offenders, and the town's prospects turned from uncomfortable to terrifying. In a small city of just ten thousand, there were more than sixty registered sex offenders within three miles of our house, a remarkable and harrowing density. Elsewhere in town, America's opioid crisis churned, along with a persistent stream of meth lab busts that indicate the rural, poor, struggling aspect of our mostly chosen home. Addicts and dealers had taken to new methods of manufacture, a *shake and bake* system that involves throwing cold medicine and shaved match tips and lithium batteries in a pop bottle, shaking it up, then regulating the gas pressure by twisting the cap. From time to time, when the reaction goes out of control, the bottles are tossed in someone's yard. One Sunday afternoon, someone chucked a smoking bottle into a four-year-old's birthday party just a few blocks from our house.

Literally up the hill from all of this, the private college where I found a tenure-track job looks to be hanging in there. It has the leafy walkways, the appealingly creaky classroom buildings, the eccentric professors, and a curiously specific sign by the library celebrating it as the "oldest college in continuous existence under the same name west of the Allegheny Mountains." But students are harder to get these days, particularly for expensive mid-tier liberal arts colleges. Experts and consultants explain this as a market problem, that the supply of high school students is dwindling in the Northeast, and there are lots of private colleges across the region. Many of these remaining students have been conditioned to expect vocationally defined educations, the neoliberal narrative of jobs-save-all so deeply set that fewer and fewer see the point in the kind of explorative intellectual detour colleges like mine used to sell. My college hasn't figured out an effective way to respond to these pressures, so our incoming classes have been short for the past four years, and operating deficits have been counted in the millions, the college's economic position destabilizing or, perhaps, starting to more clearly reflect the town within which it resides, a place I have come to call the confluence of Rust Belt and Appalachia, a nexus of two different sorts of declining fortune.

Indeed, northwestern Pennsylvania is both of these, and the dynamic of the college echoes the regions, Appalachia and the Rust Belt both places where old ways are dying and new ways are never quite built on a faith in the return of old ones that are gone, everyone struggling to pay the bills. Even the buildings on campus show a wear not dissimilar to the downtown, the ragged edges seemingly less and less like eccentric collegiate shabbiness these days and more like trouble. The building where I work carries a remarkable number of water-stained ceiling tiles, and black mold often erupts in the men's room in the philosophy wing. The college has had to cut back on janitorial service to save money, so in winter the thresholds of my building are coated in a dingy, salty residue, an obscuring haze through which fraying linoleum tiles peek through. An entire light fixture fell from the ceiling in another building, smashing into the floor of a political science professor's office.

Do I even need to mention the presidential election of 2016, when Trump signs popped up across town like dank mushrooms after cruel rain, when I stayed up late watching returns with an ever-growing sense of dread and helplessness, when more than 70 percent of the voters in my county followed the pattern of much of Appalachia and voted for a candidate that seemed at best a cartoon villain, and at worst a curious political stunt? Reality proved to be a harder truth, a deeper worse than I might have imagined.

Everywhere, the town seems to encircle us with despair. The FBI raid of my colleague's house took place a block from ours, and in the previous summer I had stopped by often with my older son to check on the basement and do general walk-throughs while the colleague spent the break at his second home in Arizona. I still had the extra key to his house when he was arrested. In fact, I think that extra key is probably somewhere on the hook of orphan keys by our front door. A day or two after his arrest, my wife got into the passenger seat of our family car and wondered why the seat had been moved. *Who was riding here?* she wondered, laughing. I couldn't bear to tell her: I'd given *him* a ride home from a poetry reading.

Rewinding to before all of this, I think about the moment I returned home on the day my colleague was arrested, when I spent hours at school making phone calls to our out-of-town chair and trying to put out the first early fires while the college offered no official response. Word had spread quickly through the students, but an administration fearful of bad publicity and, I suppose, lawsuits, said nothing at all. I walked home that night, reached the living room, and collapsed against the wall where I wept uncontrollable sobs of deep grief, fueled by the arrest and shock and also, I imagine, by many things that I didn't fully understand and still don't, or perhaps that I'm not yet ready to admit.

Shortly thereafter, I began to suffer strange physical symptoms. My wife and I chocked it up to stress, triggered by the arrest, aftermath, and troubling local response. After meals, my face would flush and my eyes would get hot, as though I were allergic to the simple act of eating. I'd be so tired after teaching that I'd have to just sit, exhausted, unable to move, think, or do anything at all. I'd also been noticing that my glasses never seemed right for my left eye, but three optometrists had checked and assured me that everything was fine, that the eye was healthy and there was nothing to worry about.

The new symptoms could not be ignored though, and my wife convinced me to see my doctor. That set off a long sequence of testing, plus a tasteless month of eating a gluten-free diet, all of this to no avail. Along the way, I gave up vials and vials of blood, collected my piss for twenty-four hours in a giant bottle, gave more vials of blood, lay awake at night thinking about my boys, then two and six, and sobbed into my pillow after a medical student allowed to offer a provisional diagnosis did so, suspecting terminal liver cancer. This proved untrue, and his guessing in front of me was unwise, unkind, and devastating. Still without a diagnosis, I endured therapeutic blood lettings once an elevated red blood count was discovered, and I scraped my own shit into plastic jars, wondering how to gracefully drop off my urine and feces at the local lab, particularly after everyone there got to know me on a first-name basis.

We found nothing to treat, only curious results indicating, well, *something* autoimmune—no diagnosis, no real treatment, just wait and see what happens. By the time we reached Prince Edward Island in the spring of 2015, I had decided to think of these health concerns as a matter of history. I doubted any future diagnosis and figured only that I'd be checking in with my new hematologist from time to time as a formality. I didn't realize that I was living in the temporary stillness between *you're probably fine* and *you're not*.

And so I come to this, the lede I have been burying for many pages in this book that is about Appalachia, yes, and particularly about Northern Appalachia, but also defined wholly and completely and unavoidably by February 15, 2016, a Monday morning when I logged in to our local hospital's internet patient portal, clicked on the latest report uploaded early that day, a radiologist's read from an MRI that had been ordered *just in case*. There, I first saw the words "intensely enhancing mass" and "the principal concern is that of a tiny meningioma."

So this is a book about the moment I felt my life fall into the pit of my belly. I didn't know what *meningioma* meant at the time, but I was conversant enough in Latin suffixes to understand that very few words that end in *-oma* are good, just as *enhancing mass* isn't a label you want to have applied to anything in your body, let alone your brain.

I remember the immediate stun of reading those words, of carrying my iPad to the kitchen where my wife was preparing breakfast for our two boys and showing her the report, the mix of confusion and immediate terror and forced, *it will be fine I'm sure* that one or both of us uttered in some way.

Soon I listened over the phone to my ophthalmologist refer to the *lesion* on the meningeal lining of my optic nerve and tried to answer his question about which Pittsburgh hospital system I'd prefer for the neurosurgical appointment he'd make for me as soon as we hung up. I was surprisingly calm on the telephone, learning about all of this with supernatural evenness that might be described as shock. This is the moment when the vague physical symptoms of my recent history got a name, when I found myself personally unhinged from the body I'd known, and when definitions of myself would change toward a life permanently defined as recovered, or damaged, or God knows what.

I picked the Allegheny Health Network, for what it's worth, named after the river that cuts southward through the western half of the state and after the ancient plateau remnant of the Appalachian Mountains, and which was also the same hospital where my grandmother learned of her terminal lung cancer twenty years earlier. That commonality didn't strike me until my wife and I drove down for the first appointment and I saw the fluted aluminum facade of the newer portions of the hospital, now old and disheveled. In some way, the metallic scallops of that facade echo the profile of the steep hillsides of Pittsburgh, the bulges and rolls also akin to the tiered recovery excavation I'd grown up seeing on mountainsides cut open to liberate coal. I had remembered that aluminum as shiny, but in the gray late winter of 2016 I was startled by its dullness, by the grime that had accumulated on the surface.

It would be both obvious and an understatement to declare that my life changed on the Monday in February when I learned of my brain tumor, but of course that's the reality of what happened. I spoke on the phone that afternoon with one of my best friends since high school, now a family-practice doctor in North Carolina, who talked me through the details of this first arc of care and also patiently corrected my consistent mispronunciation of the tumor: *ma nin gee oma,* not *manine guy oma*. In learning to pronounce this word, I began to pronounce the life I now lived. The story I'd known my life to be altered in a way that could not be taken back.

I have since spoken with many doctors who use medical language to understate the seriousness of what has been described to me as the *brain tumor you want if you have to have a brain tumor* and a *not-so-bad tumor in a really bad place*. I still often hear the words of one oncology nurse echo in my brain, a middle-aged woman filling in at the cancer center where I did radiation. She reviewed my history, thinking no doubt about the relatively young man in the room with her, my profile being a couple of decades younger than the average patient coming in for zapping. She asked about my brain tumor, and I said the now-familiar word *meningioma*, and she said, without any pause, *praise Jesus*.

In the Appalachia of my birth, you drive often among hills carrying the unmistakable shape of strip mining reclamation. The contour lines are smoothed off such hills, the angles planed into more uniform grades than the typical eroded topography of this part of the country. There are Christmas trees planted alongside grass, pine, fir, and spruce, making a decent crop in soil that's too steep and depleted for much else. They call hills like this "returned to contour," a legal requirement for the reclamation of land after strip mining. The idea is that the external signs of great gouging shovel work are removed: the term is a lie intended to suggest that strip mining is a benign act, that the land can be returned to what it was before, that it hasn't been altered by the destructive forces of extractive moving.

Strip mining came to my homeland in the 1960s as a way to both more cheaply and more safely extract coal from our mountains. Tunnels can collapse, particularly when the layers of rock overhead are not as thick, when seams of coal are closer to the surface. Deeper tunnel mines were starting to run a little short on coal by the second half of the twentieth century, so earthmoving machines followed streams along the contour of hillsides, cutting away the rock above the seam to expose coal to easier digging. That rock is known as *overburden* because it is above the coal and because, I suppose, plain old rock is a burden instead of an economic boon, like coal. The machines dug along the hills to expose the coal seam, then dug into that seam toward the center of the hill. The excavation of this coal formed what's called a *highwall*, a long sheer ledge remaining after the mining equipment passes through.

I use the past tense here, but this is a technique that miners still use today. It's different from the more nationally famous, and infamous, Mountain Top Removal, which involves removing the overburden, a tall peak, and pouring that rock into the adjacent valley with no intention to ever put the top back on the mountain. In fact, the intention is often to create a flatter area because it's cheaper and because politicians and developers can claim that such flat spots are good for shopping malls, which everyone is supposed to need and want.

From about the middle of the twentieth century until state and federal laws became a new kind of overburden, strip-mining companies finished up the excavation of seams and then simply left. The land lay exposed and transformed, denuded of trees (probably logged because that was also profitable), and carrying giant gashes, right-angle walls, and the slow-drip of tainted water. The mining left behind massive piles of carbon-black overburden—boney piles—which accumulate so much heat from the sun that seeds are fried before they have a chance to germinate. Such barren piles still mar the woods, nearly half a century after the mining ended. There was then no legal requirement for even limited restoration. Whether dug as deep open pits, or tunneled as warrens of interlocking shafts, or scraped out of the sides of mountains, mines could just be abandoned, and of course they were.

Recognizing the layered problems of this industrial history, the Commonwealth of Pennsylvania passed the Land and Water Conservation and Reclamation Act of 1968, which focused most of all on the destructive seepage of mine acid into waterways. It took more than a decade for federal law to accrue, with Jimmy Carter finally signing the Surface Mining Control and Reclamation Act of 1977. The Act outlines legal parameters to mining while still making it clear that the law will "assure that the coal supply essential to the Nation's energy requirements, and to its economic and social well-being is provided and strike a balance between protection of the environment and agricultural productivity and the Nation's need for coal as an essential source of energy."

The 1977 federal law lays out rules and declares that surface mining projects must at minimum "restore the land affected to a condition capable of supporting the uses which it was capable of supporting prior to any mining, or higher or better uses of which there is reasonable likelihood, so long as such use or uses do not present any actual or probable hazard to public health or safety or pose any actual or probable threat of water diminution or pollution." Furthermore, the mined land must be restored to "the approximate original contour of the land with all highwalls, spoil piles, and depressions eliminated (unless small depressions are needed in order to retain moisture to assist revegetation or as otherwise authorized pursuant to this Act)." Elsewhere, provisions are made to exempt steep terrain projects from having to find the original contour, with similar exclusions allowed for projects that face particularly thick layers of overburden. In these cases where mining means lopping a lot off the top of mountain, well, that's OK. You don't have to go back to contour then. You can just restore the terrain to as minimum grade as possible, as long as the new grade is not steeper than the "angle of repose." Which might be good for a shopping mall.

The act also defines "approximate original contour" as "grading of the mined area so that the reclaimed area, including any terracing or access roads, closely resembles the general surface configuration of the land prior to mining and blends into and complements the drainage pattern of the surrounding terrain." The land is dozed into the same rough shape it once had. Mathematically, I'm sure it works. You can measure the rise and run, and the new is the same as the old. But it isn't the same, and anyone looking at the hills can tell. Part of it is clear from the scrubby vegetative growth. The topsoil is gone, washed and trucked away, so millions of years of natural compost are gone too, along with the healthy nematodes, insects, and onward up through the chain of natural organisms. Walking these former hills would be an industrialized version of what Wendell Berry cites, of traversing Kentucky slopes "as if 'knee-deep' in the absence of the original soil." In this fashion, a strip mine is reclaimed, considered to be restored and healed.

When I consider the language of reclamation, I consider also the extent of need. In *Circling Home*, John Lane writes of Barry Lopez visiting the creek that Lane writes about, explaining that streams cannot be impaired. Instead, Lopez told him, it is our relationships to them that have suffered. So it is in my childhood home, Indiana County, where the marks on maps and the stains on rocks shout about a long history of impaired relationship.

In this context, *reclamation* strikes me as a violent term, even if it's the best we have. Reclamation implies a continued cycle of domination, very little change to the conditions of power that led to problems in the past. Indeed, such cycles are the unbroken history of Appalachia, where impaired relationships find new ways to hold onto old grudges. The landscape suffers, always, even while it obstinately continues to exist. Instead of reclamation, I desire the wisdom of repair. That begins with the act of recognition, self-recognition most of all, since change that gestures only outward without settling first inward is doomed.

And I recognize this: the new contour of reclaimed hills is awkward and jagged. Eons of geological uplift, natural erosion, gathered silt, and pathways of deer and people are razed, then dug through, then rebuilt with a dozer. The contour line is a best-fit line—I mean this in the sense of math again—the natural chaos of erratic dots replaced by the smoothness of simplicity, by what a human being can do in a week in contrast to what an ecosystem can do in millions of lifetimes. I might also describe looking at reclaimed hills as akin to viewing an eight-bit video game version of the landscape, everything pixelated and blocky, without nuance. The technology wasn't there, in those old video games of my childhood, to make the scenery look real. That's a reclaimed mountain too. If there's a ledge, it's tiered, limited in our infinite landscape, just as if there were sprite problems and processing limitations.

Such a rise is no longer a mountain, but we have no word for it, no new category to define the new thing that has been created. It fits our paradigm of a mountain, so we call it a mountain, pretending that what it was is what it has become again. But the past is irretrievable. We should all know that by now. Words are funny, and how we speak the world into existence is strange, imprecise, and ultimately not as useful or stable as we might think.

Consider deeper history, the very geology that made Appalachia. Some 375 million years ago, the tectonic plates shifted, and various continents and subcontinents smashed into each other with enough slow-driven force to instigate the Acadian orogeny. This is the birth of a mountain range, the slow-gathered energies of tension squeezing rock together, slinging some up, tunneling others beneath, until a great ridge begins to rise from the flatness. The Appalachians were once mighty mountains, high and craggy and snow-capped, and rivaling anything the younger Rockies boast. The Rockies are at most only eighty million years old, more or less fresh, and have not yet experienced the hundreds of millions of years of weather and wind and further tectonic events that have smoothed out the Appalachians—years during which rock entrapped and overlapped organic matter, forming the valuable mineral resources we know as the industrial markers of the region: coal and natural gas and, near where I live in northwestern Pennsylvania, the oil deposits that spawned a world-changing commercial industry.

The oil has long since played out, and the coal industry has followed its own cycles of boom and bust. In the part of Appalachia where I grew up, the big days of coal ended when I was a toddler. A few small companies still run, mostly nonunion, small-scale underground operations and various strip mine enterprises that peel back the trees to scrape away the remaining coal. Even recent attention to the pockets of organic matter trapped in layers of black Marcellus shale, formed early in the Acadian orogeny as a byproduct of erosion, has dimmed. Bust is always following any sort of boom, that cycle as tidal as the ancient sea that gathered sediments in the Appalachian Basin.

Appalachian strip mining itself can be described like this: about three hundred million years ago, in a geologic time called the Pennsylvanian Period, the vegetative matter of life drifted slowly to the floor of the great former sea that lay where Appalachia now rests. It gathered, decayed, and began the long ride toward becoming the carbon-rich burnable rock we call coal. Over time more sediments drifted down atop it, layers of silt and sandstone that hardened to sandstone. Pressure hardened the rock and made the coal beneath. More or less around this geologic instant, the Appalachian Mountains were born and immediately began eroding.

The soft sedimentary rock of those peaks became a thick layer of rock above the coal beds, forming the Appalachian Plateau, which small creeks began wearing away into the deep valleys that shape the topography of this region. That water also sometimes exposed this burnable rock, and humans started using it to cook meat and provide warmth. Then humans started digging small pits and tunnels by hand, and in places like western Pennsylvania they realized that it would be cheaper to use the machines they'd come up with—mighty tractors, giant shovels, blades, and buckets.

The point is, geology defines what the region would be for eons to come. First, the land was home. Next, the mountains were obstacles. Then they were conquered, offering a triumph narrative for America. And there was coal, gas, and the ripping of these things from the ground. For a long time, there have been people also, triangulated with the geology and the energy trapped within it. Also for a long time, the people of my region have been defined within the context of the geology beneath them, in more or less precisely the way scholar Adelene Buckland writes in reference to the rise of geology's prominence in Victorian England: "Instead of articulating the narrative mechanisms by which people, place, landscape, architecture, culture, and economics might be linked [nineteenth-century scientist J. F. W. Johnstone] relies on postulated metonymic associations between them." She identifies that familiar, still powerful move that suggests that people who live on iron ore reserves, for example, might be described as having ore mining in their blood. Such metaphors are forged in the language of industry, with people who are viewed as utilitarian agents of commerce yoked forever to the value of the natural resources they live among. Buckland is rightly suspicious of such a move: "It is less obvious how the existence of metal beneath the soil might influence the moral and social disposition of the inhabitants of that city."

Understand that I'm mentally swapping *coal* into all of these sentences, which makes them sound like lines you may have heard at any number of 2016 political rallies, where so many people were pissed off about the decline in shitty coal jobs and frustrated at the way entities like the EPA supposedly ignore the alleged deliverance of "clean coal." When coal's in your blood, and your region's importance has been defined by your ability to rip that coal out and find a sense of personal worth in the way that mining "keeps the nation's lights on," it's easy to support a pillaging industry that destroys your land. Coal is to burn, and so are you. This is Buckland's claim about the birth of geology, which she labels as a science governed by literary thinking—that rocks offer metaphors applied to people. Even more importantly, the way rocks are used and valued creates the metaphor, and the people above the geology are suddenly thought to carry those very qualities.

In Appalachia the metaphor of "coal in our blood" becomes grotesquely prophetic when the demand to dig leads to the invasion of the body by the substance itself: black lung and silicosis no longer metaphors for a person consumed by rock. We need to read metaphors better so we can understand the links that shape our implicit sense of what people are and how much they matter.

I come to my own weird personal identity as an Appalachian, as a *Northern* Appalachian, and as a Northern Appalachian who grew up on a farm with a professor father and a demure and intellectual mother from the Midwest—and with a grandfather who dug anthracite in pit mines in eastern, not-really-Appalachian Pennsylvania. I grew up as a nerd and a farm boy, as a 4-H club president and a high school thespian, with close friends who were the children of other professors, but I was also friendly with the neighbor kids who spit tobacco juice into Mountain Dew bottles in the back of the school bus during our morning pickups. I was a kid at home in both the back of that bus and the front of the classroom, comfortable with nerds and rednecks, on the farm and the stage, in school and in the woods.

I should qualify *equally at home*, though, to indicate how I never felt fully part of either side of that implied dichotomy. I've always felt a little stuck, which is to say I've always felt rather Appalachian. My metaphors are mixed, which fits because Appalachia is itself a liminal imaginary space. It is the region between north and south, east and west, past and future.

And, as it turns out, even the mountains of Appalachia are not generally mountains at all but instead mostly a "dissected plateau." In my home turf, the appearance of mountains has been acquired only through the erosion of the Allegheny Plateau, a high landmass that stretched westward from the peaks of the mountains that are no more. The mountains of my youth were actually cut out by the flowing water of streams, creeks, and rivers and were not lifted to their lofty position. There had been an uplift long ago, but the landscape that makes me me was a feature of wear and use. It is old. It is worn but not worn out. Maybe Buckland's recognition of Victorian geology as metaphor can work here, if only we can reset the way we value the things our rocks imply, define ourselves not by the value of coal but by the grandeur of erosion. We can recalibrate how our metaphors make the unknown better known.

Prince Edward Island figures in this geology as a collection point, both personally and in the fashion of sediment. Tucked into the Gulf of Saint Lawrence between New Brunswick and Nova Scotia, it is a curious, bright red sandstone Island, its geology fresher than most other Appalachian rock. The Island is described by its original Mi'kmaq residents as *Epekwitk*, anglicized to *Abegweit*, a land cradled by the waves, or by others, as a pillow on which Nova Scotia rests its head. PEI's red sandstone was formed when soft grit washed through waterways in the Permian Appalachian Mountains. This Island that I have come to love is the collection point of erosion and is quite literally built from the accumulated bits and pieces that were lost elsewhere. What washed away from those old mountains became a big pile of compressed sandstone, pancaked into a more or less stable Island that, nonetheless, chips away each year from the force of winter gales and the splintering hydraulic action of freezing ice. Its coast loses about three feet annually, so Prince Edward Island is never the same, is always in a state of flux and reinvention. You might see already why I'm drawn to it.

For Pennsylvania, geologic history is equally unstable, even if to the human eye the chipping away is less dramatic. From high above the earth, you can plainly see great long swirls of landscape in the center of the state, unique and beautiful natural patterns that designate the Ridge and Valley section of Pennsylvania, pinpoint more or less where the Allegheny Front lies and where the harder substances of the ancient Appalachian Mountains remain. Those swirls in the hard rock are what are left, the sandstone folded in a way that would not wash away so easily as the flat-layered sandstone of my birthplace, with higher quantities of quartz also offering strength and resistance.

I grew up west of the Ridge and Valley, in the dissected plateau that is not a mountain just as much as Prince Edward Island is not a mountain. We still called our neck of the woods *mountains,* or at least considered it awfully hilly. On the ground, it doesn't feel a lot different from portions of the state east of the Allegheny Front. It still takes a lot of effort to climb.

Precision demands the clarification, though, that the hills of my homeland and, in fact, of the greater bulk of Appalachia itself, happened as streams cut down from the high points of the Allegheny Plateau. All across the region, you can point to high peaks and declare, *this is not a mountain* and *this is not a mountain* and *this is not a mountain.* The peaks are all more or less at the same altitude, which is how you can tell how the geology works. There was a great flat table, high up, and the erosion wore great grooves, with rivers and streams digging ever downward. Geologists call this pattern *dendritic,* meaning the valleys were cut by the branching veins of waterways. That's why you'll find at least a small seasonal creek at the base of all of our not-mountains: that's what made them, over time and slowly.

I was born to an area where relief is produced not by uplift but through degradation. If this isn't a metaphor, I don't know what is. All that we have comes from erosion. Still, we call them mountains, another metaphor, because we Appalachians don't want to recognize where we really come from, what the land is. We think of erosion as bad, as lesser, as a geologic function inferior to something like uplift, which creates the craggy high points. We want to measure up, even if that's not what we are.

So when we arrived on Prince Edward Island in 2015, I had some unarticulated goal of renewal. We were a thousand miles away from the troubles of home, and that seemed like an important separation. We moved into a cottage overlooking the Hunter River, tucked into a quiet dead end behind the New Glasgow cemetery. There was a rusting bus in the front yard, something our landlady apologized for but that I found appealing enough to post on Facebook as a sign of rugged northern beauty. Foxes had covered an old spare tire, chucked in the bus's interior, with an impressive pile of scat, marking territory with a heavy musk. I imagined this as a war to claim the bus as a winter den.

Evenings, I drove through the national park and looked for foxes, mostly for *that* fox, the blind-eyed ghost who seemed both a reflection and a sign. I thought about landscapes and recovery, about being drawn to this place that is not so different from the place I am from, western Pennsylvania coal country an analogue to the Canadian Maritimes even in the ways that the people are stereotyped as backward, less, and hick. But I thought also about being always in exile, never belonging to any place. My parents were not from Appalachia, meaning it was not theirs by birthright. And living half a year on PEI meant I was more than just a *summer person*, but I'd still never be an Islander. In much the same way, even though I was born in Appalachia, I felt always exiled from what that would seem to mean. The prefix *Northern* makes it an exile from the broader region. The main term *Appalachian* makes it an exile from America. Lacking generational claim to the place, I can never be much more than a new resident, thus exiled from history itself.

In PEI's rockiness, its position as the residue of the eroded northern tip of the Appalachian Mountains, I felt completely at home and completely not. I hadn't yet considered the metaphorical strength of its geology, that PEI is made of sandstone, that its soil carries a beautiful red sheen akin to the creeks of my youth because the dirt literally rusts. In Pennsylvania, the rust is a stain, a result of leaking mine acid. In PEI, it is just the rock, and it figures prominently in tourism brochures and, of course, in *Anne of Green Gables*.

I prefer PEI's natural dynamic to the staining of rocks in so many Appalachian creeks, where the rusting comes because of the mining, because of harm caused and opened. The shorelines and red cliffs in PEI are fragile, and the Island owes its birth to erosion. Yes, it's part of the Appalachians, but it's not built of or on the rock that I know. Instead, it grew from the outflow of all the water cutting away the softness, became an island as the silt of erosion first gathered then was pushed higher by uplift. This strikes me as a metaphor for hope, how what appears lost can refashion itself into something beautiful, maybe even better.

Throughout our first summer on PEI, I felt as physically worn as I did at home but experienced no sense of relief at all. Some nights I'd lean against the walls of the shower and let hot water flow over me. When I read to my older son, I squinted harder and harder. I closed my right eye, left eye, right, left, and watched the images change, bright through the right, veiled through the left. Words were clear if I read with my right eye, hazy and gray through the left, an emptiness emerging in the center of my field of view. We were reading *Calvin and Hobbes* that summer, and I could make Hobbes disappear just by closing one eye. This effect finally led me to see the ophthalmologist who ordered the MRI *just in case*, that growing blindness coinciding with the accumulation of medical testing fees, bringing our expenses to the deductible threshold of our new cost-saving insurance and thereby alleviating the economic disincentive for further necessary tests. Had we not reached the maximum on our new high-deductible plan—pitched as a benefit to us, one that would make us better consumers of this more expensive health care—I would not have had my eye checked out. Maybe this is Appalachian too, economic struggle nearly preventing me from finding out about my brain tumor. I had to get broke enough to justify spending the money to find out how broken I was.

I live now with many descriptions I'd prefer not having, simply because people think they know what these labels mean and might define me by them. Or maybe I don't like them because I'm afraid of their accuracy.

I am a man permanently half blind in one eye.

I am a man who had brain surgery.

I am a man with a brain tumor, nestled into a spot that makes it impossible to remove.

I am a man with a brain tumor called *dead* by my doctors, these specialists all convinced that the radiation I received was strong enough to render inert the mass that threatened me.

I am an Appalachian, which is to say I am something understood as less than whole.

I am Northern Appalachian, which is to say I am something hardly understood at all, or even considered.

I am a survivor, of something.

None of these descriptions are labels most people want to hang on to and claim. Is it any wonder that, growing up, we Pennsylvanians more or less said, *Appalachia? Naw. That's down there,* hooking thumbs toward West Virginia and other parts south. Is it any wonder that I feel guilty and angry when someone refers to me as a survivor, me hooking a thumb toward a better example, someone who had to fight more dire growths, suffer harder treatments?

Yet I survived, and my birthplace is in Appalachia, and my home today in the northwestern corner of the state, where glaciers flattened the topography and the decline of eastern heavy industry did the job on the economy, is also Appalachia. But each of these places is also part of something different. They are *Northern* Appalachia, a place both within a broader region and distinct.

So I'm writing not just about Appalachia and not just about my brain tumor, but also and mostly about exile, about being from a place that doesn't count as a *good* place—this being the plight of Appalachia in the national American consciousness. And I am writing about being from a place that doesn't even fully count as being part of that maligned locale. Ask anyone who isn't a student of Appalachian Studies about Pennsylvania and its part in the region of Appalachia and, more than likely, the state's membership will be disavowed. Pennsylvania requires the sub-descriptor of *Northern* to Appalachia, which is a way for many to say I am not from *real* Appalachia.

Let's not dwell yet on my other disqualifications, that I have a PhD, a professorial gig, no discernible accent, and progressive politics. To wit (using that phrase disqualifies me even more!), I've been complimented on more than a few occasions for the propriety of my speech *even though* I'm from Appalachia, just as academic colleagues have joked that I'm not a *real hillbilly* because of all the things about me that go against the stereotype. This figures, at least in part, in why I've long felt that the condition of exile lies at the center of who I am and that I find myself often trying to triangulate just who I happen to be in the wake of various historical, conceptual, and personal traumas. It would not be inaccurate to say that I fancy myself in a constant state of exile or, better put, constantly in need of some kind of reconciliation. Reconciled to what, I am unsure.

Thinking about culture, language, and history, I now see connections between the collision of land masses that formed the Appalachian Mountains and the collision of culture that erodes the people who have lived in and near them. Certainly those who, like me, are accurately labeled as Appalachians have suffered literal and figurative damage because of the broader national desire for mineral wealth. But also consider that as the Appalachian range stretches north into the place where those old land masses first smashed into each other, we come to the Maritimes of Canada and, particularly, *L'Acadie*, where the descendants of French colonists were shipped out during *Le Grand Dérangement*, a moment when the British were doing well enough during the French and Indian War to deport the people in their way. And consider the anglicized Acadia as a linguistic variant of Arcadia, an ancient Greek region, mountainous and pure, where the original Greeks lived, and a term that was later used to indicate idealistic pastoralism and harmony with nature. The state of Arcadia is a state of unspoiled wilderness, our mountains imagined as a purest idea of that.

I am struck by the way that I have grown up in an Appalachia that is so narrowly and inaccurately defined, no matter how you approach it. There's the mistaken grandeur of mountains that are, in fact, eroded highlands, and there's the misapprehension that the heavy scarring of ancient land is somehow less noble than towering peaks. This matters to me, almost more than I care to admit, that I can recover and reclaim the majesty of erosion and scarring. This is, to be sure, not the same thing as reclamation, which itself would suppose not only that mountains are better than valleys but also that mountains can be measured with a best-fit-arc and formed from fill and graded by machines. Instead, I find myself urgently interested in recognizing just what I am, just where I come from, and just how that came to be. I care in mighty ways about the definitions of my region, how limiting they are, and how I have often felt pulled along the spine of the Appalachians, all along the highlands, largely to the places that are not mountains precisely, but instead to the fertile lands beneath them.

Let me put this another way: I love nothing more than looking from the peak of a high range across the lands below; it is not the mountain I love but the perspective. If I can admit it, I am drawn to regard the places like those I come from, the highlands that receive little credit for being themselves, as constantly thought of as in need of recovery, reclamation, and new growth. That's ingrained in me, the message always implied by the landscapes of my birth, which are always described as scarred. I am no fan of scarring. I am no fan of unwelcome growth. I am no fan of false definitions. I have been learning the vitality of recognizing just what things are and have been, even as I find myself uprooted from all sense of what I thought I was.

I certainly had the meningioma when we first came to Prince Edward Island, might even have had it when we lived in France, perhaps a tiny little bump creeping out of the lining of my brain. Nothing had dimmed my vision yet, but growth is slow for such things, perhaps all things. It would be three more years before I returned to Pennsylvania and recognized it as home, another three before I started thinking seriously about Appalachia, almost another decade before I started reckoning with myself as a battered and eroded man in midlife who needed to understand so many geographies, who would be ready to link both his home geology and his personal medical history and declare, half triumphantly and half beseechingly, *this is not a mountain.*

CHAPTER 3

Marginal Appalachia

On a mid-November day, warm for the week before Thanksgiving, I walked the family farm in a breeze reminiscent of spring, or perhaps the last breath before autumn gives way to winter. The brown-dried prairie grasses of the upper fields rustled as I walked the northern edge of the field, near the rusting highway fence that separates the farm from the bypass. Cars hurtled by, driving their own wind and, as I always seem to notice on return visits these days, contradicted my memory of a quiet childhood through constant whooshing, the unmuffled roar of motorcycles, and the rattling and banging of heavy trucks hauling loads. Higher up in the forest capping the farm, trees finally muffled the highway sounds. The fine ribbon of another bypass shimmered in the distance through the sun haze, the rush of those cars also carried by the winds, but lower and blending in. The grasses whispered an echo of the highways, or I hope, a counterpoint. Gunshots rang in the distance, sporadic, measured—hunters sighting-in rifles for the first day of deer season, a week away.

I walked through the upper fields at first in a nostalgic stupor, entranced by November weather that mixed hope and doom. It was warm enough to be spring, and the wind encouraged the illusion of coming good weather instead of the last twitch of autumn. I found myself thinking about how often I long for empty acres to roam now that I live most of the year within the borders of a struggling small city two and a half hours to the north. The farm always feels far away from all of that, encircled by the highways but somehow as immune from the plight of struggling Appalachian towns as it is reminiscent of foolish pastoral cliché.

My trance soon ended, however, anger replacing wonder as I began to notice scraps of plastic tape strewn about like the worst kind of litter or vandalism. Knotted and clumped and tethered in the grasses, and through the tree line that separates the farm from the neighboring Christmas tree plantation, neon orange plastic ribbon flapped in the breeze. Everywhere, I saw survey tape, markers from a gas exploration company. Marcellus crews had been measuring, preparing, readying the land for mighty thumper trucks, dynamite charges, and other rumblings covered by the term *seismic testing*. They had been here, had walked the same route I walked, and not long ago.

I came to realize that the survey tape approximated the borders of the property. Permission had no doubt come from previous owners who had retained subsurface rights when they sold the farm to the people who sold the farm to my parents. Because of the separation of land ownership and mineral rights, my parents had no say in drilling, mining, or exploration. Land remained untouched by miracle or more likely low wellhead prices. Throughout my childhood, there had been only two gas wells on the farm, the traditional straight-bore, old-school sort. There had been no need to fracture shale for these, as they just sucked up the gas from relatively shallow deposits, one in the middle of the steepest sledding hill in the lower pasture, the other in the upper fields just around the corner from my father's hunting stand. They always seemed just a feature of the landscape, something that had come with the place, markers of certain locations that helped me triangulate myself when I emerged disoriented from the forest.

At the highest point of the farm that November day, I found slats of rough pine pounded into the prairie grass, into the farm's old cornfields my father had restored to nature a few years before, switching them from the interval of crops into the regular cover of primeval meadow. Each pine slat had black numbers magic-markered across the top, together signaling where boxes should be placed, devices that would measure the vibrations of small explosions meant to create an artificial echoing eye that would gaze on the layers of Devonian deposition from the ancient Acadian Mountains. The explosions would map out long-ago seas, now turned gaseous and valuable. The plastic survey tape traced the waves of that ancient shoreline and signaled something simple: dig here.

The pine spike pulled free easily that day, straight up from the prairie. I windmilled it into the breeze-blown grasses. The pine spike flipped end over end, then disappeared into the dry grasses, gone, futilely gone because there were dozens more— pine spikes and plastic survey tape commanding someone to thump here, dig here, all will be well here. I was surrounded by the gunshots, the wind, the roads, two highways, bypasses around the farm and the town and Appalachia, asphalt rivers for the heavy rigs and thumper trucks and drilling crews and money, at least maybe for a while. The wind, still gentle. That last touch of autumn. That coming winter, the last one before I'd learn about my own seismic turmoil. That period when prairie grasses are dry enough to spark and burn.

Before I return once again to turmoil, I want to think about the rage of that day, about the contrasting moment of my walk around the uncommon beauty of an unexpectedly warm afternoon, about the peace of visiting the home that I compare all others to, and about finding that someone else had driven stakes into it. There's something righteous in my anger. I cannot feel badly about my sense of affront and outrage. How dare they do this to my farm, my home, to me? How dare they apply survey lines that mark where the cuts will be, use magic eyes to peer beneath the surface and find what they want? How dare they make plans to excavate and pretend that nothing will be changed afterward?

Yet the truth is that people have been drawing lines on Appalachia for a long time. The survey flags on the family farm, those were lines, literal ones to be used to make money. Figurative maps are drawn too, as in *lines in the sand*, about who and what matters most in the region. Most of the time, those lead to motives that lead to more maps based on money. In Appalachia, people often seem to matter only in the way they can be defined as producers of wealth, rarely for themselves but instead for the people who draw the maps.

Many maps govern what Appalachia is and how we think about it. Recently, electoral maps have mattered a lot, with Appalachia being defined by national newscasters as *those people* who voted for *that guy*, followed by lots of reporting on the antiquated practices of people who, curiously, still suffer the application of hillbilly stereotypes. Forever, it seems, people whose place on a map lies outside of Appalachia have assigned particular tropes to those who live within. J. D. Vance, he of the runaway memoir *Hillbilly Elegy*, somehow became a guide to these most recent maps, pointing the nation through familiar routes and stereotypes in the guise of explaining Appalachia to the rest of the country. And, yeah, it isn't too hard to find evidence that Appalachia is what the nation thinks it is, but you do have to find it among the many ways Appalachia is also not what everyone thinks it is—and finding it is often a reminder that plenty of lines exist in the national imagination that prevent the region from ever breaking free from its stereotypes.

Appalachia is today defined by a map, one first established by the passing of the Appalachian Regional Development Act of 1965, the culmination of the work done by the Appalachian Regional Commission in outlining a big chunk of the country that struggled economically, that had infant and general mortality far beyond the rest of the country, suffered poor healthcare access in general, lagged behind in education, had poor transportation infrastructure, and was, as the report claims, "a region apart."

Large portions of this ARC map follow the lines drawn in the early twentieth century by writers like Horace Kephart and Joseph C. Campbell, those chroniclers of the curiosity of Appalachia who wound up defining where and what Appalachia was. If you think about *where* Appalachia is, you're probably thinking about where Kephart, Campbell, and others defined the "Southern Highlands." If you think about *what* Appalachia is, you're probably also thinking about characteristics that these nineteenth- and early twentieth-century writers "observed" and defined.

Campbell's 1921 book, *The Southern Highlander and His Homeland,* includes a foldout map that isolates the region as stretching down from the southern border of Pennsylvania through West Virginia, then including parts of Kentucky, Virginia, North Carolina, South Carolina, Tennessee, Georgia, and Alabama. Campbell argues that "the lines by which the Southern Highlands are defined are not chosen arbitrarily. They correspond for the most part with boundaries of natural divisions; on the east with the face of the Blue Ridge . . . and on the west with the western escapement of the Allegheny-Cumberland Plateau." Campbell's core definition of this proto-Appalachia follows the rocks and is scoped by the way mountains figure as defining limits of the landscape.

Campbell also notes that his northern border is "in part purely political," referencing the history of the Mason-Dixon line, itself a survey line that means something far different than what people often think. If we think about it at all, we tend to recall the Mason-Dixon as the separator of North and South, a moral line between those who believed in slavery and those who understood it as abomination to humanity. Indeed, in the context of the Civil War the Mason-Dixon works as a general separator between the free states and the Confederacy, except for a couple of complications. For one thing, West Virginia is mostly south of the line, even though that state came into existence precisely because it seceded from Virginia to be part of the Union. For another, the Mason-Dixon line actually predates the United States of America altogether. Work on the line started in 1763 and finished in 1782 when America was just getting going. In fact, the line had nothing to do with morality. Instead, it was a taxation line, precisely separating the colonies of Pennsylvania and Maryland because the founders of those two places—William Penn and Lord Baltimore—were in dispute over who got to levy taxes where.

The mapping of the Mason-Dixon line was a pre–Revolutionary War plan concerning the economies of those two colonies and only later seen as the dividing line between North and South, slavery and freedom. When the line was first drawn, what we now think of as Appalachia would have been a tremendous wilderness, populated mostly by the American Indians who hadn't thought to draw lines measured in tax revenue. In a sense, the Mason-Dixon was a line of demarcation on this land by European economies, claiming it for white settlers, particularly the rich ones, and specifically claiming that the dominion of land would be defined forevermore by the dollars that it could raise. The line meant possession, even as the region would remain an outpost for many years. Appalachia perpetuated conceptually as an imaginary relic or as a contemporary assertion that those in the mountains are fallen human beings in need of reclamation and valuable only as measured by the dollars they produce from the rocks beneath them.

As Edwin Danson writes in *Drawing the Line*, the mechanical prowess of the Mason-Dixon enterprise was also about modernity, or rather modernity's triumph over landscape. Drawing this line was not easy and was in fact a solution of the long-standing longitude problem. Navigators had gridded the globe with intersecting latitude and longitude coordinates but, alas, had no way to figure out which longitude number applied to which specific location when they were actually standing on or sailing around the earth. Figuring out how to map longitude on real terrain marked a massive advancement in European methods of dividing natural landscapes through artificial borders.

The Mason-Dixon line could only be drawn because engineers finally figured out how to do longitude on dry land. As

Danson writes, "In human terms, the Mason-Dixon line was the eighteenth century's most ambitious geodetic survey, and a project without precedent. The men who finally solved the boundary line problem were astronomers, men of science." More than that, the men who figured out how to draw that line on the heavily wooded mountain terrain of the North American frontier figured out how to use a line to define commerce, and that's been what the Mason-Dixon, the ARC, and maybe maps in general have really meant so often. The Mason-Dixon meant something economic, immediately and forever. First, about taxes. Later, about slaves. Now, about areas of the country that matter more and less.

John C. Campbell himself recognized how the Mason-Dixon line suggested the exclusion of Northern Appalachia forty years before the ARC even became a twinkle in a geographer's eye. "Though our study is limited to the territory just described," he writes, "we would repeat that the Southern Highlands should not be disassociated in thought from their northern extension." Campbell suggests that certain geological similarities extend farther north, that even though "the mountain character of the Blue Ridge Belt loses itself in the modest altitude of South Mountain in Pennsylvania," he could imagine making a case for the rocks elsewhere in the Appalachian chain. He links geology and people, offering a quick riff on the ancient seas that preceded the orogenies that made the mountains. He then goes on to declare a remarkably Victorian metonymy between landscape and residents:

> Those who would understand a people must know the land in which they dwell, and a careful study of the topography of the Southern Highlands will repay the painstaking student. A study of elevations,

depressions, and slopes is a dry task in and of itself, but if the narrow winding valley and broad fertile plain, the isolated mesa and expansive plateau, the steep slope and towering peak be translated into terms of life, the study becomes of absorbing interest as the forces are revealed which have influenced some groups to face the future, and others to linger in the past.

His definitions here both ultimately exclude Northern Appalachia from consideration, as he goes on for the rest of the book to define only the Southern Highlands, and also reinforce the notion of Appalachia as a literal and conceptual barrier to modernity. The Mason-Dixon line conquered the landscape in this way first, modern science shaping geography for taxes. Delimiting the Southern Highlands pushed that further, working from the assumption that modernity is a certain thing, and Appalachia is not it.

Campbell evokes the idea that the landscape of the region presented a hardship of travel that separates settlers from people who stopped, an important distinction in the mythology of American progress. In essence, Appalachians didn't follow the westward urge and probably were the brothers, sisters, mothers, and fathers who wondered why anyone would bother struggling over such rough terrain. They dug in, scraped out homes, and ignored commands to go West and seek modern fortunes.

In a sense, Campbell sets the stage to consider the alleged insularity of the region as a relic of its settlement. This notion has been fetishized as devotion to coal, even though it is damaging to people and place, and enacted by devotion to politicians like Trump, who activate the anxiety of being left behind in the American dream. This is the backward orientation of the Appalachian Imaginary, a perversity of the American capacity for motion. Appalachia is the middle space—Flyover Country—trapped between the wealthy, foundational East and the potential for wealth to the West. Appalachia is portrayed as always stuck in itself.

When I read the text of the original 1964 report from the Appalachian Regional Commission, I find that precise sentiment established from the start. "Appalachia is a region apart—geographically and statistically," it reads. "It is a mountain land body upthrust between the prosperous Eastern seaboard and the industrial Middle West—a highland region which sweeps diagonally across 10 states from Northern Pennsylvania to Northern Alabama." The introduction goes on to briefly outline the unrealized potential economic benefits of the region—forests, minerals, coal, and gas—and the poverty of its residents. The report identifies Appalachia as lagging behind, pointing out that even the urban areas that do better than the rural portions still fare worse than non-Appalachian urban areas. The word *hinterland* is deployed frequently, as in: "Prosperity in the urban centers cannot reach desired levels unless the hinterlands also prosper." Hinterlands are to be feared, as they are unmodern, holding urbanity back, and resisting progress itself.

Ideas about Appalachians appear in the report with a remarkable consistency to the language of Campbell and Kephart. The perspective presented in the report is toward aid and development, but the images are stock, as diminishing to Appalachians as they are ultimately clinical:

> Graphs and tables can hardly relate the acutely personal story of a child in a remote valley, his horizon of opportunity limited to the enclosing hills; nor the despair of his father, who, idled by forces beyond his

control and seeing no prospect of future development, must live month in and month out with the vision of that child repeating his own history. This report can only present statistical evidence, the inanimate pictures, and hope that they are as convincing as the visitor to Appalachia finds the realities.

The statistical evidence includes poverty, little urban growth, lack of education, low standards of living, and bad infrastructure. The report also makes it clear that among the most painful realities of Appalachia is that it contains a high concentration of natural resources that have not been adequately developed. The report suggests that the "exploitation of natural resources" should be the first step to the salvation of the people of the region. I'm sure, of course, that *exploitation* was not intended to carry the darker intonations that it carries today. I am also sure that the effective meaning of *exploitation* was no different from those intonations and designated the desire to dig up the region, perversely as a way to offer progress to the people destined to be left behind in a landscape thus exploited.

This PARC report clearly shows the map of Appalachia as a map of poverty. Congress pretty much drew a thick, squiggly line around the poorest counties in the Mid-Atlantic, and that became Appalachia. The line implies that the territory is filled with battered trailer homes, abandoned and weed-choked mine portals, Confederate battle flags, and Trump signs, some still stuck in the earth more than a year after his misbegotten election. Already, the notion of Appalachia has spread. The ARC map could be seen as a warning, a demarcation that signals to outsiders something akin to *abandon hope all ye who enter here.*

The ARC map also is not stable. Comparing the map in the original report to Campbell's Southern Highlands suggests a slow creep of this anomalous border, a few new counties glommed on in the South, plus the fresh inclusion of the bulk of Pennsylvania. Just a few months after the report was approved by Congress in 1965, thirteen counties in the Southern Tier of New York were added. In 1967, twenty counties in Mississippi were added, plus two each from Alabama, New York, and Tennessee. An Ohio county was added in 1990. Another Mississippi one in 1991. Two from Alabama, two from Georgia, two from Virginia, and one from Mississippi in 1998. Two each from Kentucky and Mississippi in 2002. Three from Kentucky and three more from northeastern Ohio, plus two each from Tennessee and Virginia in 2008.

The region of the ARC remains defined by the imagery of its earliest chroniclers, even as it continually spreads in geography as politicians recognize the value of federal dollars that come with Appalachian designations. Simply put, the ARC lines don't indicate anything explicitly geographical. They're not map lines based on rivers or mountains, even as Appalachia lies above the geology of a portion of the Appalachians. State lines aren't part of the ARC design: some states have just a few counties within, and only West Virginia is completely within it. Some areas within the ARC are mountainous, some relatively flat. Nor does the ARC map really define a continuous cultural region, particularly when you compare, say, northeast Ohio to eastern Kentucky, places different from each other in so many ways.

Places within the ARC share a common feature of being broke, and many people within it struggle economically. It troubles me to think of how I and so many others are defined by an encircling line that separates us from the rest of the country precisely because we are less economically able. It troubles me further to think about how that ensnaring sets up conditions that let people outside the line do things inside the line that make them richer and Appalachia poorer. That is, indeed, the official origin of the region's designation, and the contemporary dynamic that works to maintain the poverty within. Origin stories are hard to shake, so once Appalachia was defined as poor, then poor it must continue to be.

Worst of all, the language of economy always makes it clear that the things inflicted on Appalachia are *good*. Development. Opportunity. Industry. So you might also think about the ARC as a line that gives license to exploit in the name of economic development. When I was a grad student at WVU, that state briefly changed the slogan on welcome signs near its border from the evocative "Wild and Wonderful" to "Open for Business," a phrase that I could only hear as a desire to be exploited again. Consider that back in 2015, the state of New York planned to ban fracking everywhere except in the Southern Tier, which is, not surprisingly, also the part of New York that lies within the ARC. Also not surprising: it's where the gas is, where the people are poor, and where a case therefore can be made that extractive industry is in the region's best interest, even if the wealth from that fracking would go to companies headquartered elsewhere.

Here's a funny thing: arbitrary lines create arbitrary distinctions. In a 1997 article revisiting the "Realities of Deprivation" outlined in the original 1964 ARC report, Andrew Isserman suggests that the border decisions of Appalachia distort just how far apart the region happens to be from average America. He argues that the inclusion of cities like Columbus, Cincinnati, and Cleveland—all of which are just outside the official ARC line—would have changed several standards outlined as problematic from the outset. More or less, Isserman suggests that Appalachian poverty might be more reflective of typical American patterns than the ARC implies. It all depends on what you include. With just a slight expansion of the ARC borders, Appalachian demographics would start to align with the rest of the country, make it look less like a region apart and more like a sign of more common, though still equally unjust, patterns of rural poverty shared in the Midwest, the Northeast, and the West.

This is not to say, of course, that attending to the very real problems of what we know of as Appalachia is bad. Quite the reverse. The ARC has led to considerable progress in several areas, even as the region still lags behind national averages in general mortality, higher-education attainment, and broadband access (something never imagined in 1964). Still, degraded imagery connects with the word Appalachia, and that creates a national sense of the people who are *that thing*, making it easier to think about how the exploitation of people and resources must be considered as vital to such a forsaken land and people.

This is all quite familiar, of course, and not just because the potential economic benefits and potential environmental dangers of extractive industry are a common discussion throughout Appalachia. Money over environment has long been a thing, money over people too, even though the language used often suggests that more exploitation is good for the people. The abandoned sites across Appalachia are worth noting—crumbling mine portals, rusting gas pumpjacks, and shattered-window steel mills—since the bust of departed industry suggests future departures and deeper busts to come. Still, those who get to draw the lines argue that the lines work, that all we need is a return to those good old days, that the collapse is not the thing, that the money can still be there (for *them*) as long as we recognize that the ARC shows us all where to dig. Maybe resistance sits in recognizing how Appalachia has no stable borders and how it has been repeatedly redrawn to benefit people who keep themselves safely on the other side of the ARC.

My outrage on the day of those blowing grasses atop the farm, of the distant automotive murmurs, and of the discovery of clear invasive intent lay within my own unsettled nature. I'd been roaming for a while at that point, even if my wife and I had been settled in northwestern Pennsylvania for five years. My job there had been going well, and it seemed like we would no longer be chucking things again to move to Arizona, to France, to wherever. I understand, as well, that I feel no small loss when I think about stability, as I relish the discovery of new places. But I want a home, a place, that center that John Lane finds in Spartanburg, that Wendell Berry finds in Kentucky, that Thoreau finds outside Concord, that Janisse Ray finds in Georgia, that the most famous writer from my hometown, Edward Abbey, finds in the Utah desert.

In *Desert Solitaire,* Abbey nobly rips survey stakes free from Arches National Monument, determined to at least delay the construction of a new road that would bring in his despised industrial tourists. He knew what I felt on the top of the family farm, that survey stakes establish a claim to ownership and use. The stakes on the farm claimed my home ground for someone else. Or, rather, the stakes demonstrated that the claim had been made long ago, that whatever surface designation I might feel, the truth of the deep was the truth that counts. Gas matters more than home, economy matters more than people, and so forth. This is not an unfamiliar story and is perhaps even worn out. But I see it also in terms of the recognition of the tyranny of maps, how the maps we read are the ones made by the people who won, likely by the people who won precisely because of how they defined the maps. The survey stakes on the farm made it clear what kind of map mattered, and it wasn't the one I preferred or held allegiance to. This is one way that I feel fully Appalachian. My home, myself, and the value of my body and geography have been drawn by someone else, and always the final map in some way excludes my say.

Near the highest point on the farm, I walked past one of several new gas wells recently tapped into the ground as wellhead prices climbed, this one tucked into a stand of trees, the loss of which my father particularly lamented. At one time, my wife and I had hoped to build a house there, before we learned we'd both lose the jobs we'd found in the Laurel Highlands—she because her private school decided French wasn't worthwhile anymore, informing her of that coming loss while she was seven months pregnant with our first child, and me because the university where I worked decided to hire in my field but couldn't see past the taint of my nontenure track status. For my father, I believe, losing this building site was the greatest insult. With it went any hope for grandchildren growing up on the farm or a summer cabin on the back forty or even just the maintenance of the woods my father has walked for decades.

Throughout these woods, small chunks of sandstone and shale have worked their way to the surface over time. I found a suitable specimen, then chucked the rock at the brine tank, which rang dully, unsatisfying, so unlike a bell. After cutting through the woods past the old tree stand where I shot my first and only deer, I emerged into the back field and paused to listen—first, to the chatter of winter birds, then to the background noise of the two major highways visible from the farm. Nowhere, save the now lost building spot, could I escape the sound of rushing cars. I counted the structures on the horizon: one coal-fired power plant, three cell towers, and at least half a dozen radio towers. My mood was souring, some kind of self-righteous indignation mounting even before I considered the string of high-power transmission lines that cut diagonally through the center of the upper fields, carrying electricity from the coal-fired plant on the horizon to the grid. The farm functions as conduit, part of the super-highway network that digs up, burns, and sends away the transformed landscape of our homes to light lamps and cook microwave popcorn.

It was in this mood that I found the pine stakes, and it was in this mood that I pinwheeled one of them into the high grasses. However powerless this effort may have been, I felt a certain pride in the removal of the stake. I thought about Abbey and Arches Park and the Pyrrhic victory of temporary blockade, of being able to annoy those who map the courses of new roads and resent any opposition. Here, I suppose, lies the true folly of the literary. I considered my act as narratively akin to his, and with Abbey's origins in my hometown—he was a graduate of my high school, in fact—my small vandalism made me feel, I guess, Abbey-esque and powerful.

Self-satisfied, I walked off the hilltop, down into the fields beside the house, and discovered the work of another crew, this one from the electric company, which had visited a few weeks earlier to reclaim the right-of-way for the high-power lines that cut across the farm. The fields below had begun to gradually return to forest since my father took the farm out of cultivation. Annually tilled fields of corn and hay had been ceded to autumn olive, an invasive shrub forming forearm-thick gnarls, which, elsewhere on the farm, my father had recently been working to eradicate. Throughout the upper fields, I had come across clearings where his brush hog had splintered and chopped the shrubs away to stumps. Directly beneath the power lines, however, everything had been stripped away. The electric company had brought powerful mowers and leveled a seventy-five-foot wide swath. Everything had been ground to bare earth. Grass, shrubs, trees—whatever had been there was no more. And, now, I discovered that the path gave an unobstructed view of the power plant, located seven straight-line miles away. From this lower part of the fields, the plant loomed atop the horizon in a place where it had never been visible before.

In the windbreak between the family farm and the neighbor, the crews had felled several oak and cherry trees of notable size. The trees had been cut and left to rot, which is perhaps the most ecological part of the whole enterprise. It seemed a waste to have the logs just lying there, but at least they would break down to replenish the soil in time. Yet it was hard to run my fingers along the forty-five rings of the largest cherry and not feel a heavy and personal loss. The rings dated the tree to 1967, which would mean it sprouted in the same year my parents married, thirteen years before they bought the farm.

Still, I took it as some small sign of hope that among the fallen logs at the property line, I found a half-chewed corncob and a pile of recent raccoon shit. Some kind of quiet protest perhaps—or at least a recognition of what hasn't yet been cut away. In the night's darkness, discovering the insult of the felled tree, some raccoon cartographer decided to mark land in a way that refuses to honor the right of commerce.

Maps don't measure in this way, this loss that I consider cultural: a tree felled by a sort of ecological colonialism that considers a forty-five-year-old tree only as a hypothetical cost, as an interference to future profit. The cut made it clear who owns and controls the land, and what surface rights really amount to. All I had to do was look up the hillside or down, following the path cut wide through the fields. Prairie grass and shrub brush can restore only so much; a mower reclaims as it wishes.

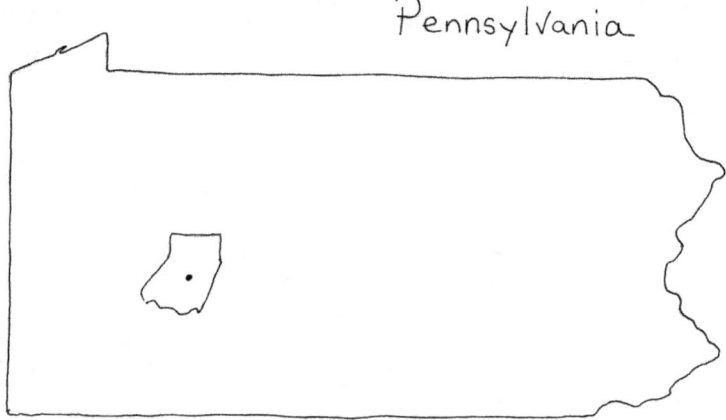

CHAPTER 4

Appalachian Flesh, Appalachian Bone

In the summer after ninth grade, my chubbiness melted and my shortness grew away. I'd stretched to five feet nine inches, no monster, but tall enough to imagine a towering future. I weighed only 120 pounds, so my own bones poked at my skin, particularly the knobs of my wrists. There, I could easily overlap my index finger and thumb, pinching across the narrow space and wondering when it might thicken into the beefy farmer's muscles of my father. I didn't know that I'd reached my full height or that I'd eventually swap the anxiety of the scrawny for the worry of middle-aged paunch.

That summer my friends and I spent many hours roaming across the family farm, exploring and fancying ourselves as something existential, or at least a sort of limited false existentialism accessible to nascent high schoolers. We all came from upper middle-class families that created children drawn to such notions of existentialism, even as our lives were bereft of the suffering that goes along with it. Of the seven in the group, six had at least one parent who was a professor at the local university, and the other had a chiropractor father and a mother who happened to be the AP English teacher at the high school. Even my father, the farmer, was really a biology professor by day.

We were all Appalachian kids by grace of our childhoods, half of us even by birth, yet we still formed a motley crew that more or less called out as not-hillbilly: one friend with parents from Greece, another with parents from India, another the child of a mixed-race marriage, one with a single mama who taught collegiate music, one from a big Mormon family, one a star competitive swimmer, and one a kind of farmer's kid (that was me).

In the brush beside the farm stream, we stumbled across bones. Hidden from the farmhouse by the steep hillside, my friends and I could easily have imagined ourselves lost in the deep woods, kicking away dried grass and carefully pulling aside spiked thistle until the intact skeleton of a deer emerged. Its grittiness offered a morbid and alluring invocation of mortality. Leathered hide clung to the bones, tatters of dried skin and bristled hair. The smell wasn't bad, just the faint sweetness of long-rotted flesh. So we wrapped our fingers around the antlers and pulled. The last fingers of grass held for a moment, then tore. We dragged the deer out of the stream valley straight up to the house. We felt this would be a possession worth the effort, even if its value was not yet clear.

When we first found the deer, it was my friends who had wanted to claim it. I'd wondered why, even balked inwardly at the rightness of the act. Partly, the deer was just another carcass to me. My father had killed many over the years, driving a neat hole through their lungs with his trusty .30-06. A dead deer hung in the backyard walnut tree each winter, its smooth muscle exposed to the air after my father yanked the skin and hide free. He hacked it first into rough quarters with a sharp hatchet and a large knife, then he and my mother used smaller knives inside the kitchen to divide the hunks into cuts of meat for our freezer. Our dogs gnawed the leftover bones for weeks. My brother and I had each shot deer too, as well as squirrels, rabbits, pheasant, groundhog, and sometimes throngs of gathering autumn starlings that fell in clumps after each shotgun blast.

None of my friends had likely ever shot a gun or even touched one, save John. Sometime during elementary school, I'd snuck him into my parents' bedroom, withdrew a leather gun case from beneath their bed, carefully unzipped it, and showed him the smooth walnut stock of one of my father's rifles. There was magic in that moment, the revelation of the dangerous, the violation of house rules to never touch a gun without my father present, the sweet tonic of gun oil, and the burl of polished wood. I couldn't possibly have known then about how my own mortality would rely later on John's gathered expertise, this boy who would grow to be a radiation oncologist and one of the first people I would call after my adult diagnosis.

As children, my friends did not know the feel of a dead animal, had never killed or slaughtered. The farm had raised me differently. I had watched chickens flop through the yard after a hatchet decapitation, had plunged their still warm bodies into boiling water, then plucked sodden feathers free from their scalded flesh. To me, the deer skeleton we found was just another dead animal, even as it drew my friends in, made them adamant. In particular, a girl for whom I still harbored desperate adolescent love wanted that deer, and so I wanted it too. My friends sensed their own magic in the unfamiliar proximity to decay. It was this, I believe, they wished to possess, maybe even contain.

We dragged the animal to the house, deposited it by the back door. My father came outside and regarded the skeleton with a level of pride that mixed hunter and biologist. *That's a big one*, he said, *and it's all there*. Immediately, he noticed the tatters of flesh clinging to the bones, smelled the unmistakable cloud of rot. He suggested that we find an anthill and drag the deer atop it. The ants would emerge, he explained, to eat away the remaining flesh. In a few months, the bones would be picked clean, and we'd be left with a pristine, entire skeleton. Ants would work as a kind of natural process of *mos teutonicus*, the medieval practice of boiling away royal flesh to safeguard remains. Long ago, bodies in need of transport had to be reduced to bone to prevent rot, as the appearance of decay was a visual reminder of the wickedness of impermanence. First boiled, then flayed, the bone became free of flesh, of putrefaction, of the reminder of ever-present mortality. Afterward the skeleton could be carried long distances for proper burial without fear of degeneration.

At the farm we followed my father's directions and dragged the deer across the driveway to the old orchard. We found an anthill a few yards away from the compost heap and centered the deer across the opening. We would return. We would check it often. We would experience the enlightenment of excarnation.

To map out is to plan, as mapping is really another way of saying you're planning to do something. What is, after all, the purpose of a map other than to bring order to the disorder of the organic—dirt, soil, rock, and the unseeable insides of your own skull?

First I went to the ophthalmologist, who mapped my vision by holding a sheet of graph paper in front of my nose. I remember it as something emblazoned with a pharmaceutical company's logo, a freebie to the office with a legitimate diagnostic function, called an Amsler grid. There is a dark point in the center where the lines converge.

Look there, he told me, and I did.

He handed me a pen and asked me to mark where the blind spot was. Just below center and to the left of center, the lines disappeared in a haze of gray. I can't say that this surprised me, since I'd been noticing the way Calvin's head disappeared in the books I'd been reading to my older son for at least a year. Still, the precision of the grid made things suddenly clear, or rather made clear what was no longer. Without looking away, I drew a wavering line around the absence. It's hard to draw a good shape without looking at it, but if I changed the focus on my vision, I'd lose the empty spot.

My doctor looked at the grid. In a film, he'd have stroked his chin. Maybe said *hmmm*. In real life, he launched into his rapid-fire Brooklyn accent, explaining the terms of what this first map showed. *Retinopathy*, he said, which meant he suspected a bubble on the back of my eye. No big deal. An easy repair, he said, then referred me to a specialist in Erie.

The specialist in Erie mapped my eyes with two machines, one of which involved an injection of dye into my veins, something to colorize and create contrast that would make trouble easier to find. He warned me that it would stain my pee to a shocking hue, but I still wasn't prepared for later that morning when I hiked through the dunes of Presque Isle State Park on the shores of Lake Erie, zipped down behind a shrubby tree, and let forth a stream of highlighter-yellow piss that left a fluorescent puddle on the ground that I feared would get me in trouble for marking territory so unnaturally.

The specialist found nothing remarkable during his tests. Still, he peppered me with a series of questions.

Take any drugs?

No.
He persisted. *Cocaine?*
No.
Meth?
No.
A little Viagra for fun?
No.

Satisfied that I hadn't wrecked my eye through bad behavior, he continued in a breezy way, unconcerned. He suggested that maybe an MRI was in order. In all his years of practice, he'd only once seen an issue like this wind up being neurological, but it would be worth checking. On the way out, the office clerk somehow found a way to tell me that President Obama made her ashamed of her history as an army veteran.

The MRI meant lying still in a plastic tube for forty-five minutes at the local hospital. The giant magnet spun around my head, and I listened to the macabre hip-hop beat of the sensors and motors. I did not then liken myself to the ground beneath my family farm, but I recognized the sudden turn toward personal cartography, the electronic eyes and computer extrapolations that have become one way that my very self is defined. I am as I am mapped. The moment before I crawled onto the MRI tray, I was a man with a vision problem. As soon as the resonance of my own internal water fed data to the computer, I became a man with a brain tumor, a *meningioma* that I would struggle to pronounce for at least a week and, then, struggle to recognize as my permanent self.

About a week after the MRI, my wife and I drove the hour and a half down I-79 to Pittsburgh. We snaked off the highway right after the skyline appeared around a bend, the mountains no longer blocking the view of the skyscrapers. We entered the portal beneath the hospital to park in the garage undergoing renovation, jackhammers rattling constantly and billowing construction tarpaulins hiding the work from view.

Upstairs, we sat in a dingy exam room at Allegheny General Hospital. A white-haired doctor used trembling fingers to click through nearly a hundred images from my brain scan, slice after magnetic slice of my brain. I remember worrying about those hands. I thought about tremors and scalpels and the sensitivity of my own brain: this seemed like a bad mix. I remember impatience also, this surgeon seemingly unable to find something that had been made so clear in the radiology report: *intensely enhancing mass; the principal concern is that of a tiny meningioma.*

Eventually, he remarked calmly that he wasn't used to seeing MRIs with such low-level resolutions, rebuking the small town where I live, the quality of its equipment. This was that part of Appalachia, after all, that did not count itself as such, and he was a neurosurgeon, and I'd had my scans taken at a regional outpost, an *Appalachian* hospital or, just as bad, a *Rust Belt* hospital that struggled to manage its new billing system, which would often not send bills until a year after treatment. It suddenly seemed like a bad idea to have trusted their MRI equipment, even if ARC funds were supposed to improve community hospitals like the one in my home.

The surgeon clicked on quietly. We watched from the chairs beside his computer, an uncomfortable stretching of my neck while I tried to reckon what I was seeing. On the screen, ghostly images of my brain flowed into one another, the neurosurgeon's navigation moving the view deeper, shallower, back in for a close-up. My brain seemed fluid and animated, melting into itself, surging almost as if alive.

He found it. Just a little speck, a brighter white than the vessels around it. He clicked back and forth, pointed it out to me. He spoke calmly. He stepped out and brought in another surgeon, one whose expertise was more suited to the particular location of my tumor. His name was Aziz. He seemed in a hurry, as I would learn he often was, even when he stuck around to patiently answer questions. That first day, his phone kept ringing, and he had to step out to take a call, then return. Eventually, I'd think of E. M. Forster's Dr. Aziz, and worry about the literary overtones of shared names, of mysterious violent actions in dark caves, of despair and alienation both literary and alive.

Aziz shook our hands. He pulled out his cell phone and made a few calls, then disappeared to meet other patients. We now had an appointment in just a couple of hours to see Happ, the neuro-ophthalmologist downstairs. He and Aziz would later work in tandem to slice me open and do the work that needed to be done. We also earned a third appointment for later that afternoon, after finishing with Happ, to see the oncologist who would oversee my radiation treatments: this had been coordinated seemingly all at once, and we were on our way. When we left Allegheny General Hospital, we merged into the line of traffic rushing across elevated highways heading north, up the hills and out of the Allegheny River valley into the new, prosperous spread of suburbs where I would meet the third doctor in my new team.

I saw my own bones frequently as a child, backlighted and ghostly on the dark films of periodic X-rays. I don't recall myself as particularly clumsy, but I did find myself often perched atop an examination bed at the ER. I have recently thought of this often, as my middle-aged life has been measured in no small part by hours atop similar tables.

I was six years old the first time I broke an arm. We hadn't moved out to the farm yet, but I spent plenty of time there while my parents worked to make the house livable. A friend had come with me one day, and the two of us crawled around the barn, eventually winding up hanging on the front paddock gate. We began by perching our toes on a lower slat, falling back, and catching ourselves with fingertips on the top board. I remember the giddiness of free fall, then a slight twist in the stomach as my back rushed toward the ground followed by the solidity of my fingers catching wood.

I don't remember falling or precisely how it happened—whether my friend shook the fence in an act of fervor or whether I simply failed to catch the gate and instead flung myself on the concrete threshold between barn and yard. While I cannot remember the impact, I can easily recall what followed: a sharp pain, then the dull sensation of a heavy, useless limb, an arm suddenly external from my consciousness.

In third grade, I climbed onto a fallen log that crossed the stream at the bottom of the hill below the farmhouse, not far from where my friends and I later found the deer skeleton. I stuck my arms in the air, walking as if on a balance beam, then slipped on the mossy bark. Moments after landing on a stack of rotting boards in the grass of the lower pasture, I raised my right arm into the air and felt the unmistakable heft of a break. I walked back to the house, tearless, and informed my mother that I'd broken my arm. She did not at first believe me, considering the calm in her nine-year-old. But she knew my arm hurt enough for a trip to the emergency room, where a doctor confirmed broken arm number two, a chip in my elbow.

A few weeks later, still wearing the cast, I chased a ball into the wood-mulched flower garden surrounding my friend John's house. It had been raining, so the wood was slick and my balance was compromised by haste and plaster. I slipped, could not catch myself since one arm was occupied by a ball and the other was out of service. I banged my head on the glass cover of their electric meter.

Dazed, I walked into the driveway, where John looked directly at me and began to cry. When the first drips of blood fell across my face, I began to cry too. His mother was a nurse, and she dragged me into their bathroom and began pouring water onto the wound. Blood filled the sink as she assured me in her heavy Greek accent, *one stitch only, maybe two*, explaining that head wounds always bleed this way.

For my third broken bone, I merely fell out of bed in the middle of the night, smacking my right arm against the heat register. My father called home from Wyoming, in the first leg of a sabbatical tour of the western national parks. My mother filled him in on the news. *Your daughter bought a new puppy. Your youngest son broke his arm again.* I was in the sixth grade, and when I returned to school I listened, mortified, as the teacher explained to the class that *Matt got into a wrestling match with his bedsheets.*

Break number one was on the radial styloid process of my right arm, called a chauffeur's fracture. My age and the severity of the break meant that the arm had to be set under general anesthesia. I lay on the hospital bed, watched the black mask approach my face, smelled the rubber as it covered my mouth, then drew in fumes, a brief spinning in my head before I quickly slipped under.

Break number two was on the radius head of my right arm, which by imperfectly healing helped me learn my right from my left. Faced with the question of turning one way or the other, I learned to check orientation by bending my elbows to reach each hand toward its respective shoulder. With my left, I could lay the palm flat. With my right, the arm stopped short, caught up by new bone, so I could barely brush the shoulder with my fingertips, a permanently limited range of motion.

Break number three was a hairline fracture of the left radius. At my first visit to the emergency room, the doctor guessed that my description correlated with a break, even though the X-ray appeared fine. My prior experience of fractures convinced him to trust my intuition, so he applied a temporary cast. The next day, the orthopedist sawed off the cast to shoot another X-ray. Enough time had passed to allow the thin fracture to open and appear on the film as a bent worm. For the first time, I received a fiberglass cast instead of a plaster one. While light enough to let me almost forget its presence, its gnarled surface also resisted signatures, the ink soaking into the dents and making my friends' practiced scripts as ghostly as the vision of my own bones on the wall of the ER.

On the day that I became a neurosurgical patient, thirty years after my last broken bone, the visit to the neuro-ophthalmological surgeon included several more tests to measure the damage of my optic nerve. I stared into a machine that sent out the report: a thinning in the nerves of my left eye, a sign of atrophy or, better put, nerve death.

I also stared into a semispherical machine that tested my visual fields by projecting tiny dots of light onto a white field. Each time I saw a dot, I clicked a handheld remote. The computer mapped these responses and produced a chart showing each missed flash as a gray X, the accumulation building a gray mass in more or less the exact area I'd circled on the Amsler grid a week before.

An ophthalmological fellow administered the Ishihara test, familiar to anyone who has ever had a decent eye exam. This is the test that shows a circle filled with dots of varying colors and sizes. Within that circle appears a number or shape made up of contrasting dots. The purpose is to test for color perception. I'd always considered this test a breeze, the numbers as clear as if written in bright felt-tipped marker. It seemed that way this time also, until the fellow had me close my right eye. The numbers disappeared. I knew they were there since I had just seen them, but they might as well have been vanished with the wave of a magic wand.

Until this point, I'd remained largely unshaken by the day, determined to show my surgeons how rational and controlled I was, a doctor myself, albeit in literature instead of medicine. The invisibility of these numbers rattled me. Not seeing them was visceral proof of something terribly wrong, proof that the territory of my vision had shifted and could not be ignored.

Indeed, color saturation had been something I'd complained about for years with at least three separate Rust Belt optometrists. The world had just started to seem duller through my left eye. Each time, I'd been rebuffed. Each optometrist had peered into my eye with handheld scopes, and each had said the same thing, *everything's fine* and *you're just getting older.*

The test at Allegheny General confirmed the end of *fine.* Even if the optometrists had seen nothing, had discounted my own sense of the world, the truth of my embodied experience had been reality. In the office at Allegheny General I felt a strange, terrifying, yet still somehow satisfying magic. My eye was color-blind, significantly so. I had not been wrong. But something certainly was wrong, this color blindness a sign of irreversible damage to my optic nerve. The defect seemed so obvious too. How had I not noticed? Or rather, how had I not insisted on the urgency of what I had noticed?

I think of this now as the moment I realized that part of me would always be defined by a new cartography, that diagnostic maps would define the immediate arc of the surgery that, already, I knew would be coming. Indeed, there would be more diagnostic maps.

A full-body CT to check for systemic cancer, requiring that I yank my pants down below my knees, but told to do so beneath the sheet to preserve my modesty, even though I knew the entire corps of whom I am, brain to dick, would soon enough be laid out on display for a team of surgeons and nurses.

An EKG, wires and leads taped to my body and spitting out a ragged line showing my heart's baseline function.

A chemically induced stress test, me walking slowly on a treadmill while an IV dripped an unknown fluid into my veins, flushing my skin, goosing my heart, and making my stomach lurch as if I'd just run as hard as I could.

A second EKG, rushed at my home hospital after the first one was lost, a congenial tech hooking me up to a plastic briefcase contraption and reproducing what had already been determined, that my heart works.

An impromptu Reiki treatment, administered by a shifty yet kind unlicensed practitioner, who ushered me behind the counter to the dim back room of his trinket store in the city where I live, gonging the bell beside his table, then cupping his hands against my left temple to focus energy on my tumor, real heat appearing, maybe just from his hands but maybe not: I hoped against knowledge. *When they do the MRI tomorrow, I wouldn't be surprised if they find nothing,* he told me when I left.

A navigational MRI the next day, the day before surgery, for Aziz to use as a map to reach the tumor that was still there, despite the Reiki.

A CAT scan shortly after surgery, which I remember only as a haze of pain and disembodied voices, technicians looking to make sure the surgeons hadn't slipped up.

Another scan a few hours later, when the aids presented questions to gauge my awareness: *Do you remember being here a few hours ago?* they asked me. *Well, you see, I just had brain surgery,* I said. And they laughed, understanding the joke. They asked me who the president was (still Obama, thank God), what day it was (Wednesday), friendly questions designed to see if the surgeons had nicked anything catastrophic during the surgery.

The walls of my eventual hospital room were covered in charts, time stamps of when I received pain medication (always too late), the volume of spinal fluid dripping through the tubes punched in my skull and back and gathering in a catch basin tied to my bed frame, the slow creep of the clock on the wall, time measuring how soon I could be freed from the hospital and released to long, painful months in the guest bed at home.

I wonder about maps and reality, whether something fails to exist when it hasn't been charted, which I recognize as a desired fantasy. I want it to work like this, that the brain tumor didn't exist because it hadn't been found. It lay in weeds, wrapped and hidden, a skeleton yet to be discovered. Yet of course it was still there, the gathering confusion of my unclear symptoms leading to my first MRI, *just in case,* and then the jarring phone call of what I guess I should also italicize: *that day.*

My friends never looked for the deer skeleton again. I checked on it occasionally, looking in on the ants' progress. My father had been right. By the end of the summer, the tattered flesh had been eaten away, leaving only sun-bleached bone. My friends never saw this, never asked about the skeleton nor, apparently, ever thought again about the deer after its discovery. We considered the deer differently. To them, it had been the find of the moment, the excitement of a singular occasion. It had been about the thrill of a deer skeleton. For me, who cared little for the specifics of deer, the thrill had been something else, a threshold of mutual discovery and connection and of future excursions into ourselves. The farm had long thrust isolation on me, reinforced by the usual sense of adolescent awkwardness. The deer skeleton was about the group, about being part of a group.

In retrospect, living on the farm might have signaled me as the only real Appalachian among them. As adults, nearly all of them would move away from the region, to cities and suburbs that would never suffer Appalachian designation. Even the one who remains in the region lives in Pittsburgh, and is therefore exempted. Only I live in the rural places that would seem to count, or not count, depending on how you view Appalachia. As a ninth grader, before all of that came to pass, the group that even then was beginning to melt away just as late summer afternoons gave way to chilly fall evenings, had offered a welcome sense of community. These were my people.

Soon enough, we started tenth grade, and though we stayed friends, even in some ways close friends, things were different. The others found upperclassmen who practiced a clearer and more direct sort of alternative artiness. These new friends were professors' kids too, but ones whose greater age and clearer sense of self had more appeal. Those boys had a band also, and to this I had no defense. My friends started hanging out in town.

They included me once, long after the new relationships had been forged. We spent a Friday night driving dark streets in a rickety van. We snatched a shopping cart from the parking lot of a grocery store, feverishly pulling it through the rear doors of the van before speeding off. The older boys wanted to stash it in a weedy ditch, then return another day to take moody photos. This was an aesthetic sophistication with which I was neither familiar nor fluent. They laughed and marveled at what they would do, while I bounced on the floor of the van's cargo space. I was bored, and it became clear to everyone that I wasn't really part of this new collection.

Though there came no moment to pinpoint the exile, I felt cast out. This exclusion felt inevitable to me, a consequence of growing up on the farm, where location posed a problem. My friends could walk to each other's houses, and they enjoyed spontaneous gatherings, street hockey, neighborhood games of mass tag, and trick-or-treating by foot instead of by car. I always needed permission from my parents to see friends, always needed a plan and a schedule, and someone to drive me. This was an imposition, however unintentional, that created a certain childhood loneliness and expectation of being left out, partly because I often was. As a grade-schooler, I wandered the farm by myself, playing a game I called German 88s, carrying one of my arsenal of toy guns as I pretended to be a lone GI dropped off behind enemy lines to destroy Nazi positions. In high school, I just wandered.

In many ways, my feelings of high school exile were common. We all felt that way, I'm sure, even if I considered my geographic isolation as different and more profound. In the years that followed, the others were part of the crew of friends who often visited the farm, particularly once they could drive. We played nighttime tag there, where I donned camo pants and a black T-shirt and distinguished myself as expert at hiding, never to be found. Eventually, such nights always wound to a sleepy close, my friends driving down the valley back home while I watched the flash of headlights disappear around the bend of our dead-end street. I stripped off my dark clothing and felt the quiet of a farm night as equal parts solitude and loneliness.

The deer skeleton lingered in the weeds of the old orchard, long freed from remnant flesh. Night animals crawled among the same low branches where I had spent hours hiding, crickets, katydids, cicadas, and frogs sounding the dark. On some nights, I listened to the ethereal chirps and screams of a raccoon, the lowness of a distant owl, or the rustling of unknown creatures searching the shrubs beside the house. Each seemed to reinforce a sense of separation that, even now, I find hard to embrace, that there is a difference between bone and flesh, that what lies at our center may make us ourselves, yet we live our lives mostly chasing tattered flesh. And high school remains forever the place where flesh is tattered. Eventually, the deer bones began to scatter, pulled apart by raccoons and coyotes, until nothing remained.

On another warm February afternoon, twenty-five years after we found the deer skeleton, and a year after I walked the farm and found survey stakes, and less than a week after I learned of my diagnosis, and four days after northwestern Pennsylvania suffered a typical lake-driven eight-inch snowfall, winter started to signal its disappearance. Bright blue sky arrived, and the coming spring asserted itself with nearly sixty degrees of heat. Rivers of water ran from underneath the snowpack in the neighborhood, flooding the street gutters. A riot of water headed downhill, eager for the final thaw. Cascades tumbled from roofs.

I remember this because the night before the wind had been high, the storm front passing through. Great violent chunks of snow roared off our roof, startling releases of thawing ice. The shingles seemed to rattle. I lay in bed, thinking, unable to sleep despite weariness, having spent the day with all my specialists.

Eventually, my younger son woke up. He was two weeks shy of turning three. I remember walking through the dark bedroom over to his bed, crawling in and pressing my head to his.

I need a snuggle, I said, which he took as a comfort toward him, even though the equation had flipped and I needed his closeness more. I hadn't yet cried in front of my wife, but I was terrified that I would die. I was terrified that I might be rendered blind, at least in one eye. I was terrified about the brain surgery, which I had been told must happen, because not having it would be worse.

The night before, in the wake of my visits with the surgeons, I had my recurring stress dream, always something about my teeth falling out or, occasionally, breaking them by eating china plates. Beside my son, I lay awake, fell asleep, awakened from another nightmare, then lay awake, returned to a nightmare, again and again. One nightmare involved me telling people about my tumor, and everyone cried: I was as afraid of that show of emotion as anything else.

In another, I was with my mother, who in real life had come to visit and watch the kids while Jen and I went to see doctors. But in the dream, we were in a pasture next to a lake, and there was a baby moose. We tried to leave through the gate but found a full herd of moose, the adults. A giant bull approached and blocked our way, so we doubled back. I found a fence, and my mother was suddenly gone, just disappeared within the strange logic of dreams. I cut the barbed wire at the top of the fence, hauled myself over, and wound up in a beer store. There was no way out except for stairs, which I ascended, only to find a tavern full of sleeping, pale people, dangerous in an unknown way. So I returned to the basement and then to the field, and I had no way out and no map to guide me.

The day before my older son's seventh birthday, I saw Aziz by myself. He went over the surgery, the details of his planned operation. *Decompression* surgery, he called it. The main goal was to remove bone to make space for later swelling, not to actually remove the tumor. Great if they could, but he doubted it. I was surprised and disappointed but listened as he ran through the risks. The bone removal would place him close to the carotid artery. It could be repaired if he nicked it. *Five percent*, Aziz assigned to the risk, repeating that his concern was primarily about vision loss, but I understood that the number reflected what his physician's assistant relayed in terrifying detail later: that in rare cases anesthesia can lead to a cascading hyperthermic reaction in a patient's body, organ failure, and death.

Aziz remained careful in his discussion with me, using the comforting obfuscation of numbers instead of narrative to describe risk. Later a Philadelphia neurologist I would visit for a second opinion would rupture that illusion, dismissively asking how any surgeon could know what percentage risk a procedure carries. *Had he done a hundred of them, lost precisely five patients?* I didn't appreciate that kind of disdainful frankness, preferred how Aziz talked through the surgery holding a resin skull, which served as a three-dimensional map of the surgery, a stand-in for my own idiosyncratic skull that he would saw through.

Aziz spoke slowly, carefully. He lied, perhaps, about percentages, deploying the typical confident delivery of physicians who, more than anyone, understand the mystical nature of the body, that numbers rarely apply. Still, I see this as a mercy. And it is, for the most part, even if the discussion of the surgery was also the worst portion of sobering. There was no getting around the reality of it at this point.

He asked about my wife, who couldn't come to this appointment. Would she want to meet with him before the surgery? I heard his question as a great kindness but assured him that no, it was better if only I knew the details. I understood how having her with me might have helped, but I held a certain level of guarded possession to my surgery. I also knew that my wife could not have helped her own cascading reaction of worry, had she heard the details of the plan and the risks. This might be categorized as my own sort of lie, the omission of detail meant as another mercy.

Worry is, of course, not built on reason. Though firm in the desire to protect myself from further damage or fright, I couldn't quite shake the fear that we weren't proceeding as we should.

Proceeding.

Procedure.

The precise language of medicine facing off against my growing recognition of the imprecision of life. I came to realize that the question of surgery was not one of proper procedure but of philosophy. Too often, disorders, diseases, and all sorts of medical diagnoses appear technical. The body takes on the appearance of a machine, with breakdowns attributed to worn or faulty parts that can be swapped or fixed. Physicians, then, function much like mechanics. Diagnoses are made, followed by repair or replacement. The soul of the machine is a secondary consideration or, more often, irrelevant.

A body is structure and soul. I think about the structure of our bone as the finest metaphor for our truest self. Bone is alive, hardened and apparently rigid, yet teeming with a marrow and blood. Bone is alive as a soul is alive.

I think, too, about the misdirection of flesh, and appearance, and the temporary satisfaction of something that appears meaningful. I think about the old deer skeleton and the rotting away of skin that accompanied the erosion of friendships, my own inability to recognize the difference between surface and depth. I think about the surface knowledge of medical tests and how it compromises the desire within bone, that it seeks to boil away the flesh to see permanence. I think about how bone is not the end, that within it lies more life: cells, blood, and soul. Tests and maps seek the rigidity of the absolute, implying first that the absolute can be known and, further, that charting is both necessary and helpful. Tests cannot find a soul, which merely desires the space to find itself.

CHAPTER 5

Learning to Say Appalachia

For a long time now, I've been designating the region of the ARC and the mountains that run through it with two disparate pronunciations, a soft *sh* for the region and a hard *ch* for the rocks. That seemed to fit, since the mountains run north all the way into Atlantic Canada, the rocks of the old range twisting upward in an artful swirl of geological pomposity in Newfoundland, the earth's very mantle exposed at more or less the point where the old Appalachians end in the subarctic flourish of the Long Range Mountains. My linguistic strategy has been as precise as it is priggish: the mountains and the region are different and so should be pronounced differently. And *correctly*.

I'm thinking also about the hand-lettered magnet hanging on my refrigerator even today. *It's pronounced App-uh-latch-uh*, the magnet declares, something else I had to learn. Growing up in Pennsylvania, if we pronounced it at all, we did so with a long *a* and a quiet shushing: *App-uh-lay-sha*. When I became a graduate student at West Virginia University and actually started studying the region, I soon learned that how a person says that word signals much.

Novelist Sharyn McCrumb describes this well in a YouTube video, identifying pronunciation as a way to identify insiders. She explains (as have many others), that people from Appalachia say *App-uh-latch-uh* and people from elsewhere say *App-uh-lay-sha*. The pronunciation matters, she argues, and there's little to no excuse for defending the outsider version, unless you want to signal that you're against the people of Appalachia.

Yet when I think about my childhood, and even my current home in the northern regions of Pennsylvania, no one pronounces the entities of region or mountain range differently. That means I grew up among Appalachians who pronounced ourselves as *App-uh-lay-shuns*. What does it mean when you grew up as a boy saying the word *wrong*? What does it mean when you're from a place where everyone did? We all said it *wrong* in southwestern Pennsylvania, even if we weren't trying to signal anything about being from or against the region we failed to recognize as our own. I suppose that means McCrumb and the others are right, at least in part. We are bad Appalachians, deniers of our heritage, willful self-exiles. We said it wrong because we were outsiders to ourselves. Still, I find it difficult to accept that we all had it and ourselves wrong, that our pronunciations meant we were outsiders to our own place and selves, even if until recently that's how I had learned to feel.

In *Ecology of a Cracker Childhood*, Janisse Ray makes a compelling claim for the dual revaluing of the Georgia longleaf pine forests and the rural people who lived among them. She argues for the viability of her childhood as the daughter of a junkyard family and so too for the recognition of the vitality of people discarded as trash. She writes, "It has taken a decade to whip the shame, to mispronounce words and shun grammar when mispronunciation and misspeaking are part of my dialect, to own the bad blood. What I come from has made me who I am."

I am interested in how a strange inversion of exile happens when you grow up pronouncing your region the way the outsiders do, or at least when you come to think of it that way. That's one of the things I learned as a graduate student in West Virginia, that App-uh-latch-uh is *correct* and, à la Sharyn McCrumb et al., saying it the other way means you side with the outsider. The truth for me is that it feels funny saying the word either way now. Both sound wrong and are wrong, depending on who you talk to. Put another way, being from Northern Appalachia is what the theorists might call a double bind: you are and you ain't, or maybe you really just aren't ever. That is, you don't quite fit as prototypically Appalachian just as you don't fit as properly mainstream. You're doubly exiled. Reclaiming the rightness of App-uh-lay-sha is a way to recognize who I am, and what this place can be.

I also am interested in applying notions of palimpsest and pentimento to this sense of exile. What happens when there isn't a right, just a lot of rights? Or when wrong and right lie atop and next to each other? This is what Appalachian linguistic scholars say about the regional title, that pronunciations vary and none has any particular claim to correctness. Yet at the same time, plenty of people agree with McCrumb, that how you say the word shows which side you align yourself with, local or conqueror.

Both are probably correct, even if finding a definitive pronunciation would seem more satisfying. Perhaps in the overwrought manner of an English professor, I think of this difficulty of bothness through the lens of the historical fate of David Livingstone, the famous nineteenth-century British chronicler of Africa. He was a writer of palimpsests, stuck in Africa and afflicted with dysentery and malaria, running short of paper but determined to continue taking notes. He wanted to profile the people and the place, driven by an idea of liberation and freedom for Africans. Finding the source of the Nile would matter, he thought. He sought it as an act of goodwill that, in the end, wound up working as a tool for the colonial enslavement of an entire continent, directly contrary to Livingstone's stated desires of emancipation and end to the slave trade. That's how empire goes, of course, whether on the grand scale of British Colonial conquest in Africa or the smaller scale of Appalachia. Colonialism functions as the denial of conceptual palimpsest, Livingstone's perhaps noble desire layered on nefarious result but, in true Colonial fashion, stable truth still presumed to exist.

As Livingstone ran short of paper, he started writing over old newspaper sheets using ink fashioned from local berries. He wrote on an angle to the newsprint, reinscribing words over words over words, until he'd created an unintelligible jumble. To the eye, there might be occasional phrases that stick out, but the overall narrative thread is gone, the sentences consumed by each other until all that's left is paper and a kind of ink smudge Rorschach impenetrability.

Technology to the rescue! Scholars in the Livingstone Spectral Imagery Project have been applying digital spectroscopy to these texts, having figured out how to use a tool of science to identify and then electronically separate the compounds of Livingstone's inks. Essentially, they figure out the wavelengths of light that correspond to the different inks on the paper, then use digital tools to electronically separate layers of text on a computer without having to disturb the fragile paper. As the computer separates the inks, scholars can figure out what Livingstone actually wrote, the implication being that they're able to access the *truth* of what Livingstone meant.

I am awed by this technology, by how scholars determined how to use techniques applied to astronomy and planetary study and other big-ticket science and use it on words, which are themselves a fascinating duality of physical ink and intellectual meaning. Yet I don't actually care much about the discoveries that the researchers make, and I'm more than a little suspicious about the impulse behind it. I get it: we want to know what Livingstone wrote. That matters. But I think also the desire to know *precisely* what he wrote is also a betrayal of the arc of his life, demonstrating our insatiable desire to find stable, original ground and to recover and reclaim what was intended to be lost forever. And I further think that denying the jumble as a thing in its own right is a tricky conceptual problem. Ignoring the jumble of the palimpsests Livingstone inscribed in his field diary is a way to ignore the mess of empire and his part in it. Of course I can throw out a version of Canadian philosopher Marshall McLuhan here, that "the medium is the message," that the fact of the illegible newsprint is more important than whatever the lost words actually say.

But *lost* is the wrong word here. Or, even if Livingstone himself was lost in a certain way—succumbing to the double-impact of malaria and dysentery, perhaps out of his mind and certainly suffering—the solution to the palimpsest of his writing is not about the recovery of what is lost. Instead, the final product, that artifact created by his desire to keep writing and reinscribe the world over other texts is the reality and, in the end, the most striking aspect of his legacy. That's the real text, indecipherable in sentences but clear as an object piece. It is a testament to his struggle—no paper, a futile desire to do something no one could really achieve—and a visual representation of his urge and desire. To write. That's what drove him to reuse his own sentences.

The jumble is, in fact, the message. Livingstone's legacy is a colonial mess, a man who wanted to do one thing but instead unlocked the opposite of that thing. He may have been devoted to abolition and the dignity of Africa, but his desire overplayed the structure of his time. Confused meaninglessness, dramatic jumble of disparate desires, that's what his overwritten texts mean. His words needn't be unlocked to see that. Worse, trying to determine what he *really* said is to deny the full spectrum of his narrative, which itself played out as overlapping lines of fractal confusion that became both less and more meaningful as they accumulated. More tragic too. That's something I don't wish to deny: Livingstone died a failure to his own desire, if not a failed man. He didn't intend to create a nonsense layering of his thoughts, I'm sure, and I imagine he was more interested in exactly the same kind of narrative fidelity that scholars are now trying to unlock. I doubt that Livingstone was able to see himself in transformation, that he was becoming a confusion of overlapping aspects: palimpsest and man, hero and villain. He likely remained steadfast in his desire to do what he set out to do, not recognizing the loss of the self that first traveled to Africa. That's probably the biggest tragedy of Livingstone.

Maybe it's curious that writing my way into Appalachia means writing also about places very much not Appalachia. But I am writing most of all about recognition, about trying to find the name of a place, defining it and me and how the place and the person coexist. Sometimes focusing on a spot elsewhere has to happen first, and it's only through the contrast of the distant to what you have always known that you begin to recognize what it is.

I'm thinking about names and calling places by their right name, about relationships to land and how Scott Russell

Sanders suggests in *Staying Put* that, "Loyalty to place arises from sources deeper than narcissism. It arises from our need to be at home on the earth." I've learned a great loyalty to place over many years, the family farm serving as epicenter to that, the kind of spot Sanders calls "a holy center, not because it gives you special access to the divine, but because in your stillness you hear what might be heard anywhere." Furthermore, I've come to think of it as a place within a place, part of Appalachia, a fact I hardly knew, certainly never admitted until I was in my thirties. Yet I also find myself wanting to cut tethers to this place, the weight of it carrying too much baggage. Appalachia signals decline, traumatic health, and ensnaring stereotypes, no matter how you pronounce it.

There's certainly significance in how often I turn toward Sanders when I want to think about place, even my own place. Coincidentally, he writes extensively about my mother's home state of Indiana, even though he was not originally from there. It also matters that he had an itinerant childhood in many locations and had to make a conscious effort to dig into the hills of southern Indiana once he settled there as an adult. He became placed, localized himself through an act of conscious will to the town where my parents met as graduate students at Indiana University. They later moved together to a town named Indiana in a different state, each falling in love somehow with Wendell Berry and the concept of resurrecting a farm that had fallen into the clutches of suburban avarice. This is the palimpsest of our lives: we can find our home as much as be born to it.

I was a kid who lived on that farm, who moved there after spending his first six years in a suburban split-level in a subdevelopment across the highway from the town's mall, and who existed from the beginning in some sort of marginal space between what was and wasn't *redneck*. On the farm we raised goats, hogs, sheep, horses, and chickens. I even slept at the county fair once, guarding the animals in what I think of as a comical situation now: someone had taken to paint-bombing the sheep, to sabotage the upcoming judging, which was based in part on the cleanliness of the fleeces. Weekends on the farm I mucked out stalls, and during the week I took calculus. I shot a deer when I was twelve, played my way to all-state band in saxophone, and fished each opening day for trout with my father. What was I?

You probably see where I'm headed. I was and am Appalachian, a more complicated term than I realized, even when I took to the *right* way of saying the word. Even then, this first blush of recognition came with a sense of exile. Being from Pennsylvania meant I was the wrong sort of Appalachian, not quite full-fledged, a sentiment shared by my friends and neighbors from home, as well as with many people who grew up in a different sort of more-readily named Appalachia in West Virginia, Kentucky, Tennessee, and on down through what Kephart and Campbell called the Southern Highlands.

"To circumscribe territory and give it a name is one thing; to call people by a name not of their choosing is quite another," Campbell writes. He continues:

> Obviously, if the term Southern Highlands be allowed for the land, native-born residents of the region are Southern Highlanders. Yet within the Highland area are many native-born inhabitants of urban or valley residence who do not regard themselves as mountain people. The writer has two friends, one living in the Greater Appalachian Valley and one in a prosperous mountain city, and both devoted to the interests of their

> own people, who refer in conversation to "those mountain folks," although at other times jocosely alluding to themselves as "mountain whites." This opprobrious term, coined as a term of distinction by well-meaning advocates of the mountaineer, is resented by all who dwell in the Highlands, by whatever name they may be designated.

Written in 1921, the text illustrates the contemporary problem of both *being* and *not quite being*. Across the whole span of the ARC, the appellations—externally applied to residents and usually with a negative connotation—grate. Campbell might as well be writing about Pittsburgh, the mightiest city in Appalachia, where residents have very little concept of themselves as being Appalachian. Such exile becomes more complicated when you're not quite sure where you come from, when both geography and parentage deny a clear identity.

This brings me back to the question of pronunciation, of *App-uh-lay-shun* versus *App-uh-latch-in*. I learned at WVU that I had been wrong for quite some time, and I therefore sought to rectify the ways that I defined myself as being from *not there*. Yet as Kirk Hazen, a WVU English professor and director of the West Virginia Dialect project, has explained, both are correct pronunciations, as are many other ways of saying the word. But correct and right are sort of two different things. It's hard to shake the notion that the way I say the word means something about my sensibilities. In fact, I only have a *mountain* accent if I try to put one on, which is to say I don't actually have that accent, never did. My midwestern reading-specialist mother made it a point of pride that her children spoke *well*, by which she meant *standard*, which meant learnedly. My eastern Pennsylvanian father shucked his Pennsylvania Dutch accent to gain acceptance in school.

I learned my flat accent from them. Is this a denial of home region? Does it mean I can never be Appalachian because my roots aren't sufficiently deep?

Appalachia is a palimpsest, a state of layered fullness that strikes me as a more useful and accurate definition of place than any measure of stable, common, clichéd, frustrating, hateful, or notion of *the authentic* ever can. My state of exile lives within the way that I don't fit the terms supplied to me. And it's important to note that the terms I fail to meet are defined also by other Appalachians, that just as I balk at the sorts of tropes and caricatures that the broadest American culture assigns to the eastern mountains, so too do I bristle at the defined ideas that come from within.

At a recent annual meeting of the Appalachian Studies Association (ASA), I heard this feature defined with great humor. A roomful of scholars and students chuckled as someone remarked that the annual meeting sometimes seemed to include a competition of *hicksters*, offering a tremendous portmanteau of *hick* and *hipster*, thereby defining the impulse as one to wear the best flannel, or love the fiddle more than anyone else, or make artisan moonshine, or have the most amazing well-groomed grizzly beard. Embedded in the word is, of course, a pejorative tone, that just as hipsters aren't quite what they seem, neither are hicksters. Each exaggerates features, puts on the clothes but isn't necessarily the thing.

This implication struck me as I sat at the conference in a room full of people wearing such beards and flannels and carrying accents that seemed to outshine one another with mellifluous flowing mountain stream vowels. Throughout the weekend, there were frequent planned and spontaneous jam sessions of bluegrass music. Everyone seemed to be carrying a guitar. I remember lots of straw hats, and feathers in some of those hats, and more overalls than you'd think would ever show up on a university campus, particularly for a scholarly conference. I loved it, even as I felt excluded.

Indeed, I marvel at the level of pride so many feel and are willing to demonstrate for their heritage. The ASA meeting offers a safe place for this kind of expression, where you can fly your hillbilly flag and no one will think less of you, even while serious scholars dress in much the way they might at, say, the Association for the Study of Literature of the Environment or even MLA. As such, the self-caricature becomes akin to the way all sorts of subcultures reclaim the precise markers that have been used against them. They celebrate the stereotype as a way to defuse it. But I am trying to say that none of these markers are mine. I wonder if my way of dressing and being—no overalls, more of a Victorian Snidely Whiplash twirled mustache than a mountain-man one, and my lack of accent—expose me as somehow less legitimate, if I seem out of place in such gatherings or, worse, like an outsider.

I would be putting on airs if I tried to enter the hickster pageant, would be faking it as *that* kind of Appalachian. Plus, I recall seeing these sorts of gestures even the year the conference happened to take place in my hometown at the university where I then taught, where my father had taught, and where I had been an undergrad. The conference had been promoted as the northernmost gathering of the organization, a sort of curiosity since the location was not typically considered to be part of Appalachia. Nominally, sessions accenting that aspect of the region were foregrounded. In reality, most of the sessions were exactly what you would expect of an Appalachian Studies Conference, focusing on the parts of the region more readily available to the social, cultural, and intellectual consciousness. *Northern* seemed just to be a token word, a kind of marketing schlock that differentiated that year's conference from all the others. So in my hometown, looking and acting like I was from my hometown seemed more like an exclusionary identity than a participatory one.

There's a surface notion of Appalachia, certainly dominant, accurate, and complex in its own right. But I was struck then and continue to think about how homogenous Appalachia seems to be at these conferences, even as association scholars produce lots of fascinating contemporary work about the many different sorts of communities, less noticed but important and integral to the region. That's the palimpsest: thinking about the many overlaying narratives that make up the ecological, cultural, and narrative history of the region. It might seem to be a "thing," but it is really many things written on one another.

Ultimately, the problem of a palimpsest is that you want to figure out what the original image is (or it seems that's the right way to think). Original implies best—the baseline, the thing that matters above all else or that mattered first. The surface visuals of ASA meetings offer the perceived stable core of Appalachia, the identity that *is*. They're akin to the digital stripping away of words that are not Livingstone's in order to see what Livingstone's experience of Africa actually was. It's the desire to believe in the authentic, to seek it out, and to imagine foundational experience as both obtainable and desirable.

But what about that? Even in our typical sense of a palimpsest, the original text or striving isn't the real baseline. To be technical about it, the substrate is the only stable thing: the stretched vellum, papyrus, paper, rock, or even the physical human body. This is the thing that also is, always has been. And let's not be hyper-technical here and think about originality itself, that impossibility, and how atoms, molecules, and the history of the universe play into all of this. So, yes, nothing is precisely original or reducible to original, the Big Bang itself more conceptual than actual, the birthing of our entire celestial existence rendered in terms we can understand precisely because the thing itself cannot be understood.

Still, we think of that original text as the thing to be unearthed. I take too much meaning, as usual, in the figurative sense of the Latin term *scriptio inferior* applied to that original text, which seems to imply that the original is somehow less important. And, really, to me that seems like a good way to think about it. If the impulse is to think of the original as better, then my reading of *inferior*—really just a designation of position, not much different than left versus right—readjusts my thinking to consider the revision as the more important text.

And yes, historically there's great fascination in famous palimpsests, like what Seneca had to say about friendship (and, really, a warning against a palimpsestic sort of friendship in which a person acts both with and against a friend), those lines written over by portions of the New Testament, which are all about being a friend to everyone. And that connects to the weird forgery of a friendship between Seneca and Paul, texts produced as a palimpsest of Stoicism and early Christianity, trying to gain power for the latter by pretending that the former wanted anything at all to do with it. But I'm interested in that totality, not just in recovering the stable *ground* but, instead, recognizing the combo as the thing, that Christianity isn't an inevitable top-end philosophy, nor was Roman intellectualism the baseline we should move toward. We should no more drill toward the original and remove the overlaying words than presume that the top layer is the only layer.

You do damage when you seek to separate. That's a lesson learned by the literary scientists of the nineteenth century, when various chemicals were used to try to physically separate the parts that make the palimpsest, to seek the original and thus destroy the substrate, melting away the integrity of the paper, rock, or whatever. The act of recovery is caustic, weakening the literal substrate as a way to get at the primacy of the foundation.

The full reality is in the layering, in how Seneca once was, then was effaced by something else, and then recovered. There's a newness formed in the entirety that takes parts of both, introduces questions of why and how and for what purpose, and lets a reader of the whole palimpsestic reality think about a larger arc of human intelligence, avarice, foolishness, hope, and love.

Let me put this in the context of a mountain: neither the peak nor the valley is the thing. Or think of that mountain's geology, that it isn't a uniform monolith; nor is it possible to separate all of the sandstone to get at the trueness of granite. Instead, the mountain is built by layer upon layer upon layer, then those layers twisted, then those layers flattened by rain and wind, and eroded into new sorts of mountains that are, indeed, my Appalachia. I am from and I am a dissected plateau, each made of the way time and event has worn through the layers that accrued. Pre–brain tumor me is not the real me. I am the palimpsest of now. Mispronouncing Appalachia is both things, each wrong and right, and that is the best way to voice the state of being Northern Appalachian. Palimpsests all.

"We late twentieth-century creatures think suburban," John Lane writes.

> We express this worldview in terms of the five units of suburban growth—tracts of houses, office parks,

institutions like schools or churches, strip malls, and roads, lots of roads. The measure of suburbia's success is housing starts. When we drive out of our "resident clusters" to shop or go to school (for one of the laws of suburbia is separation), we drive through a built world projected by our minds, constructed by our dollars, and protected by our laws.

I like to think of Appalachia as a mighty resistance to this suburbia, which is also perhaps why it is always defined as *backward*. Appalachia refuses the suburban ideal, and in that it becomes a protest obstacle to American blandness. Appalachia defines itself and is defined by a rugged rurality: hollers, trees, hunting, and dark forests. This would explain the desire to act Appalachian, to foreground the overalls, fiddle music, and ridiculous transcendent mountain beards. Such a manner of being is the opposite of suburban, where flatness of identity owns all, where beige is a state of ecstasy.

Yet suburbia is far more prevalent in Northern Appalachia than in Southern, precisely because the parts of the region closest to my home are defined by the urban center of Pittsburgh. This might be why, when I took an informal poll on Facebook about what Appalachia meant to my friends and whether they identified as Appalachian, the responses were rather uniform. Appalachia was always somewhere else, and, no, they were not Appalachian. Friends from high school repeated stereotypes of what Appalachia is, creating a contrast between our own rather suburban childhood and the region as typically defined. One friend suggested that we couldn't have grown up in Appalachia because she remembered collecting money in church to send *to* Appalachia.

These responses connect to a definition of region that Karl Raitz and Richard Black explain as "Cognitive Appalachia."

They cite their 1981 study of college students who were asked if they were *in* Appalachia. The results are shown as an isopleth map—kind of like a contour map—with concentric ovals of declining percentages. The highest percentage of respondents who said they were in Appalachia actually were at the most southern part of West Virginia, a circle more or less around McDowell County that corresponds with more than 80 percent answering, *yes, Appalachia is here.* Quite surprisingly points both north and south of McDowell County show diminishing rates of response. By the time you reach the Mason-Dixon line, respondents only say they are in Appalachia about 40 percent of the time. My home county in Pennsylvania is near the 20 percent line. My home now in northwestern Pennsylvania is outside the chart, at less than 10 percent identifying as Appalachian. For most people, Appalachia is always elsewhere.

The idea of Appalachia is an idea of a location somehow outside America, while the idea of suburbia is the idea of America itself. I don't say this with any pride, as track homes and anonymous box stores are the worst kind of cultural flatness. That blandness is precisely what Appalachia resists. You might not like a fiddle, for example, but you wouldn't call it *bland*. Growing up in a Pennsylvania college town meant growing up in blandness, without the fiddle and without the sense of being something definable at all. The trouble of Northern Appalachian identity, then, is a trouble of absence. We might have thought of ourselves as living in just America, since so many friends grew up in split-levels surrounded by other split-levels, all of which had been built in what was once a farmer's field.

A similar aspect dominates in southern Ohio near Cincinnati, in central Ohio near Columbus, and in northeastern Ohio near Cleveland, these other large cities lying just outside the region. The suburban growth of these places is starting to creep toward the ARC, which is part of why such locales often feel less *Appalachian*. Suburbs exist throughout Appalachia, of course, even in places we might not expect and even though track homes and commuter-culture aren't what we think of when we hear *Appalachia*. To wander into the anonymity of a housing development is to feel far away from the mountains, far away from anything regionally specific or distinct.

I take foolish pride in the origin of the family farm, that it took the land back from suburban development, that my parents did that whole Wendell Berry thing to redeem it. They preserved a farm from suburbia, protecting its Appalachianness. Yet I'm also a close miss, since the home I was born into was itself a track home in a small development near the mall. This was the house that my parents could never love, that they abandoned for the farm and a life far different in concept. I share that emotion now, unable to love the house where my wife and I live in northwestern Pennsylvania. There, we're in the city limits in a pleasant neighborhood that feels so suburban. And I hate it there. I feel ungrounded, living in a house instead of a place. I long for the view from my parents' house, where I sit at the kitchen table and look at the rise of the hillside, the layered view of lawn, the orchard, the tall grasses, and the sky.

I wonder now if I should think of these layers of life as pentimento instead of palimpsest, considering the visual layering of image instead of the textual layering of words. Renaissance artists painted over old images on their canvases, sometimes as part of the simple practice of making art. Other times, the pentimento is about correction. A part of the image looks wrong, so the artist scratches off the paint and repaints, or just repaints without removing the original. And other times, the pentimento is a full covering of an older work, sometimes a beautiful one like a hack job over a Rembrandt, sometimes a worthless attempt that the painter decided needed to disappear. Or, I imagine, sometimes it was just easier for an artist to find a used canvas and start there, instead of stretching a new one.

In all of these cases, the concept is the same as the palimpsest: there's an original beneath the new. But one of the glorious aspects of the pentimento is the way that old images reassert themselves—a phantom limb will reappear over time, covered but not gone. Layers of paint find a way to creep forward, the hidden revealing itself eventually, always there and refusing to be forever invisible. And even when not yet visible to the human eye, inner layers exist, ready for new technologies that let art historians use computers and cameras to unearth the original without damaging the top layer.

Scholars may think of these layers mostly as discrete things. The intellectual interest lies in seeing what was there before, either to reveal a hidden gem or to confirm that, yes, the master painter made a good choice with that new coat. To my mind, it's once again the totality that matters most of all. The layers are fascinating individually, but they are not things to be recovered or weighed out, one better than the rest. The first layer of paint is no better than the others and certainly doesn't indicate the purity of achievement, which is then besmirched by later development. No, the final product is the final product, final also being a term without definitiveness. A painter can always paint again, covering even an old Rembrandt today, if we so choose. Yet the paint beneath asserts its presence in the final product: I will always have been born in the suburbs of a small town—no matter where I live, no matter how wild I become, and no matter what version of myself I most want to claim. But I also will have always been born above sedimentary rock, in a region of erosion and flowing water. Best that I remember this, because the trouble with layers is that it can seem impossible to know which one matters most. They all matter. And the layer you're in, that's the layer you live, even as you need to know what lies beneath, how far you need to go to find bedrock.

A few years ago, I took a class of first-year students to the rare books room of our college library to examine old illuminated manuscripts. I'd titled my class "Analog Writing in a Digital Age," a course that focused on the mechanics of physical text in a digital world. To that end, we made paper, bound journals together with needles and cotton thread, and wrote with old-fashioned fountain pens. A colleague from the art department came and taught my students how to whittle bamboo pens that they could load from ink he made by boiling down the husks of chestnuts from my parents' backyard tree. We made our own calligraphy text art and illuminated them with colored pencil and aluminum foil. And the students hung in there, most not really caring that much or being moved by my devotion to the archaic. One student fought me every inch of the way, arguing that Twitter and texting were a much more powerful form of writing than stodgy old ink.

"If a person turns from print—finding it too slow, too hard, irrelevant to the excitement of the present—then what happens to that person's sense of culture and continuity?" Sven Birkerts writes. He argues in the *Gutenberg Elegies*—a central text of that class—about the "durational reverie of reading," that the method by which we engage information has a lot to do with how we process that information. I see this as linked to what I'm trying to say about palimpsests, or what Birkerts suggests: "To enter the work at all we need to put our present-day sense of things in suspension; we have to, in effect, reposition the horizon and reconceive all of our assumptions about the relations between things."

My point in the class was never really about the either/or, a nuance that can be a hard sell to late teenagers. I have a smartphone, text plenty, and am probably addicted to Facebook. I've even read a few e-books despite my preference for paper, and certainly when I research I'm happy to use digital tools and pdf versions of journal articles. So my frame of reference in that course was not about rating the modes of communication, but rather about studying their differences, examining how text is not just text, understanding that there are differences in our approaches to the physical and the electronic.

This is another kind of palimpsest or pentimento or geological inquiry. The digital subsumes the hand of the individual, presuming the objective, even as it makes change much harder to glean. Consider fracking. To get the gas deep beneath Appalachia, geologists predisposed to the aims of resource extraction see not a palimpsest but discrete zones of rock. Busting them with fluid pressure can be done, and the gas that makes part of the whole can be extracted and burned. Yet it comes as no surprise that earthquakes have started to spike in places thusly fracked, the earth itself functioning against the affront to the palimpsest. Layers exist, yes, but together they are the whole. Broken apart, the totality suffers.

Books are not rocks, of course, as they accrue through the idiosyncratic application of human hands, particularly ancient texts scribed and scrawled on long ago. As with rocks, we must read these layers to understand the whole. In the rare books library, that became visceral to my students. They touched twelfth-century Flemish illuminated texts. They saw the pinholes in the vellum, the residue of the work, where the monks had driven metal though the paper to hold it open while they worked. They saw the precision of the inking, the magnificent attention to detail that makes a hand-lettered book appear mechanical: the scribes were that good.

One of my favorite aspects of these old books, though, are the ancient marginalia, proof that the texts belonged to and were read by individuals who had ideas. This is a shock to students as well, that some people write in their books, a lot, and that they have been doing so since the birth of writing. Part of student surprise is likely a residue of high school classrooms, where you check out the textbook at the beginning of the year, and you're obligated to cover it with something to protect the book itself (I used to use paper bags; now you can just buy covers on Amazon), and you're warned to avoid even the smallest pencil mark in the margins. The original matters here and must be preserved forever in a way that implies no human hand has ever touched or engaged or altered it. Part of their surprise might be at how we can learn from such marks, even if they would seem to deface the page.

I remember in high school seeing the old, snide remarks that disobedient students penned in the margins. I resented them, superior little shit kid that I was, but I also often found them funny. Later in college, I liked buying used books for classes both because they were cheaper and because they came pre-highlighted. Sometimes, that mark of the previous student helped guide my own studies. Other times, probably more often, it let me chuckle and feel, once again, superior: I certainly wouldn't have marked that passage!

The passages we mark are who we are. There might be a wrong passage to cover with yellow highlighter, in the context of preparing to answer questions to arrive on some future test. No doubt about that. But what we see and care about is a mark of who we are, regardless of what will be on the test. Maybe that makes some of us dumb and some smart, but really I think that's a puerile distinction best left to the sort of insufferable good student I used to be. Instead, the marking of lines is an indication both of who we are and how we are engaging the world—that we are engaging the world at all. It's this last aspect that matters most. Each of us makes moves that affect the world around us. We make our marks, literal and figurative, and those tell us a lot. If we think of Appalachia as a text, the person who highlights coal is different from the person who highlights mountain streams is different from the person who highlights romance is different from the person who highlights a suburb.

The literal marginalia I love most of all lies in the top left margin of a musty old book in the college's rare books collection. There, beside the Latin text outlining world religions, someone long-dead sketched an image of a dude in a top hat, a giant dick hanging beneath his legs. It's always been that way, hasn't it? The urge to draw a penis cannot be denied, and probably shouldn't be. Everything isn't as straight ahead and serious as we think, texts marked and changed by how we see them, how we add to them.

I see mercy in that marginalia, a sign of a serious mind bored and benumbed, maybe just horny, maybe concerned about his own tiny dick and wanting to make up for it on the page. No matter the reason, it's a mark made that says, *I was here, I am, I contain Whitman's multitudes of seriousness and sexual desire*. And, no, I have little desire to track down the provenance of that sketch, to see who made it and why and if it means something. It's the entire artifact that matters to me, that my college has as part of its collection a book of serious import that contains marginalia of base urge. That's the artifact of life, the indicator of what we're really examining, that life matters. We are profane and serious, old and new, always many things at the same time.

Appalachia is a palimpsest, a pentimento, and a geologic process, a place inscribed with marks that indicate the fullness of what we are and reveal the values of those who write upon it. Appalachia is also covered with marginalia, the truest markers of what the people of the place have been thinking and what the people from outside the place have been thinking also. Boney piles. Ball fields. Libraries. Crumbled Ruins. Gardens. Red streams.

Consider the desire to get to Appalachian baseline, and consider the bifurcation of purity that lies at the two poles. In one, Appalachia is nothing but a wide swath of coalfield and gas deposit. In the other, Appalachia is a purified locale of a certain sort of valuable mountain culture. Borders lay claim to what they surround, and baselines tell us how to read what has been contained. Appalachia is dream and commodity, depending on who you ask. The people within are noble or fallen, fitting one of the extremes of identity allowed for those called *hillbilly*.

I fit neither extreme, of course. No one does. That's been my point for a while: that the only absolutes are individual, the marks of the person, the marginalia of the writer hidden as part of the text itself. I'm mixing the metaphors I've drawn here, but my point is that we've come to think of Appalachia, like all things, as something reducible. Worst of all, the mechanism of reduction is often, maybe always, hidden just as it is driven by a certain frame of reference. That's why the narratives of the region are so hard to shake. They are real, part of the history, some lived and some applied, but all useful. We don't see who's been scribbling those margin sketches, though, and over time they've become part of the palimpsest even as they are thought of as foundational and definitive. We can't discard the history of our region and must accept its violent settlement, its violent industry, its struggle to imagine its way out of stereotype.

We also have to consider and weigh the history of Northern Appalachia itself. Recall that Pennsylvania was not included in the Southern Highlands that serve as proto-Appalachia, and consider that Congress first identified it as part of Appalachia only in 1964. Is this perhaps an origin point for at least my sense of Northern Appalachian identity? Is it possible that Pennsylvania did not exist as Appalachia until that date? The peculiar absence that I recognize in my Northern Appalachian identity, and that so many high school friends still feel when they hear but do not connect to the word *Appalachian*, develops from the reality that a Congressional designation is not a cultural position. When the striking of a gavel turned my homeland into Appalachia, nothing changed. This makes any connection to southern inflections even more alienating for people like me, since claiming my own sense of being Appalachian as being *that kind* of Appalachian is to claim an identity simply not consistent with my own regional history.

When the ASA conference came to Pennsylvania, *Pittsburgh Post-Gazette* writer Brian O'Neill wrote a piece titled "Yes, We and Yinz are Part of Appalachia." Within it, he argues for the recognition of Pittsburgh as part of the region and lauds the presence of the conference in the state. He also suggests that polka music be considered alongside mountain fiddle music as legitimately Appalachian.

While I agree with O'Neill's impulse to champion the local recognition of Appalachian identity, I also raise an eyebrow at the idea of polka music inhabiting the same cultural space as more familiar sorts of Appalachian culture, partly because embracing polka music as a regional identity seems as anachronistically limited as other stereotypes. And I think of the deeper problem of Northern Appalachia not even existing until 1964, long after polka had become folk. One of the problems of defining Appalachia is that we seem always hasty to define it only through history, in the resurrection of some gloried past instead of recognizing the present. Whether polka or mountain fiddle, the past is only part of what we once were, a small element of who we might become or have become already.

Northern Appalachian identity is a contemporary identity, perhaps very much connected to suburbia itself, since Congress declared it part of the region in the same general period that saw the explosion of split-level ranches. Maybe our suburban lack of hollers, lack of fiddles, and apparent lack of *identity* is instead what we are. Yes, we are part of the ARC. And, yes, we share an industrial history of degradation and abuse. And, yes, there are places within Pennsylvania where folk music matters deeply, and the hill cuts are steep enough that some coal patch towns are really within hollers. And, yes, like all of Appalachia, we are not ahistorical, or just historical, or stereotypical, or what everyone thinks. And, yes, like Appalachia everywhere, our identity seems always built on the foundations of industrial pasts: steel mills superseding coal in Pittsburgh, the Steel City, for example, and everyone loving being that moniker, even though steel is not who we are now. The mills have long been dismantled.

App-uh-lay-shun is an identity we can claim. This is the stable ground to which we must return, not to the legacies established by Campbell, Congress, or even Appalachians elsewhere who might mean no harm but, really, exclude us from the region when they suggest that we say our name wrong. Here's the thing: I learned to call myself App-uh-latch-in when in fact I am not. Pronouncing that way is against *me*, as claiming heritage that way is both appropriation of a culture not my own and a denial of the complexity of what I actually am. This is why I seek an App-ul-lay-shun identity that's actually mine, a desire troubled by the seeming absence beneath it.

Appalachia is all of it. Appalachia exists today as the overlapping scribbles that create not a meaningless but a new totality. Hollers, banjos, split-levels, Run DMC, flowing streams, strip malls, dulcimers, electric guitars. Still, it's worth thinking about what part of the scribbling each of us belongs to. Do we just read the whole thing and say, *this doesn't make sense*? Or are we actively shaping and defining which of the layers will matter? Do we think about what the layers mean, and maybe how the ones that are given weight indicate a certain underlying value?

Scholars have examined this, in the ways scholars do. Many have approached Appalachia in very much the way that scholars approach the texts of Livingstone. They apply the spectroscopy of theory, interview, literature, cultural examination, history, science, religion, all of that. In so doing, they tease out the different aspects that make the whole. I fear and resent, of course, the ways that certain definitions are declared as *real* or *true* or *authentic*, particularly since so many of these definitions leave me out: weirdo Northern Appalachian, former pro golfer, highly educated and nonaccented Maritime-loving me.

We have to think, also, about the marks left in the margins, those big-dicked scribbles that give us a sense of how the readers and writers of Appalachia have approached the enterprise. Slag heaps are big-dick scribbles. Abandoned mines are big-dick scribbles. Opioid abuse is a big-dick scribble.

Poverty is a big-dick scribble. Stereotypes are big-dick scribbles. *Deliverance* is a big-dick scribble. The books I have read that told me who I was and where I was from even before I knew it are big-dick scribbles. Not knowing what I was or where I'm from are big-dick scribbles. *App-uh-lay-shuh* versus *App-uh-latch-hh* is a big-dick scribble. Brain tumors, poisoned water, dirty soil, extractive industry, Donald Trump, these are all big-dick scribbles. Loving it all is also a big-dick scribble, loving it as you hate it, seeing the gouges even as you see a flash of fading winter light dart past the Homer City Generating Station that dominates the horizon behind the family farm, a whole landscape for just a moment glowing in ethereal light, hills, trees, and steam rising from the cooling tower stacks, what the power plant represents and what the ground has always meant, and what it all maybe could be if we let it.

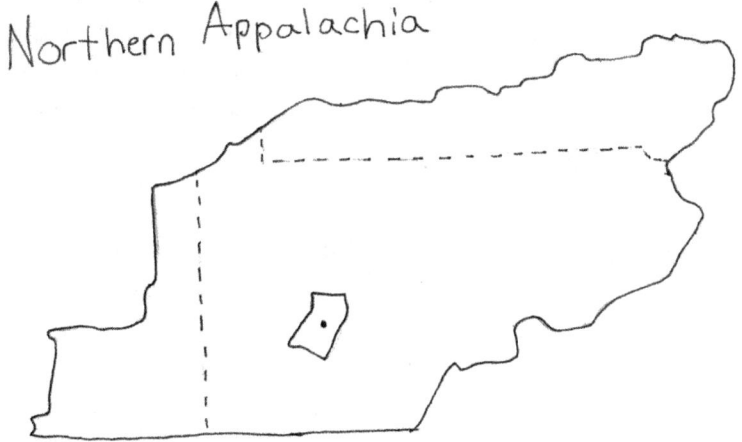

CHAPTER 6

The Molt

There's a great problem in writing a health memoir, particularly one dealing with a brain tumor. There are really only two possible narratives. In one, the author learns to overcome a great obstacle in the face of immense peril, then survives, wiser and more thankful. In the other, the author dies. This narrative is also somehow supposed to be uplifting: powerful lessons learned from a voice crystalized by coming death, refined even more because the text on the page is a *memento mori* and, therefore, wiser still. And from a purely literary perspective, I think we are supposed to prefer the second sort. It's more ambivalent, so better (this is what I teach my students, after all, about happy endings in fiction and nonfiction, and how they are ultimately less satisfying). There's more drama in death. Plus dying makes an author more reliable. His analysis of the lived life has been made finer by the specter of death, purified in the end by its actuality.

I have not participated in that mortal narrative, however, nor do I wish to have done so. I was a forty-year-old man when I learned I had a brain tumor, and I am now a forty-two-year-old man who still has a brain tumor, unremovable because of risk to my vision but rendered dead—my doctors assure me—by a sequence of surgery and radiation. Yet when I first learned of that tumor, when words like *meningioma* and *optic glioma* came into my vocabulary, one term delimiting the state of benignity and the other malignancy, I understood that all narratives were possible. And that might have been the hardest thing to absorb: to imagine that I was living a story with an undefined ending. Nor did I then know how long I had to write this book. Should I have been hurrying? Was there a clock ticking, or could I take my time and check Facebook?

Here's the first gloss of my narrative, built from notes I jotted down in the days after my diagnosis:

I shocked my local friends by telling them I had a brain tumor.

I emailed old friends, doctors now, and shocked them also by telling them I had a brain tumor.

I shouted at a faculty meeting about the financial crisis of my college and how the trustees' failure to draw down the endowment to cover several years of struggle was nothing more than a lack of faith in us, the untenured faculty. I thought about the tumor in my head while doing that, and I'm pretty sure I wouldn't have said anything if I hadn't had one. What did I have to lose?

Just a couple of weeks before surgery, I interviewed for a job at another college, in the same city as my pending surgery.

I told small lies to my children, and I wept, often, thinking about the various and deep injustices of death, shortened life, transformation, and how we want to think of transformation as a positive alteration, the hardening of fresh wings, the shedding of a restrictive body for the new, better, transcendent.

But transformation is neither easy nor always necessarily positive. L. A. Paul writes of this troubling reality in *Transformative Experience*. In categorizing human moments of upheaval, she explains that such periods "can be epistemically transformative, giving you new information in virtue of your experience. And they can be personally transformative, changing how you experience being who you are." The trouble enters when we think about those moments in their most dramatic sense, when the transformation is both epistemic and personal, when we become a *new* person on the other side of a change that radically alters how we think of ourselves. Paul writes, "You cannot know what it is like to have that kind of experience until you've had it. In this situation, you cannot determine the subjective value of any outcome that involves what it is like for you to have or have had that experience."

The comforting effect of narrative is that it presumes the ability of choice, which is precisely what Paul writes throughout her book, arguing that the trouble of making rational decisions in the context of radical transformation is that the decision is predicated on becoming something different from what you are. And that is, of course, impossible. In essence, the tension of transformation is the tension of narrative collapse. There's no story like this one because the story belongs to us and has not been lived yet. In the case of medical drama, is it any mystery that so many turn to the pabulum narratives that already exist? They're easier than the messy reality of living on, forever suspended in a semi-buoyant space of *not anymore* and *now what*.

I search, then, for metaphors as a way to bring the unknown into the context of the known. And I think about the remarkable creature of the periodical cicada, the creepy, dramatic bug that is found nowhere else on the planet other than the zones around my Appalachian home. Of the roughly three thousand species of cicada in the world, all of which experience long life cycles, most of which are spent as nymphs underground; only eastern North America's periodical cicadas act on mutual clocks. There are six species of the periodical cicada, half of which live on a seventeen-year cycle and the other half on thirteen. These species are further separated into broods, geographically grouped populations that emerge together in certain years. In Pennsylvania, all of the periodical cicadas run a seventeen-year cycle, with respective broods appearing en masse only a few times within the scope of a human lifetime.

The periodical cicada holds one of science's greatest genus names: *Magicicada*, a term I can only imagine was coined because of the apparently occult nature of their appearance. For sixteen years, nothing—then a sudden explosion of singing, clicking, flying bodies. Individually, they are red-eyed and sinister, appearing together as a conjurer's trick, a plague that does little harm beyond surprise and volume but that looks like the end of the world.

In the summer of 2008, a brood of *Magicicada* emerged in southwestern Pennsylvania—my home then, a few years before the job in the northwestern corner drew me away. The cicadas' cast-off, too-tight skins soon filled the underbrush, clinging to the eaves of homes, and latching on to stems, leaves, and trees. A biological magic wand had been waved somewhere and, presto, the early summer was filled with a flying circus of rare creatures. Their crushed bodies, too numerous for cars to dodge, slickened roadways, and in some places, great stenches of rotted cicada accented the presence of death in our cycles of life.

In his influential, *Magic, Science and Religion*, Polish anthropologist Bronisław Malinowski argues that magic

> enables man to carry out with confidence his important tasks, to maintain his poise, and his mental integrity in fits of anger, in the throes of hate, of unrequited love, of despair and anxiety. The function of magic is to ritualize man's optimism, to enhance his faith in the victory of hope over fear. Magic expresses the greater value for man of confidence over doubt, of steadfastness over vacillation, of optimism over pessimism.

Malinowski arrived at this conclusion based on his studies of magic in "primitive" cultures, examinations that led him to argue against the then current wisdom of cultural binaries. While Malinowski unselfconsciously labeled his non-Western study subjects as *primitive*, he also made the case that magic was not derived from irrational, simplistic minds but, instead, works in concert with a deep understanding of the world within which people live. He argues that magic cannot be easily divided from the scientific or rational since the cultural practice of ritual, myth, and indeed all religion comes from studied observations of the nature of existence.

I think, then, of *Magicicada* and the root of its genus name, *magi*, and also of magic, of the Persian prophet Zoroaster, whose followers were the first to be called magi, and of the Magi of Christianity, those three wise men from the East who followed the stars to visit a newly born Christ. I think of the emergence of *Magicicada* and of those European immigrants to North America who must have lain in shock as the magic creatures dug free from the ground, apparently released from their tombs to live again. I think of how many would have been frightened at such emergence, would have decried such appearances as work of the devil and further sign of the cursed lands to which they had moved: first famine, now this. And I consider how the appearance of fear comes about because of a failure to know the land itself. Anyone who knows the place understands the periodical cycle, can predict the cicadas' appearance and recognize it as mere biology.

Yet I find myself not interested in the biology, but rather am moved by the confluence of the cicada as Magi, as early monotheists, as wise voyagers who pay homage to an incarnation of optimism and goodness. Indeed, I think about the long periods underground and the miracle of cyclical emergence. In the discarded husks of thousands of cicada, I see the improbable magic of nature, the ridiculous good faith to figure that something deeply buried will emerge and crack out of ill-fitting shells to perpetuate the brood.

The year 2008 marked an important moment in our return to Appalachia. My wife and I had returned home from France just three years prior and made a prototypical move of early middle-age by buying a house and saying, *this is it*. Yet 2008 also marked our first encounter with the specter of loss, a simultaneous act of connection and violent uprooting, Appalachia welcoming and denying us. The cicadas buzzed and died, and it is no lack of rationality for me to consider these deaths as a tragedy of some order. I know now about the depths of my own cycles, or at least am beginning to understand.

No one really knows why meningiomas form, but they do, and much more frequently than you'd expect. Many people carry them, unseen, and also without effect, hidden within their skulls. I don't like thinking about that, partly because the prevalence of tumors strikes me as terrifying, but also because I am troubled when I think of myself as commonly afflicted. That's a weird aspect of serious illness: the desire to be special in affliction. This might just be a personal character flaw, but I can't help but feel trapped in a bizarre competition of illness. I feel slightly superior when someone complains about suffering a *lesser* problem, a bit chastened when someone perseveres against a disease more serious, say something defined as malignant instead of benign, something that precisely threatened life instead of just vision.

This is a strange kind of guilt. Since my diagnosis, I've found it hard to take my tumor seriously, even as it has always felt absolutely overwhelmingly despairing. Since my treatments, friends have referred to the tumor as cancer, and I never correct them. I don't because, really, that's not the conversation we're having, and it's too hard to stand back and say, *well, let me run down the pathology of this, the structures of the brain, quick biology lesson here.* Even more than that, the question of whether it is cancer or not confuses me, since I'm not a medical doctor. Since it's *not cancer*, which is to say it is a tumor that has so far showed no signs of malignancy, it seems not to matter, something I know to be true even as I know it not to be true. I'm creating too much of an equation here, I realize, weighing the severity of affliction again, worrying that correcting people—*nope, not cancer*—would lead to the dismissal of the severity of what I faced and continue to struggle with.

Technically, no, my tumor is not *cancer,* since it has been designated as benign. A meningioma is a lesion growing on the meninges, the thin wrapper of the brain, and mine is on the inside of the optic sheath, the meningeal membrane that coats the optic nerve. It is small, just 11 mm by 6 mm, but the optic nerve is also small, just the thickness of a hair. My tumor is tucked against the optic foramen, the tiny hole through which the optic nerve passes through the skull into the brain proper. That's why it's a bad spot, because any growth means more pinching of the nerve, more blindness, and, eventually, optic nerve death. Untreated, it would keep growing, taking my vision, eventually even growing outward as well, leading to a bulging eyeball. There could have been some risk that the growth could have headed inward also, through the foramen. Tumor growth is by definition out of control, even when the tumor is benign. All it wants to do is grow. It is growth for growth's sake, growth also being uncontrollable when it has no purpose beyond itself. Here's another way I see myself and Appalachia and native molting cicadas as metaphorical echoes.

Think about the sudden inundation of flying, shouting cicadas, their bodies coating every surface, mad with their instinctual desire to propagate. They do it, perhaps, for a reason called *predator satiation*, the notion that a huge population means creatures that feed on cicadas will get their fill without decimating the species. A fast explosion means there's no defense, no way to stop things, even if cicadas are *benign* and do little damage other than causing annoyance and fright in their emergence.

Think about economic growth, how that's a purely accepted need in our national consciousness. The economy must grow or things are bad. But growth is never without negative impact, even if you can't know who will suffer it. Think about who benefits from economic growth, particularly in the Appalachian context. Usually, the people who host the growth—the people of Appalachia—suffer the most. Yes, they get jobs, but rarely great ones, and pretty much always people other than Appalachians benefit. And once the growth ends, Appalachia is left with a big hole, and nothing to fill it with. Growth turns on Appalachia, just as mine might have turned on me, so even if we don't call growth-based capitalism a cancer per se—and I find myself a bit uneasy with that term of reference—economic growth is at the very best *benign,* which is not to say it is good.

Think about my benign tumor and how even calling it *benign* is a leap of faith, since its sensitive spot makes it impossible to even biopsy. I learned about that after the surgery, when Aziz explained that he and Happ found it tucked inside the sheath and agreed that doing anything to the tumor would have placed my vision at serious risk. They still considered the surgery a success, as their primary goal was to remove bone and tissue, slicing away the sphenoid process in order to open space in my head. Goal two was the biopsy. Goal three was to remove as much tumor as possible. Only goal one could be achieved, the two surgeons deciding the area was too sensitive. Eight hours of surgery just meant a little space for swelling, an inevitability during the summer of radiation that followed the surgery.

Ultimately, the goal of my surgery was to disrupt cycles. Tumors grow, and the measurement of rate designates their existence as benign or malignant, cancerous or not, threat or just there. The rads I took broke that cycle, stopped the wad of tissue in its tracks, or at least was intended to. I live now in a perpetual state of clock watching: Has the tumor stopped growing or just slowed? Is it dead or just dormant, lying in wait to spring to life by some unknown call, digging out from beneath my optic sheath to emerge anew? And I tell you, I cannot help but think about the tumor as red-eyed, sharp-clawed, and winged, a beast that will forever shock in its appearance.

Molting is a widespread phenomenon. Snakes leave behind dried skins like ghost reflections. The tiny hairs of our long-dead beagle that remained throughout our house for years, that traveled on our clothing to work, stuck to peanut butter sandwiches dropped on the floor, that we still found on her favorite blankets, were part of her constant molt. Humans slough off skin in a steady process that resembles a sort of molt. We're built of layers, an outer dermis and underlying epidermis, which work always upward from the core, raising new cells from the depths into fresh air while old skin cells litter our bedsheets and the insides of our sweaters. Deeper still, nearly every cell in the body cycles through life spans. Our skin is renewed, our bones are renewed, the greater bulk of our physical being replaces itself. With the exception of the rigid permanence of our brains, a human being who has reached, say, twenty years of age is a completely different physical object than when newly born. We constantly renew ourselves, whether we think to or not.

Yet when I think of molting, I think of the more dramatic and obvious process of arthropods, creatures trapped within shells that don't grow with them. Insects and crustaceans outlive the usefulness of the armor they produce and must escape. Videos of this process are jarring, otherworldly, and appear painful. Time-lapse images of cicadas show a slow expansion of an apparently resting organism, an inflation, like a tire pump left on too long. The shell cracks, and a new cicada emerges, wings crinkled but otherwise fine. During their molt, crabs appear to ooze out from the midline of their carapaces until the tops flip open and the animals withdraw each soft leg from the old chambers. Crayfish lie on gravelly bottoms, writhing inside their shells until they suddenly explode outward in a startling and violent release. In each of these cases, molting doesn't seem like a process of growth. Instead, to my eye, which is used to the slow softness of mammalian physiology, these molts look like death, as if one creature has consumed another from the inside and must make a fast getaway.

In fact, the biological process is described in far less dramatic terms. It's simple enough: The creature grows too big for its shell. Molting fluid weakens the bonds between exoskeleton and soft epidermis and then fills the new spaces in the old shell. The arthropod wriggles, sucks in air, sometimes raises the fluid pressure of its body until the old exoskeleton cracks, then it crawls, climbs, or shoots out. The chitin of the new shell soon hardens, and the creature resumes life in its next stage—bigger, older, and once again covered by a rigid protective suit.

I feel now like a creature who has undergone a molt, or perhaps one who is still halfway through. The shell has broken, and I'm exposed to the world with a softened and vulnerable middle. I find myself quick to cry these days, maddening in its frequency: the manipulative swell of music in a mass-market film, the sudden thought that my four-year-old will not always be four, the pleasure at watching both of our boys play together kindly, sharp words from either me or my wife and that terrible lacuna between anger and regret, the news every night. I long every day for the hardening, for either the new or old me to calcify.

What's hardest to equate is that all I'm doing now is living my life, and that the treatment of my brain tumor is not separate from my life. It is my life. There is a rough concept of the narrative of medicine, that we go in with the notion of cure, magic in essence, to be made what we were before we were sick. But the body doesn't often work that way. We might be returned to contour, or repaired, or our cycles realigned, but we are not fixed, restored, back to what we were.

We all carry scars. I have many from childhood falls, and they grow with me. I carry a bald streak in the front of my hairline from when I hit my head on that electric meter outside of John's house in third grade, his mother the nurse, their white porcelain sink splashed red as I bled, freshly scarred forever. Then there's the divot on my knee when I wrecked my bike, and when later that night I awoke to see the terrifying omen of a bat flying around the ceiling of my room. The hairline traces of the three broken arms I earned while in elementary school, each a memento of healed fractures clearly visible on X-rays. The screws now in my skull, which airport agents can see each time I walk through security. The headaches. The perpetually thinner hair on the left side of my head, where radiation damaged follicles as it destroyed my tumor. The drooping of my left eyelid as I tire. The new philosophy of scarring. The antibodies we develop after a cold.

Our bodies record everything that threatens, or maybe the body is actually defined by the things that threaten it. We become us by the way we heal from damage or, better put, we become a new self constantly by stacking on the history of our own injury. We are made in how we struggle against the difficulty of living; we are soft and vulnerable, but somehow resilient, not bouncing back but forward.

In 2005 my wife and I decided to dig in to our home ground in southwestern Pennsylvania, not far from where each of us grew up and where our parents still live. My wife liked the job she found there at a small school in the Laurel Highlands, and I liked the one I eventually found teaching at the university where my father had taught and where I had been an undergraduate. We decided that, yes, we were Appalachians, and there we would stay.

Late in 2008 Jen became pregnant. Satisfied with our rootedness, we soon bought a house, and it was to this home where we would carry our first son as a newborn, where he would learn to walk, where he would grow rapidly into himself. We thought wisely of our decision to move from France to southwestern Pennsylvania. That summer, Brood XIV of *Magicicada* emerged, their eerie buzzing lament filling the summer air.

Shortly before our son was born, a new head of school arrived where my wife taught, bringing new ideas from her job at an affluent private school in California. Within a year, she blithely axed the French program and, with it, my wife's job. Late in the fall of 2010, my department chose to ignore my application for a tenure-track position, a snub I found particularly demoralizing. I had worked there for three years, teaching well and shouldering more responsibilities than required, and the job had been a good fit. I received no interview, not even a quiet word in the hallway from friends or professors that I'd not passed muster.

When I received a new job offer elsewhere in early 2011, doing precisely what I had applied to do at the old job but at a far stronger school, I felt vindication. My wife and I saw the moment as a turning point. She became pregnant again. I remember declaring 2011 the year when we would, for the first time in twelve years of marriage, begin to feel truly settled.

Early on the morning of St. Patrick's Day, I awoke and noticed the absence of my wife in our bed. Our son lay quietly asleep beside me, snoring lightly. Barely, I heard sobs from downstairs. I rose and found my wife, distraught, clutching her nightshirt to herself. She told me about heavy clots, which I tried to believe were nothing to fear. Our midwife, godmother to our son, was out of town. By the middle of the day, we sat in the office of an unfamiliar midwife, who confirmed what we both already knew to be true: we had suffered a miscarriage.

This was a mourning for which we were unprepared. Well-meaning people, relatives among them, assured us of the blessing of the occasion. Miscarriages, we were told, were a natural sign of an unviable pregnancy. But this sounded to us like an indictment of the child we felt we already knew. Such declarations call forth a narrative I refuse to accept, called that child unviable, a nonperson, mere blood and tissue that *didn't take*. This is, perhaps, biologically accurate, but it is also not comforting. We mourned an absence, a person we didn't quite get to know, who certainly felt real enough. Our son had referred to the new life in my wife's womb as *she*. A few nights after the miscarriage, he told my wife that he had heard a baby crying in the middle of the night, and we couldn't help but wonder what he felt or knew. He told us later that he missed his sister.

"Man has to live his life in the shadow of death," Bronisław Malinowski writes, "and he who clings to life and enjoys its fullness must dread the menace of its end. And he who is faced by death turns to the promise of life." This is itself magic, the ability to bear loss, even the capacity to live when we are conscious of our own finite limitations. Yet loss presses hard against me. It is a shell I cannot shake. It is a suit of armor one size too small, whose receipt I have misplaced. It is the slowly drifting body of a dead bug in a quiet pond, revealing the quiet of its heart through translucent flesh.

Magicicada is a show-off, a genus that practices coy absences and dramatic entries. It is perhaps no exaggeration to call *Magicicada* a diva, intent on making each appearance an event, determined to, beyond all else, be noticed. And while the great scientific mystery of harmonized cycles remains, less-ostentatious annual cicadas appear each summer. It is these insects whose discarded bodies I find most often, and it is their August call that marks the truest sign of summer and the constant reminder of cycles.

I am a man who has spent the greater portion of his life in school, subject to that schedule, and as a professor will continue to do so for most of the rest of my life. As such, my years are divided between the intensity of semesters and the broad languid freedom of summer and winter recesses. As a child, the annual appearance of the cicada always inspired a certain level of dread. Such is the feeling of August: excitement at warm days that encourage swimming but also a foreboding reality of the coming school year. Were I a better adult, I would now claim an inversion of that emotion. I would explain how the presence of the cicada signals an exciting moment of cyclical renewal, that school will soon be upon me, and that I enter that period with vigor and enthusiasm. Soon I will enter anew into the intellectual arena, where I draw energy from the invigorating exchange of ideas. Instead, I am forever a boy, standing beneath the trio of tall cedars in my parents' backyard, listening to the cicadas sing of shortening days, coming books, and the end to aimless wandering.

More or less every summer I find the dried husk of one of the insects clinging in an unlikely place: the bottom of a table, the swinging gate of the backyard, the thorny stalk of a rose bush. These are either stragglers off the clock or a different species of cicada, nonperiodic ones that do their buggy metamorphosis more frequently. Each discovery comes with a shock because a cicada is a startling creature: red eyes, high-volume buzz, sharp legs. They mean no harm, and once they're out from underground, they commit no crime more serious than their appearance. The adults don't even eat much. That's left to the nymphs buried in the soil, who suck juices from roots. Even that causes little damage to trees.

I find the emptied out shells of cicadas somehow creepier than the real thing. The translucent shell, the split down the centerline of the back, the perfect, indelible facsimile of the cicada's face, legs, eyes, ridges, and claws, its life-cycle clinging, dead but clinging to something. The shell signals desperation as much as it does renewal. It is a husk from which life has emerged, but that is also an apparition of violent end. This is a transformative change, and one I cannot know whether the cicada anticipates, intuits, or understands at all.

L. A. Paul writes:

> A life lived rationally and authentically, then, as each decision is encountered, involves deciding whether or how to make a discovery about who you will become. If revelation comes from experience, there can be value in discovering how one's preferences and lived experience develop, simply for what such experience teaches. One of the most important games of life, then, is the game of Revelation, a game played for the sake of play itself.

For the cicada, change just is, this natural molt and growth. There is no decision for a cicada, just the automatic violence of molting. I do not molt, of course, at least not in this way, and for my own back to split open would be disaster. I cannot ever crawl out of myself. I cannot ever leave my husk behind, to walk on larger and more mature. Perhaps, in regarding the husk of a cicada, I feel envy: if only I could do this.

In the rapid period leading up to my surgery, diagnosis in February and anesthetic by the end of March, I hustled across the state to visit one of my oldest friends, John. He lives in the leafy suburb of Swarthmore, in a townhouse abutting the grounds of his alma mater there and near the train station that ushers him daily to the University of Pennsylvania hospitals where he is a radiation oncologist. The night before the appointments he arranged for me to gather second opinions in a world-class hospital, we sat around the table with his family, including his mother, the former nurse who observed my first, most obvious head wound, that cracking against her outdoor electric meter. We ate a casserole, John, his wife, his cousin from Greece, his mother, his kids, and me gathered around the dining room table. John and I had not spoken at length in more than a decade, and we launched into our childhood stories.

Once we were on Matt's farm, John said. He turned to me. *Do you know what I'm going to say?*

I held back the laughter that arrived, this joy of common mind forged by our original histories, this first best friend of mine. Long ago, we had been thrilled by how our phone numbers shared every digit save the last two. In second grade, we often were confused, offering each other's numbers instead of our own when asked.

The tree, I said, and John was laughing too.

He told the story to his wife and his children about how we found a hatchet in my father's workshop. We carried it to a small stand of spruce trees and took turns hacking it into the bark until fresh sap began to flow. My father discovered us. Of course he did. There was yelling, anger at the destruction we wrought in our desire for boyish who-knows-what. There was embarrassment, John for falling from grace in front of my father and me for getting in trouble in front of a best friend who I always considered better than me. I still feel that way. I have to admit that our later loss of closeness has long haunted me, a pain with no reconciliation, even within the warm closeness of a visit to his home, sharing a meal with his family, understanding that who we once were together remains always, even if there isn't quite a now to us.

Early the next morning, John and I drove to the hospital and talked in comfort, old friends who had not seen each other in seventeen years, since my wedding in 1999, a year that happened to coincide with the emergence of *Magicicada* brood V, which would lay dormant beneath Pennsylvania soil until shortly after my brain surgery in the spring of 2016. Eventually, John and I got to the kind of directness only possible in the intimacy of permanent friendship: *we hate to use radiation on forty-year-olds*, he told me, *because you're almost guaranteed to get a tumor later in life from the treatment itself.*

This turns me again to my own strange sense of guilt, when people refer to me as having brain cancer. No, I haven't, but I don't know what to say in response because cancer is conceptually hard for me to weigh. At heart, I suppose it's about proliferation and spread. A cancer will grow out of control (but so might a benign tumor), but it will spread and metastasize to other parts of the body in a way a benign tumor never will. I am supposed to be reassured by the full body CT scan I received during my diagnosis, which found no proliferation of tumors elsewhere. My tumor is benign medically, something contained.

Yet my tumor is certainly still impactful. Benign is still a risk, to vision in my case. Worst of all, the containment of my benign tumor meant choosing to establish an undefined cycle of likely cancer: my choice to treat something that had to be treated meant defining myself as a future cancer patient. The meningioma may be benign, but to mitigate its risk I had to roll the dice for my own future. And, as we all know, the house always wins. I essentially decided to get cancer to defeat the tumor, for now. Maybe I should put this another way; I decided to take ownership of my own personal definitions—regardless of what that might mean down the road—instead of relying on the preexisting narratives that often govern us. You don't want cancer, ergo you shouldn't want radiation. But I did, and I'm glad for it. Mostly.

I didn't really think about my self-selected fate until more than a year after my treatments ended. That's when I had to accept the easy lie of choice. I erupted again into the sort of heavy sobbing that I hadn't felt since I was a child but comes back so easily now that I have become a man with a tumor. Dormancy functions in so many aspects of our lives. Clearly I'm not over all this, and how could I be? I do not know the period of my dormancy, whether cancer will lie in check for ten years, twenty, eleven, or seventeen before its red-eyed fury arrives, animation coming again to the dead husk I know lies within the lining of my brain.

That's my problem of *reclamation*: treatment back to baseline more or less determines that I introduce the circular nature of boom and bust to myself, that I step on the medical treadmill and submit to being a brain tumor patient forever. In fact, that fate was delivered to me precisely at my neurosurgical one-year follow-up. I quipped to the scheduling nurse that, no offense, I looked forward to the day when I could see her for the last time. She's a lovely person, and we had been chatting a moment before about how she and her husband were hoping to buy a cabin in the heavily wooded territory near my northwestern Pennsylvania home, an hour and a half north of Pittsburgh.

I have bad news, she told me, *you'll be seeing us every year for the rest of your life.*

That's my fate, since there is really never recovery from having had brain surgery. The surgery is over, the radiation is over, but there's no going back. I'll never be a man who didn't have a brain tumor. The six weeks of radiation I received should have killed the tumor, but unlike other kinds of lesions, meningiomas don't disintegrate and disappear. My tumor remains in my skull, ready to be photographed once or twice a year. We'll watch it forever to make sure it doesn't reawaken or switch to some long cycle of dormancy and then mad growth. There's no escape from my surgeons or from the reeling kind of seesaw conversation I had with the nurse. One moment you're living your life and the next you're having a crushing epistemological conversation about medical fate, understanding that the biology of meningiomas and the geography of my tumor's location means I get to keep the souvenir, the tumor itself dead and lumpy, a sort of startling relic husk forever clinging to the inside of my optic sheath like a translucent carapace, claws frozen perpetually to the underside of me.

The act of the molt is an act of life, entry into a new cycle nearer maturity. Yet the molt also places us into an indefensible position of vulnerability. In growing, we weaken ourselves, shed the armor that helps make us formidable. We become little more than raw flesh, forced to wait for our chitin to harden once again.

How, then, do I choose to live? Maybe like this: Saturday mornings, my older son and I used to drive into town for swimming lessons at the YMCA. He preferred when we rode in the pickup truck, when the center perch of his car seat commanded a fuller view through the windshield and, I think, when he appreciated the vehicle the same way I did, as some kind of antidote to middle-American respectability. I teach environmental literature, so a four-wheel-drive pickup isn't the sort of Prius I'm supposed to drive.

THE MOLT

We were in the pool together on these mornings, a blue swim float clipped around my son's waist. The added buoyancy tended to hold him upright, so his first gleeful leap into the water left him nearly standing. He kicked his legs and grinned, reaching forward to dig the water as his teacher taught him, and shot off into the pool. I used to follow, submerged to the neck, and offer only the sort of gentle encouragement I imagine I could bear in his position. The truth is, I hated swim lessons as a child and recall clinging to the side of the university pool with tears streaming into the chlorinated water. I didn't like being told what to do, and, a sensitive kid, I was likely felled mostly by the high-volume shouts of the college students teaching the class.

I hear that same tone in the teachers who direct the older kids at the Y, the local children who were just a few months older than my sons when they learned to swim, who have graduated into the class that lets them be in the pool without a parent—or forces them to be in the pool without a parent. One of the goals of the class I took with my son is to give the children the confidence to swim by themselves, to eventually pluck the parents from the water and plant them on the hard benches, left to choke in the humid air of the room. I watched a few kids work through that hurdle in our class, tears and cries while their parents crouched on the deck, with swimsuits bunched, cleavage gaping or beer guts squished by the angle of encouragement.

My son and I swam on, half listening to the directions of our teacher. For a professor, I've turned out to be a pretty poor adult student. But we swam, and we did so with the sort of baleful joy that draws me to open water. He raced me, commanding that I swim underwater while he swam above. He laughed and even sang to himself as he pulled his body from one side of the pool to the other.

He was three and a half, just a few months away from finally being a big brother. My wife was pregnant again then, she and I having silently passed the moment in the pregnancy when, just a little, we could relax. Her belly had reasserted itself. The bloom of the pregnancy inflated her breasts, accented the curve of her hips. Inside, our son swam in his own fluid. He was active, just as our first son was, flipping constantly, a hand or foot occasionally reaching out to dent the skin of my wife's belly.

I glided in the water beside my son, reached a hand up from the depths to support his back when he tried to float. For months, he refused to do so, jack-knifed so his legs pointed at the sky. He flailed his arms and demanded to be released, to be flipped back over onto his belly so he could swim again through free water. I remember keenly the day he lay still for the first time. I felt the tension of his body release just enough, his backside inching in line with his torso and legs. With the tips of my fingers alone, I supported his body as he stretched out, ears in the water, nearly floating by himself. But I mark it as a great victory that my son refused to be still. His feet kicked, just so, a flutter of motion that belied his refusal to give up. I'm not sure I could take it if he did, if he lay flat on his back or, worse, facedown in the position swim instructors call the dead man's float. I could not bear it if his own body took on the nature of stillness. Quiet matters, more to me now than ever before, space to gather and recover strength, to reflect, to hold onto flagging energy. Yet I want always something to move—a finger, a foot, a mind—some signal that all is not lost, that we haven't given up on becoming something anew. That my son always moved cracks me open, just enough, so I can wriggle free from that which holds me back. There is life here, his kicking feet signaled. There will be life here tomorrow.

CHAPTER 7

Conduits

When I drive to the Northeast, I prefer New York's slower Southern Tier Expressway to the roughly parallel thruway, even though the older road is rougher, longer, and lacking in official rest areas where you can stop and get fuel, coffee, and overpriced snacks. Instead, the expressway winds between small Appalachian towns not far above the Pennsylvania border and through the sovereign territory of the Seneca Nation, signaled most clearly by the glittery structure of the Allegany-Seneca Casino. Recently, a friend referred to this building as "an abomination," a criticism likely formed by the way a casino is not the same thing as the mountain behind it, its peaks reflecting in the dark green-blue glass walls, and its topography something the casino seems to echo at least in part. Certainly, the parking garage is hideous (aren't they all?), yet the casino itself displays care, a design that might not be invisible but, at the very least, interacts with its place.

I'm thinking of what David George-Shongo Jr. recently told me about the place where the casino resides: *People are surprised this is the reservation. They say,* but there's a McDonald's. *Yeah, McDonald's are in how many places around the world?*

David is director of the Seneca-Iroquois National Museum, a modest, low-slung block building within view of the casino and just around the corner from the tidy, striking, modern administrative offices of the Seneca Nation. Money from the casino helped pay for that office building, helps support highway repairs and schools, and will contribute funding toward a new building for the museum itself.

I had driven along the Southern Tier Expressway to get here, taking the exit near the gleaming casino, and steered into the administrative offices parking lot to talk with David and Tribal Councillor Steve Gordon. Steve is an energetic man of about sixty with an office that looks out on the mountain and the casino and whose walls are covered with various artifacts. I came to ask them a deceivingly simple question: do the Seneca see themselves as Appalachians?

Politically, the climate does not allow that, Steve said.

That's the short answer, one that links to long histories of regional identity, tribal identity, colonial exploration, and reneged treaties. Steve approached the longer, more complicated answer by explaining that when you look at the landscape around the headquarters of the Seneca Nation near Salamanca, New York, you see tall ridges to the south and flat earth to the north. He referenced glaciers, how they came down from the north and sort of stopped, right where we were sitting.

That's why I believe our people came here, he said, *because the glaciated ground was fertile, and flat land was easy to farm, and the openness allowed for good sun.* On the other side of that flattened plain, mountains provide water and, in fact, a sense of self. In their own language, the Seneca are the O-non-dowa-gah, the people of the Great Hill, as David explained.

We identify that way, he said.

As long as Appalachia is here, we're here, Steve added. *If it is to go under for any reason, we're probably next.*

And this is about the mountains and the land, which are very much part of the whole deal. Steve meant to explain that we cannot be separated from the mountains, the plants, the animals, the rocks, the water. This is Appalachia, a connection between the landscape and the people, geology and culture. The mountains reflect in our windows, are part of us, are layered upon us, just as we are layered upon them, casting our shadows across their shapes. We are the mountains and they are us.

I recently learned about the academic study of a certain kind of mapping called "persuasive cartography." In the online introduction to Cornell University's P. J. Mode Collection of various propaganda and message-centric maps, the curators set things up this way:

> In fact, no map provides an entirely objective view of reality. Even the best-intended cartographer must decide what projection to use, what features to include and what to exclude, what colors, what shading, what text, what images—all of which shape the message communicated by the finished project. Every map is somewhere along a spectrum from objective to subjective, from science to art.

Maps are simply narratives inscribed on the land, dependent on the whims of the mapmaker and, more so, the person hiring the mapmaker. Consider the underground maps being made on my family farm by thumper trucks. Such maps would offer an accurate location of gas deposits, but they would not necessarily be accurate maps of what the Two Lick Valley is. Or, at the very least, I wouldn't share the values of those maps. Such maps persuade toward a perspective I don't share, imply a relationship with the landscape valued in dollars and measured by the wealth beneath the surface.

Consider as well how ancient maps were quite different from contemporary ones. Nautical maps, for example, don't always list the names of landmasses, because the point is to navigate the water: useless if you have a car, pointedly applicable in a boat. Some western transcriptions of traditional oceanic maps show only the currents of the oceans, and some ancient maps from this part of the Pacific were just bits of coral tossed on the ground to teach navigators how to follow the stars or sticks lashed together to form a concrete model of the ocean swells that signal land masses. Consider the difference of perspective that emerges when you conceive of a map for an outrigger driven by wind and a map intended to guide a giant ocean freighter efficiently between ports. Currents matter less in the second case, maybe affect fuel cost some but don't dictate the route you take. The currents are the route for an ancient Wayfinder, the night sky the actual chart.

Or consider the Southern Tier Expressway, that often-buckling ribbon of asphalt that winds its way through Appalachian New York and over the Seneca Nation's ancient Forbidden Path, a fact of history signaled in I-86's official route markers, which feature the stylized profile of a clichéd American Indian. The highway does not carry the name Forbidden Path, probably a title that would make any local chamber of commerce wince. I'm sure that the Seneca who still live here would not look favorably on such a name for a highway that effaces their own history.

The Forbidden Path carried that name because travelers needed permission from the Seneca to walk it, so there's deep dishonor in the presence of the stylized American Indian on the I-86 road signs, intended likely as some commemoration or acknowledgment that the highway runs through the Seneca Nation. Yet, of course, the logo fixes American Indian existence in a romanticized past, and it certainly does not acknowledge the Seneca right to decide who gets to walk or drive their territory. Not surprisingly, this highway arrived in conflict, as the Seneca opposed the construction of I-86 through their land, but some kind of deal was reached, land exchanged for some insufficient sum of money, and now there it is.

Steve Gordon has been active in Seneca politics for a long time, and he's old enough to have remembered when close to seven hundred people lost their homes to another federally driven exchange of land for not-land. In 1965, the same year that the ARC was defined by Congress, the United States declared eminent domain on territory of the Seneca Nation, when the Kinzua Dam was built in northern Pennsylvania. Construction of the dam blocked the Allegheny River into its present state as a flood-control reservoir. Some ten thousand acres of Seneca farmland were lost forever to the backup, despite a 1794 treaty identifying the land as belonging perpetually to the Seneca. Still, the Seneca had to move. On maps, the river became a large blotch, miles of backed-up water making an artificial lake flooding fertile ground no longer available to farm.

Eminent domain strikes me as a violent exertion of persuasive cartography, maps now reflecting the way one sovereign nation can claim precedence over another. It would be unthinkable for the United States to claim territory upriver from Niagara Falls in order to build a dam and create a new lake in Canada. Yet that's what happened with Kinzua, a replication of hundreds of years of conveniently mutable definitions of sovereignty as applied to American Indian nations. Definitions, like maps, are created by those with power.

Do you know why it's called Turtle Island? David asked me, referencing North America. He pulled out his smartphone and called up an illustration of the continent overlaid by an image of a crawling turtle. Perspective matters. The shape of our maps designates the shape of our world. If we see the world differently, we can draw the maps to show different realities.

Our conversation continued this way, Steve speaking often of spiritual aspects of the Seneca while David periodically asked questions and found images to show me on his phone. Each of these brief exchanges presented a different cartography of the landscape within which the three of us sat. David and Steve were drawing maps—literal, historical, figurative, and mythological—with a different set of guiding principles than the ones sold at truck stops or filed away in state planning offices.

Do you know about the Covenant Chain? David asked me, flashing the image of three links of silver chain mounted on wood, the words *friendship*, *peace*, and *respect* affixed behind it. He explained it as the sequencing of the mooring of ships. First the Europeans tied their vessels to the shoreline branches with rope, a link to this continent that was both weak and loose. Later they moored with steel chains to rock, indicating a tighter cinch to North America. Finally they used a silver chain to affix the ships to the mountain, representing solidity and permanence. Steve then emphasized that the chain *joins* instead of *binds*, verbs so important in conveying how a relationship is supposed to function. I see his verbs as optimistic, perhaps overly kind.

A more clinical history describes the Covenant Chain in legal terms as an agreement that began in the seventeenth century between the Iroquois Confederacy and the British Empire, then was declared broken in the mid-eighteenth century due to various thefts of land, but then soon renewed. David's story instead declares the representational power of narrative and the agency of the Seneca, who were traveling pathways through Appalachia before Appalachia was a word with any particular meaning. He did not mention how Europeans broke those chains—on their own terms, for their own reasons.

Do you know about the Trail of Trees? David asked.

His phone came out again, and he showed me pictures of various mature trees with unnatural kinks, the branches serving to point out water or the path, each bend meant to communicate with walking warriors. I remember lessons on this subject vaguely from elementary school, about bending saplings to mark trails. David explained that these markers—the Trail of Trees—run between southern New York and Harrisburg, an expanse of some 220 miles, an ancient and well-developed trail network for pre-Columbian and early-American Seneca.

When our warriors walked, Steve added, *their boundaries were marked when they couldn't identify trees, plants, or animals.*

I wonder most of all about this, about how we might think of biome as a different sort of mapping philosophy, a way to move beyond the historical-political histories that limit Appalachian membership in so many ways. The mixed hardwood forests of Appalachia are distinct, but they are not limited to the ARC; nor are they about poverty or racial division. Indeed, the presence of trees, animals, and even rock beneath the ground offers no particular claim to economy or politics. Instead, it suggests a more contiguous and underlying recognition of our place in the world. Or perhaps we might think about different sorts of conduits, different lines, different motions that have governed not the development of the United States or the economy of regions, but instead something deeper, rooted in us and in the land.

Highways figure prominently in mapping Appalachia or, rather, the trouble of their lack figures prominently. A significant chunk of Appalachian Regional Commission funds is ushered into infrastructure projects intended to improve the conduits of travel. In response to the way rough roads prevent economic development and access to health services, more than three thousand miles of highway have been built under the auspices of the Appalachian Development Highway System (ADHS). In Pennsylvania, money was spent on US Routes 15, 20, 219, 220, and a handful of state highways to shore up connections to the interstate system. In a sense, Appalachia itself might be defined by its roads, where, as always, it falls short of the American ideal.

I certainly can't begrudge the benefits of easier travel. A good road to the hospital, for example, is handy when you break an arm or when a baby is on the way. Certainly part of the success of the ARC has been the improvement of travel; the things I value most—improved infant mortality rates, access to education, and health care—come about in part because of the improvement of roads. But I can't help but be bothered by the way the region winds up being defined by these concrete lines and by strange declarations of triumph, like this one that appears in the 2015 report on the ARC in its fiftieth year: "It is impossible to drink water, flush a toilet, or drive down a highway in Appalachia without seeing firsthand the result of an ARC investment." Such ideas suggest that the road itself becomes the desire, that the transportation of people ceases to be the point. Success is measured in tons of asphalt, not in lives improved.

Official Northern Appalachia is cut and defined by I-70 in the middle of Pennsylvania, by I-80 farther north, that massive transcontinental highway that runs literally coast to coast, and by the New York Thruway, I-90, running along the Great Lakes and through New York State. The thruway is the cap, the fast road north of Appalachia, a way to avoid having to drop in and bump along the Southern Tier Expressway. This is the point of the ADHS, after all, to improve access to the interstates that crisscross the region.

Consider the point of interstates though. As they cut Northern Appalachia into vertical tiers, these connecting points serve primarily to usher people through the region, not into it. There are far fewer interstates in the region running north and south, just I-79 in western Pennsylvania and the spur of I-99 that runs along the ridges near Altoona and State College. The truest purpose of these roads is not to connect points within Appalachia but instead to allow travelers to travel through, as fast as possible. It's only when someone wants to see the locals, partake of some history, that they get off these conduits and ride the named roads, the charming ones. More poignantly, fast highways are all about cutting, flattening, and making inert a landscape ill suited to speedy travel.

Maps are defined by what matters to the person making them, and they seek to dictate the way the reader of the map views any given space within the cartography. You notice the currents, not the islands. Or you notice the gas, not the people. Or you think of Appalachia only as a monolithic, stable, concrete place, a caricature of backwardness and poverty invented by America and continually reasserted by the very existence of the maps everyone uses to navigate the region. Or you think about Appalachia as the place where several interstates form a grid, and points off those lines cease to matter just as the realities of the lives of people in the place vanish into fantasy and politics.

I want to draw new maps of Appalachia because I don't think the old ones work very well. I want to draw new maps of myself because I don't fully understand who I have become. That links up to my own sense of exile, no doubt. Even as I've come to know myself as Appalachian, I have come to know myself as not seeming to fit in. Part of that is the imposition of the super-Appalachian, the *hickster* fetish of countrified mode that places me outside definitions of my own region. And my desire to imagine new cartographies certainly links up to my life as a man who has had brain surgery, because that's a marker on a map that can't be ignored. I don't yet have the key, though, and I sense that it lies in relationship, somewhere, to the places I count as home.

My friend, poet Erica Charis-Molling, put it this way in a Facebook post: "Each of us has a map of ourselves, with the Self as the center. Detailed as it is fictional. How far away is the next self on my map? Is there a path from one to the other? If we never make a path, do we slowly forget the rest of the map? What would I be willing to lose in the center to remember the rest?"

The existence of a seemingly stable map persuades us to think in static terms. If a place is mapped in a certain way, we see it that way. If we map and delineate ourselves in certain unchanging ways, the outcome is very much the same: we don't see the capacity for new ways through or new ways to be. We define ourselves through certain permanent

Mason-Dixon lines, or interstate lines, or even as existing only as Appalachian if we live within the borders of the ARC, which is to say we exist only as Appalachian if we accept ourselves as being defined by a map that designates poverty. If we fail to remember why a line has been drawn in the first place, and we fail to consider how arbitrary, temporary, or even useless a line is, we start to think of the regions of ourselves as immutable. Worst of all, we begin to lose sight of how the routes we once took no longer exist, and the who we once were has been redefined, and that this is not, in itself, a problem. Maps can and must be redrawn. We aren't only access roads to clearly defined interstates set up with a particular national, economic, and crushingly intractable definition.

How about this: better highways let thumper trucks move more easily in the Southern Tier, the part of the country where deep gas gets its name, and where the Marcellus and Utica shale geology are ground zero in the fracking of landscapes, and where actual Southern Tier towns carry the names adopted for these shales. Better highways mean better maps mean better industrial extraction and, even the ARC would say, result in exploitation.

Appalachia is defined by the desire to build faster, smoother roads through the region, and roads symbolize the fate of the place, how development brings America through but never into the region. Roads are just another way to say what the 2015 *Appalachia Then and Now* report declares, that this is still "a region apart."

Devotion to seeing Appalachia through the lens of highway development has consequences. Roads matter more than people; that's what I'm saying. In the Seneca-Iroquois National Museum, David told me a story while we looked at a diorama of a Seneca longhouse village. When construction crews were excavating land for US Route 15—just across the border in Pennsylvania, they found longhouse artifacts precisely where an exit ramp had been planned. David had been in college then, an anthropology major, and he had the opportunity to be part of a brief project studying that find. He told me it was the largest Seneca longhouse village ever discovered.

But development can't be stopped. It would have been too expensive to relocate the exit ramp, so the artifacts were buried under the road. That's what the dominant map said must happen. Sure, the project leaders understood that this ancient village mattered in some way, so they decided to install a geoplate beneath the tons of soil that lie under the asphalt. That plate is meant to signal the presence of the Seneca, who defined themselves as the very mountains that shape the region. The Seneca were Appalachia long before the ARC decided that roads matter so much, that they mattered more than people. Maybe, David suggested, someone will dig up that exit ramp some day, and the geoplate will signal a longer, richer history than can be currently recognized. For now, there's just a concrete highway that lets drivers pass through without pausing to consider what lies beneath their tires. An Appalachia defined by highways is defined by numbers—routes, speeds, and dollars—that care little about the history, people, and culture forever buried. We can hope such things lie ready to be unearthed and rediscovered and made more whole than has been allowed. Better that we decide not to bury them in the first place.

In a sense, erasure makes the Seneca Appalachian, but only if we disrupt apparently clear delineations of cultural definition and make space for several coexisting kinds of Appalachian (which I am pronouncing *App-uh-lay-shun*). I mean this to link people more distinctly to the mountains, to suggest that, like the Seneca, we can recognize the power of the rocks that shape our lives. We can embrace the roughness of landscape and the value of geological and cultural history. We can recognize that the maps we internalize fixate our attention on money and commerce and things that have hurt Appalachia immensely. We keep defining ourselves by the profit we can pull out of the ground instead of thinking about how we, too, live in relationship to our geology. That's been a bad relationship for too long. Fixing it might be a productive first step toward escape. Appalachia must exist, as itself, in the form of its landscape, if Appalachians are to exist. Without the reference point of place, there is no such thing as an Appalachian. A wounded landscape strikes me as leading to a wounded sense of self.

Water marks natural borders. In my Northern Appalachia, the water you pour on the ground will find its way through streams and small creeks to the Ohio River, then the Mississippi, then the Gulf before it makes it to the Atlantic. The half of Pennsylvania on the other side of the Allegheny Front drains toward the Susquehanna, then the Chesapeake Bay, then the Atlantic. In this difference I define the two halves of Pennsylvania, a border drawn not by politics or economy but by watershed.

Yet water is also used in drawing artificial borders. From a natural, pre-map perspective, rivers and lakes offer an easy way to identify territory: yours is on this side of the river, mine on that side. On a map, the river is rendered as a ragged line, which I see as a signal of the artificiality of typical cartography, that the organic refuses to be portrayed in right angles or even in long straight stretches. Still, the line representing the river becomes the clarified separation of territory, an artificial permanent thing, not at all like the river. On the ground, the touching of two frontiers is forever cleaved apart by the flow of water, and the territory shifts daily. On the map, the line just is.

There's something chaotic in how water denies the absoluteness of a map, and I like that tension far more than the permanent, stable, straight-drawn lines of dry state intersections, like the western border between Pennsylvania and Ohio or, worse, the flat line of the Mason-Dixon or the surveyed territory of the Allegheny Reservoir. These are lines built by straight-edges and compasses, surveys and concepts. They exist because we agree that they do, and they only move if we decide so. They are, at heart, built and maintained by the ideas we construct, not by any stable reality. A river, instead, can't help but move, ripping land away at one bank, building on another. Rivers spread out, slowing themselves over time and carving broad paths as they find new ways to navigate space.

As a border, a river must be considered technically tangential, though modern surveying establishes defined and stable borders permanently marked in numbers—latitude, longitude, degrees, minutes, and seconds. But when I look at a river as a border, I can't help but see the constant shift and the contingency of forever, how the landscape presents a resistance to our desire for stability and dominion. Today, the river is here; tomorrow there, taking with it the clarity of separation. A highway is better from the perspective of a mapmaker, as it's more stable. A highway serves as a more permanent border, built as a monument of concrete and stone, which makes highways worse in my book, particularly when their presence and quality are used to measure the validity of human lives.

Highways broken by water, by the force of ice and rain, by the same erosive strength that shape the mountains beneath them, well that's a sign of hope. The water takes back what cartographers cannot maintain, and if we follow our water, and maybe start to think about a deeper ecology of cartography, regional territories shaped not by commerce, or racial separation, or national borders, we can begin to think differently about ourselves.

I admit here to an overly romantic decadence, but part of my affection for the Southern Tier Expressway is the roughness of its surface. There's something hopeful in its decay, suggesting a potential for a different sort of rebuilding or, even, recognition. The thruway gets a neat coat of pavement frequently, NYDOT presenting a facade of permanence to so many miles of asphalt and concrete. The state seems to mostly ignore the Southern Tier Expressway these days, so even in a car hurtling along at 65 mph you can feel the forces of winter and summer, geology and erosion. You get to ride the landscape in a way more fully felt than on a better-maintained road. In that, at least, this highway is more a part of Appalachia than a conduit passing through. Driving it is always an exercise in pothole dodging, since each winter the region teeters between deep cold and brief warmth, a freeze-thaw cycle that buckles asphalt until the road craters deeply and pushes car suspensions to the limits of their own tensility. In this way the Southern Tier Expressway feels always like the mountains are working in earnest to take it back.

CHAPTER 8

Reading Like an Appalachian

While visiting home, just as I was nearing the end of my MFA in Pittsburgh, where I failed to distinguish myself as a fiction writer and faced prospects even more limited than the usual twenty-three-year-old with an advanced degree in creative writing, I ran into an old college friend at the grocery store. Standing beside the rack of shopping carts, we chatted about the last couple of years, during which he had been working as an assistant editor at *The Indiana Gazette*. He'd also been the editor-in-chief of our college newspaper, for which I had written various smug columns, into all of which I somehow worked the word *heinous*, a running joke that, yes, proved me to be just that kind of insufferable. Somehow our conversation turned to my pending joblessness, so he put in a good word at the paper and, for reasons that I have never understood, the *Gazette* cleared the junk off a desk at the back of the newsroom and I suddenly had a job.

As an accidental journalist for my hometown newspaper, I wound up with a newsbeat covering the far-flung rural parts of the county, places where regular reporters rarely traveled unless there was a big car wreck, a barn fire, or something particularly newsworthy. I drove my rickety Plymouth Reliant along dirt roads in search of greasy township garages where I'd explain to the road crews who doubled as elected supervisors that I'd be writing up their monthly meetings for the paper. Many were suspicious but shrugged. I was welcome to sit in their battered folding chairs and listen to them rattle off the tonnage of road salt they'd purchased or make plans for which roads needed an application of brine water harvested from gas wells to keep the dust down.

Maybe because of the aesthetic that comes with having an MFA, I also wound up specializing in human interest features: a rural doctor's bat-infested attic, a tongue-in-cheek theological inquiry into the presence of a chicken in the shrubbery outside the Anglican church, keg races at a local firemen's carnival. That disparate range, coupled with the MFA, probably explained why our editor appeared at my desk one day and thumped a large PR package from Viking Press on my desk. Tawni O'Dell, a woman who had grown up in town, was releasing a book called *Back Roads*, and it was about to ride the bountiful wave of Oprah's book club.

A book review? I asked.

Not a book review, Sam said. He wanted a feature story emphasizing the local-girl-makes-good sort of angle. Focus maybe on how the book is set in a kind of version of Indiana.

So a story, but with some review of the book? I said.

I don't want a book review, Sam snarled.

I still remember opening the book, a little thrilled but mostly jealous that someone from my hometown had beaten me to the punch. Somehow I felt a small place like Indiana couldn't expect to produce two novelists of more or less the same generation. Then, while reading *Back Roads*, I experienced a strange, disorienting sense of where I grew up, and for the first time I consciously realized I was Appalachian. Something rankled in O'Dell's portrayal of Indiana, which appears in the novel not as itself precisely but as an indistinguishable type.

This disorientation would have figured as the center of my review had I been able to write one back then and is part of why almost twenty years later I still feel the drive to weigh in. While the local chamber of commerce likes to lean heavily on Indiana as the birthplace of Jimmy Stewart, the rest of the world thinks of us as flyover country, hillbilly land, coal country, or lately, with the pejorative neologism of *Pennsytucky*. The signs outside of town champion Indiana as "The Christmas Tree Capital of the World," even if the sociological signs of a collapsed coal industry signal it as just another played-out Appalachian community. That it also harbors a doctoral-granting state university of thirteen thousand students seems often a footnote, except for robust local support for Division II men's sports.

Back Roads skips the Christmas trees and university and, instead, sides with the tropes:

> I close my eyes and picture it. The roof with gaping holes. The rotting floorboards scattered with broken window glass, used screws and bolts, and pieces of flattened iron that used to be part of something bigger a long time ago. When I finally took her there, she didn't ask me to sweep it out. She said she didn't want to change anything about it because she knew it was a special place for me. She said she loved the calm of decay and desertion that reigned there. She liked art and sometimes the way she talked sounded like a painting.

This is the second page of the novel, a fine example of the knock-out gorgeous language that fills the first few chapters before the plot collapses into a blend of stock genres: romance and dark hillbilly murder mystery.

Back Roads is about a love affair between a young man named Harley and Callie, a middle-aged woman whom he describes in the passage above. The novel is also about a kind of love affair between O'Dell and Northern Appalachia, a landscape she consistently links to herself but also writes as a troubled relationship. O'Dell can turn a sentence, and she builds that shack with precision, offering the kind of freighted, double language that helps a good reader understand that decay and desertion are external and internal, her main character a tortured Appalachian soul, the novelist likely that also. There's a complexity here that I want to embrace, even though the ultimate pessimism of the novel bothers me. I read her description of that shack as a description of Appalachia, and I do not like the ways the image is recognizable and false at the same time.

Certainly, the resonance of O'Dell's descriptions throughout the novel exist in the register of decay. The location of *Back Roads* is dark, perhaps evil, certainly troubled. She writes of "quiet, wounded hills" and how "blue-gray tree branches crawled against the white sky like veins on Betty's thighs." Our narrator Harley is nineteen years old, and he makes love to Callie, a beautiful, depressed, wealthy, middle-aged neighbor in that shack, where she is later found murdered, killed by Harley's sister in a jealous rage. Harley assents to fucking his own sister near the end of the novel, an echo of the external conflict of the book: Harley's mother is in prison for murdering her husband, who was actually shot by one of Harley's other sisters in a jealous rage because the father was fucking his daughter and the daughter tried to kill her chief rival, the mother.

Oprah describes her admiration for *Back Roads* this way: "Tawni O'Dell's heartbreaking and at times humorous portrayal of the Altmyers, and her dead-on description of rural Pennsylvania is sure to mesmerize readers." I admit this is what bothers me most about the novel, not so much what it is but that the response to its action is to say, *seems accurate*.

To know who you are, you need to know where you are. Or maybe to know who you are you have to figure out how you learned who you were, and how where you're from has been drawn and defined. As a kid who read a lot, I learned a lot about myself from books. Much of what I have come to know about Appalachia has also been built from writers, which is a general condition of knowing Appalachia at all. The region is as much a literary construction as it is anything else.

Back Roads is a novel about Appalachia, or so it claims. More specifically, *Back Roads* is a book about Northern Appalachia that Oprah declared authentic. I grew up where the novel is set, just like Tawni O'Dell did, in the deeply rolling hills of the southwestern portions of Pennsylvania, where coal mining once ruled the economy until flatlining in the 1970s. The industry's departure left flooded shafts, abandoned portals, and fresh unemployment. Surface mining stuck around, the hills of my home county often gouged out with big shovels and dozers, great scars seared into the landscape.

All of this seems consistent with what you probably think about Appalachia, which thanks to the election of Donald Trump has been thrust once again into the spotlight of a confused public attention. Every few weeks, my Facebook feed blows up with a link to some national think piece explaining

Appalachia to the world in the palette of decay and backwardness, and comments from my own non-Appalachian friends chime in with versions of *yep, seems accurate.* As it has for centuries, my home region continues to be considered as curious, strange, backward, and somehow malevolent. How you describe it depends on who you're talking to, as the broad strokes of Appalachia have pretty much always depended on how an outsider wants to define it and for what purpose. Lately, we're stupid and vote badly. Right now, we suffer the guilt of blame for a national political disaster.

"I may be white, but I do not identify with the WASPs of the Northeast," J. D. Vance writes in *Hillbilly Elegy*, his improbably successful, ham-fisted memoir of semi-Appalachian life. He continues:

> Instead, I identify with the millions of working-class white Americans of Scots-Irish descent who have no college degree. To these folks, poverty is the family tradition—their ancestors were day laborers in the Southern slave economy, sharecroppers after that, coal miners after that, and machinists and millworkers during more recent times. Americans call them hillbillies, rednecks, or white trash. I call them neighbors, friends, and family. . . . To understand me, you must understand that I am a Scots-Irish hillbilly at heart.

Vance begins with this declaration of a long-debunked and simplistic origin myth of Appalachia, one built on an erroneous but oft-repeated stable homogeneity of the mountain Scotch-Irish. He then goes on to happily accept the mantle of insider explaining Appalachia to everyone else. Vance explains nothing other than conservative talking points and old stereotypes: hillbillies are lazy, and you get ahead in America by hard work alone. Poverty is simply a sign of moral failure, he argues, and regional economic struggles borne of the inherent laziness of Appalachia. "Too many young men immune to hard work. Good jobs impossible to fill for any length of time. And a young man with every reason to work—a wife-to-be to support and a baby on the way—carelessly tossing aside a good job with excellent health insurance," Vance writes.

This is the Appalachia that *Hillbilly Elegy* portrays, Vance offering sweeping assessments in a memoir of his own personal triumph. He writes of somehow finding a way out through grit and luck and being nothing special, just an average Yale Law School graduate who learned good values from his grandmother and a stint in the Marines, and whose literary career received a boost by connections he made along the way. *Hillbilly Elegy* is essentially a conservative wet dream about Appalachian struggles solved by the bootstrap mythos, overlaid with a veneer of racial-social purity. And it all begins by Vance's nodding assertions that, yup, Appalachia is what you thought.

A quick condensation of Vance's shallow characterization of the region yields a troubling window into his sense of the place:

Point 1: "This is the reality of our community. It's about a naked druggie destroying what little of value exists in her life. It's about children who lose their toys and clothes to a mother's addiction."

Point 2: "This was my world: a world of truly irrational behavior. We spend our way into the poorhouse. We buy giant TVs and iPads. Our children wear nice clothes thanks to high-interest credit cards and payday loans. We purchase homes we don't need, refinance them for more spending money, and declare bankruptcy, often leaving them full of garbage in our wake. Thrift is inimical to our being."

Point 3: "We choose not to work when we should be looking for jobs. Sometimes we'll get a job, but it won't last. . . . We talk about the value of hard work but tell ourselves that the reason we're not working is some perceived unfairness: Obama shut down the coal mines, or all the jobs went to the Chinese. These are the lies we tell ourselves to solve the cognitive dissonance—the broken connection between the world we see and the values we preach."

Vance admits that his book "is no academic study," more or less the only sentence in *Hillbilly Elegy* supported by evidence or accurate interpretation. The book's vacuity is made clear by a notes section that lists nine websites and only four sources that *might* be considered acceptable in a high school research paper. His best seller is built entirely on shallow anecdote and the shittiest, most cursory research possible.

In that, Vance might indeed fit neatly into the long history of writers who sought to define Appalachia. Pretty much always, these writers came from the outside, and pretty much always they sought to define Appalachia from preexisting claims. Vance happens to be sort of from Appalachia, growing up in the Rust Belt portion of southern Ohio just outside the ARC and spending time with extended family in Kentucky, even if his arguments smack of precisely what people from outside Appalachia want to think about rural poverty. Still, to Vance's credit, he has recently announced a return from Silicon Valley to Ohio to try to contribute to the region's recovery. I do fear the kind of recovery he might imagine, though, as it likely will be built on a foundation of stereotypical nostalgic industrial exploitation fantasy.

That sentiment isn't far different from many of the early chroniclers of the region, most of whom seemed to approach their work from a perspective of generosity, even if they failed to understand how their work used the people of Appalachia as tropes to defend prevailing social-industrial modes. So much of what we think we know about the region now comes from the late nineteenth and early twentieth centuries, when missionaries of religion and commerce traveled into the mountains to write about the oddballs in the hills.

Consider how Horace Kephart kicks off his 1913 book, *Our Southern Highlanders,* one of the seminal texts on the region:

> Time and retouching have done little to soften our Highlander's portrait. Among reading people generally, South as well as North, to name him is to conjure up a tall, slouching figure in homespun, who carries a rifle as habitually as he does his hat, and who may tilt its muzzle toward a stranger before addressing him, the form of salutation being:
>
> "Stop thar! Whut's you-unses name? Whar's you-uns a-goin' ter?"
>
> Let us admit that there is just enough truth in this caricature to give it a point that will stick. Our typical mountaineer is lank, he is always unkempt, he is fond of toting a gun on his shoulder, and his curiosity about a stranger's name and business is promptly, though politely, outspoken.

Beyond the language, this might as well be written in *Hillbilly Elegy* or portrayed on the screen of any horror movie fixated on the demon rednecks living in the woods. The passage also bears striking resemblance to the answer you'd get on the street if you stopped anyone and asked them to describe a person from Appalachia. *Guns. Suspicion. Rough clothes.*

They'd probably be written as obese instead of lank these days, but otherwise the timeless stereotype of the Appalachian holds sway.

"In his veins there still runs strong the blood of those indomitable forbears who dared to leave the limitations of the known and fare forth into the unknown spaces of a free land," wrote John C. Campbell as he, also, set out to describe the Appalachian type in 1921. He writes extensively about the terrain, seeing in it some reflection of the people fated to live among it. Even that, not surprisingly, winds up teetering toward the negative, as he also revels in nostalgic mountain romance: "There is nothing austere about the rural Highlands save the simplicity of life within them. There is a softness about the wooded heights and hollows, a beauty of melting curves, of lights and shadows, of tender distances wherein the hearth-smoke is a part and the cabin is at home."

Campbell writes ultimately of the region as cursed with obstacles of literal and philosophical progress, about "thickets of rhododendron and laurel" and "echoes still sounding of half-remembered traditions, folk-lore and folk-songs, recited or sung before the fire by 'granny' or 'grandpap.' " And then he makes the move, offering words to hang onto the place and defining the region specifically and absolutely as "the Southern Highlands." Such a title means it is separate from the rest of the country, and the narrative constructions aligned with it reinforce and perpetuate that separation.

History is tricky, and Appalachia has suffered for it. Ever since it became identified as the Southern Highlands, and then later as Appalachia, the place has been defined by the needs of the economic engines of the nation. To describe a place and to assign it a name is to fix it permanently in relation to the one doing the describing and naming. The value of the place lies implicit in such characterizations, nearly always subordinate to the locale of the namer, who also nearly always has ideas of how the now-named place could be made better. This is another kind of persuasive cartography, one built by words as much as maps. Campbell, for example, ends his book with extensive discussion of commerce and economy. "The situation is not to be improved, moreover, by decrying industrial development," he writes. "It is not possible, nor is it desirable to arrest this. The store of treasure is of value only as used, and ability, if dormant, is useless."

Pretty much forever, Appalachia has been defined within such terms, whether as a site for missionary fund-raising, or a place to be timbered, mined, fracked, blamed for the election of Donald Trump, or used as an example of the economic downside to not poisoning the air by burning coal. Recall how government documents like the PARCS report and the Surface Mining Reclamation Act also make it clear that one of the national priorities of the region is to maintain its position as the ground where coal and gas can be extracted. Consistently, Appalachians have suffered negative, or at least distorted, portrayal at the services of these ambitions. Degraded people are easier to exploit, so the definitions work always to position the people as in need of something that can come only from the outside. Development is always the answer. At the same time, the region has long persisted in the American imagination as an ahistorical, Rip Van Winkle sort of temporally frozen wilderness. Appalachia is at once an ahistorical mountain fantasy and a giant coal mine.

Campbell, to his credit, recognized that Appalachian development was "at times of questionable benefit to a native population," and that "the social salvation of the mountains will not be won by putting its people forward as pawns to advance others, nor by using them as filling to make the highway of progress smoother, nor will compulsion from without, however benevolent, ever be a substitute for self-direction under the impulse of ideals voluntarily accepted." Yet he, like others, was unwavering in his belief that the people and place were both in need of development, each a sort of primordial version of America.

I don't see Vance as much different in that, as he simply gloms on to the prevailing stereotypes that offer excuse to the suffering Appalachia, which has been caused by the presence of economic development, rather than its absence. I don't see O'Dell as much different either, as her characters are written as trapped in an inescapable cycle of degradation, lacking the agency or wherewithal to change things. Campbell's words are sage, of course, that when industry benefits only the out-of-region owners, things don't go well for the locals. These are the books that taught me to read myself. They taught me to accept decline as the only potential for my home.

O'Dell writes of herself, on Oprah's website, this way:

> I was born and raised in the Allegheny Mountains of western Pennsylvania, a beautiful ruined place where the rolling hills are pitted with dead gray mining towns like cigarette burns on a green carpet. My hometown is Indiana, PA, which was also Jimmy Stewart's hometown. Half the streets are named after him and we have a bronze statue of him in front of the courthouse that looks suspiciously like Henry Fonda. My roots: I'm half Pennsylvania redneck and half southern white trash. Growing up, I never really fit in. I always thought I was a freak because I liked books and living animals. All my childhood girlfriends wanted to be Farrah Fawcett or Christie Brinkley. I wanted to be Roald Dahl. This greatly concerned my

family. Especially after I explained to them who he was. I'm the only member of my family to go to college. I have a degree in journalism from Northwestern University. My high school guidance counselor advised me against going there because they had a bad football team. Even after I explained to him that I wanted to be a journalist and NU had one of the best journalism schools in the country, he said, "Well, sure, but you'll still want to go to the football games." I went anyway and graduated with honors. All my life I have struggled with this particular identity crisis: being an educated woman saddled with a biker chick's name. A theme that often appears in my work is one of characters struggling to define themselves among people who already defined them wrongly because of a stereotype, or their own inability to look past a person's surface and see inside them. I've frequently had to deal with the danger of being mislabeled.

After the publication of *Back Roads* and her quick ascendance to the status of best seller, O'Dell also wrote in the *Pittsburgh Post-Gazette* about being treated poorly as an author, how at first her publishers wanted to just use her initials so her book could appear to be written by a man. Once they found out that she had worked briefly for a party company jumping out of cakes, they devised the character of her authorial persona, which she describes as a "stripper with a thesaurus." O'Dell writes about doing a photo shoot sponsored by the publisher, where a stereotypically New York photographer took her into the woods, asked her to strip naked, and shot gauzy wood-nymph photos of her.

I'm troubled by the pain O'Dell writes, and I'm bothered by my own response, that of disbelief. I don't fully trust O'Dell, can't help but think of the ways she might have been complicit in the degradation of Appalachia or, at the very least, understood how she was trading on the currency of local trope. Didn't she also shape this authorial persona? Didn't she write a novel that hews closely to the line of Appalachian stereotype? But I also don't want to discount the difficulty of her position as an author of a book being marketed as authentically Appalachian and as a woman who, as she laments, would find a hard time being taken as seriously as male writers. But she does spin the image, and I wonder why.

O'Dell writes:

> I'm a novelist and I'm a woman and I'm considered to be a serious author whether I like it or not. I write literary, not commercial fiction, or so I've been told by my publishers who are proud I write literary fiction but secretly wish I wrote commercial. I've been well-reviewed throughout my career, even by *The New York Times*. (Granted, it was a decade ago, but my agent says it still counts.) I've been compared to such writing luminaries as John Steinbeck, Clifford Odets, J.D. Salinger, and Emile Zola. To my knowledge I've never been compared to a female writer. Probably because none of the reviewers could come up with one he took seriously.

I remember one day at *The Indiana Gazette*, after I'd received the novel and started working on the story about *Back Roads,* a trim, tall, well-dressed man waltzed into the newsroom, escorted by the owner of the paper. The man wanted to talk for a second, say hello. This was O'Dell's father, the president of a local banking corporation that had been growing for decades, buying up smaller banks and becoming a significant player in regional finance. When he retired a decade or so later, his buyout was measured with seven zeros.

You have to understand, O'Dell's father told me, *Tawni exaggerates.*

He didn't say this in anger, but as a serious businessman. Her father wanted me to know that their family wasn't like the one in the book—fiction too often understood to be autobiographical in his buttoned-up mind. Clearly, he didn't want anyone thinking that *he* was Appalachian trash. I later happened to meet Tawni at his house, part of the interview for the coming story. Her father then lived in the largest, most-expensive McMansion development in town, where I also met his much younger second wife, saw how he'd become a father again in his late middle age, living that cliché instead of the dark Appalachian one he'd feared.

Later, I attended the hometown release party for *Back Roads*, an opulent affair the banker likely sprung for. The town's business elite—lawyers, car dealers, and other bankers—gathered in a downtown bar built to recreate the feel of a British pub. The owner of a nearby British roadster restoration factory had flown in timbers from England and knocked down an old building to replace it with a waddle and daub recreation. The sign outside carried the red, blue, and white bull's-eye of a British Spitfire, and inside the decor emphasized rich leather chairs and a gigantic fireplace. The glasses were heavy-cut glass, filled with the town's perhaps first Guinness tap. Other nights, the same crowd that attended the party gathered in their sportswear to listen to local jazz players and drink Scotch.

At the party, we downed succulent beef tenderloin, drank from the open bar, and hobnobbed with the idea of the New York literary scene. O'Dell's editor was there, a young woman dressed in an easier, smarter way, clearly a different sort of elite than the town's rich. I made a fool of myself by mentioning my MFA, and the idiotic novel I was then writing, and I imagine it took much self-control not to roll her eyes and call me the bumpkin I likely appeared to be. I wonder now how she saw all of this. Did it seem like a counterpoint to *Back Roads*, this collection of local aristocracy, or did it offer confirmation, all of these hillbillies dressed up and pretending to be something akin to sophisticated? Still, if you squinted in the firelight, and imagined the cuts of the suits in the room being just a tad finer, the night was about as anti-Appalachian as you could get.

The most famous author from my hometown opens his most famous book with a declaration of connection:

> This is the most beautiful place on earth.
>
> There are many such places. Every man, every woman, carries in heart and mind the image of the ideal place, the right place, the one true home, known or unknown, actual or visionary. A houseboat in Kashmir, a view down Atlantic Avenue in Brooklyn, a gray gothic farmhouse two stories high at the end of a red dog road in the Allegheny Mountains. . . .
>
> For myself I'll take Moab, Utah. I don't mean the town itself, of course, but the country which surrounds it—the canyon lands. The slickrock desert. The red dust and the burnt cliffs and the lonely sky—all that which lies beyond the end of the roads.

This is Edward Abbey, writing at the beginning of *Desert Solitaire*, a book my father gifted to me when I was a college intern at Assateague Island National Seashore. He had known Abbey in a peripheral way, the author having spoken at some gathering at the Lutheran Church, for reasons I cannot fathom, and my father seeing him as far too brusque and crass. Still, *Desert Solitaire* mattered to my father, as it made clear declarations for the value of wilderness, a perspective my father shared.

On one of our many drives together, heading toward a farm sale, out hunting, or fetching supplies for the sheep, my father also pointed out the old rock shop Abbey's father had owned near the small village of Home, just outside Indiana. I remember the word *communist* applied to Abbey's father, not bitterly, but clarifying the outsider status of the family. Maybe for that reason, it took a few more decades before even a simple roadside sign appeared near Home, announcing it as the birthplace of one of the most famous and revered environmental writers ever. It took a professor from far away—Jim Cahalan, author of *Abbey: A Life*—to move to the area and motivate the historical society to recognize the birthplace of someone who has mattered deeply to the world, even if his views might not have been consistent with the typical perspectives of his fellow denizens.

Abbey seems to have shared that uneasy relationship with his native landscape. I find it curious that he centered himself in print far outside of his birthplace, could write of Pennsylvania only sort of and just twice at length—first in his novel *Jonathan Troy* and then in *The Fool's Progress*. Notably, Abbey hated his first book, and the protagonist hated where he came from, some thinly veiled version of our shared hometown of Indiana. Even in *The Fool's Progress*, the main character (another thinly veiled Abbey) is returning home to West Virginia but is really at home in his adopted West. Abbey is known for his devotion to the hardscrabble landscape of the desert, a place where the writer found himself and a geology that reflected his philosophy of life: punishing, dry, and beautiful.

Maybe this estrangement is why Abbey had very little influence on my notions of being Appalachian, particularly as I have come to recognize that I am inescapably an Appalachian writer, through birth and sometimes subject. Certainly, few would count Abbey as an *Appalachian* writer, just as few would count Annie Dillard as such (she's from Pittsburgh, after all, and Tinker Creek is in Virginia), since neither writer delivers subject or style typically coded as Appalachian. Yet each writer was born to the region, and Abbey in particular wrote sometimes about it, even as his reputation is decidedly linked to the desert. The limitations of stereotype prevented me from seeing writers from my backyard as such.

But Annie Dillard is also who first allowed me to take seriously my prospects as a writer. When I was in college in Indiana, my freshman composition professor took me aside after class and invited me to her office. Rosaly was a poet, and one who carried the aspect of brilliance, at least to a young guy who didn't quite understand his own literary potential. She had a shock of dark hair, one gray streak near the front left, and she moved and talked always in an ecstatic jumble. I only ever half understood her, which to me seemed to declare *poet*. I was both enthralled and afraid.

I remember entering the fascinating tower of paper and disorder of her office. Books were stacked this way and that, sheaves of paper atop the desk, atop other sheaves, atop books, and sometimes books atop sheaves.

Are you a reader? she asked me.

Oh yes, I said, as I always had been.

What do you read?

Louis L'Amour, I said. I had stacks of his novels, passed on to me by a widow at my childhood church after her husband died, plucked weekly from his bedside stand. I relished the Sackett series most of all, the tracing of that frontier family on through L'Amour's romanticized western pulpiness. I couldn't get enough.

Not anymore, Rosaly said.

She directed me to Dillard, and to *Pilgrim at Tinker Creek*, a book I wish I could say I devoured. Instead, I struggled through it, understanding that I was close to something powerful in her words, was living in the presence of a lyric genius who both saw and delivered the world differently, yet grasping to understand what I was reading. In truth, Dillard was a slog, even as I loved every moment of it. She writes with so much density, so much elliptical form, so much lyric imagery, and so much startling wisdom. Yet reading Annie Dillard is also my origin story as a writer, *Pilgrim at Tinker Creek* an epiphanic depth of language that led ultimately to my longer reckoning of what taking writing seriously can mean.

I wonder now if taking Dillard and Abbey as models differentiates me from Appalachian authorship. Each is, of course, a *Northern* Appalachian, like me. And neither is ever really counted in the canon of Appalachian literature, perhaps because of subject. One writes too much of the desert, the other with too much mysticism. Yet each of these authors influences me as a writer and a thinker, more so than any author labeled as *Appalachian*, including Dorothy Allison, James Dickey, Denise Giardina, Lee Maynard, or Lee Smith. Those writers come from farther south, are always writing about *Appalachian* things that don't fully connect to my own experience, even if I take pleasure in their language and imagery.

Obviously, this is a terrible imposition of title, and a moral failure of my own imagination. And, let's be fully honest, I don't often really think of myself as an *Appalachian* author either, even as I write through a book trying to make claims about what Appalachia can mean to a soul. I wonder, then, about commonalities of judgment, about the ways that Tawni O'Dell rails against the limitations placed on her. She chose a subject and style that reads pretty clearly as *regional*, and pretty clearly within the parameters the book market—whatever that is—likes to think about *regional*. Think Dickey here, and *Deliverance*, a novel that is less about its stereotypes than a recognition of the suburban mind that lives within a world shaped by them. Still, when you think of the novel you think about banjo music, whistling like a pig, and getting buggered in the woods. Well, you probably think about the movie, not the book, which is probably half the problem. Still, the greatest danger of the woods is that readers will find and leave you there, see you only through the lens of what an Appalachian writer is supposed to be.

If I am writing through the recognition of myself as Appalachian and also through the process of seeing myself as an Appalachian writer, I have to think about journeys, which are themselves built from the relationship between beginning point and end.

"In the moments before you begin a journey, you are something less: less complete, less aware, less developed, less sure of where you are going or what you will find," writes Sean Prentiss, in his love letter of a book, *Finding Abbey*. Dissatisfied with his own city living, and long connected to *Desert Solitaire*, Prentiss tries to find the grave of Edward Abbey and, in fact, himself. Spoiler alert: he finds both.

These words struck me when I read them, resonated even more when I met Sean at an impromptu writers workshop organized by a mutual friend. I'd just bought Sean's book on a whim in a Johnson, Vermont, bookstore. This was the August after I finished my radiation treatments, during a trip that I used to restart another part of my life paused by the constant presence of my own necessary medical recovery. I holed up for a week with another writer friend, each of us hammering away at stalled projects that meant much to our senses of self. We were both determined to take ourselves seriously again, to finish what we'd started and prove life had not gotten in the way.

We drove way out into Vermont's Northeast Kingdom for the workshop, itself a standing group consisting of Sean, our mutual friend, and a poet-farmer who offered her house and hospitality. We sat in her back room with a long view of a flat valley between mountains, ate a potluck lunch, and sipped beer. Sean, for his part, turned out to be affable, energetic, kind, quick to laugh, and a generous and enthusiastic reader. He drove a small pickup and beamed about the recent pregnancy he and his wife had just learned of. He could not wait to be a father. Sean's always up for journeys, loves the anticipation, and I can't imagine a better trail partner. I wanted to be his friend immediately.

About beginnings, he writes:

> But you are also less jaded because you don't know of all the dead ends ahead, less burnt from the days scorching beneath that black sun, less weary because you have not yet walked the hard rock road through those harsh deserts.
>
> Afterward, you become something more: more aged from the years spent searching for whatever your heart needs, whatever made you begin this fool's journey. More weary from the fretting of failure, from the glances at the map to ensure you are on a right path. But also maybe, if you are lucky, wealthier for the surprises seen breaking over those serrated mountains and the new friends you've met along the way.

But can a person precisely point, as if on a map, to the origin of a true, transformative journey? Is there any proper beginning?

Sean begins the journey of *Finding Abbey* at the crossroads in Home, just around the corner from a corrugated metal utility garage where I used to often meet with the Rayne Township supervisors to write articles about road aggregate and bridge repair for *The Indiana Gazette*. Sean describes the town, not inaccurately, as "small farms with barns of peeling red paint and corn growing tall in the fields. Cars rusted in the driveways and tractors rusted in the fields and huge trees in deep bloom casting afternoon shadows across it all."

Sean finds the graves of Abbey's family in Home, the launch point for a cross-country search for the hidden desert grave, meeting with still-living Abbey friends along the way. He also journeys into himself, something I doubt he understood at the beginning of his project, even if it lies at the center of his book.

"I'm after the essence that people leave behind, the traces of themselves that linger upon the land," Sean writes. "The essence of who Edward Abbey was remains out there, and I intend to find it, because maybe his essence, his secrets, can teach me how to best live my own finite days here in cities and in deserts, in lifetime jobs and in thirty-year mortgages."

Abbey's grave matters, that's for sure. Sean weeps when he finds it, satisfied with the discovery of this conceptual idol, even as he necessarily keeps secret the location. We all need to follow our own winding paths toward what we seek, and predetermined destinations do not equate to useful internal discoveries. You have to search if you are going to find. Not long after his discovery, Sean also quits his job at a midwestern urban university to take a new one at a smaller school in

Vermont. He does this to live in mountains, the place he recognizes as being at the center of his notion of the beautiful. I envy his self-recognition, his commitment, and the house on a lake in the mountains that he now shares with his wife and daughter.

"A decision needs to be made on which road we take. Every journey, no matter how deep into it we have traveled, no matter how close to an ending, requires a choice. Which road to travel, which branch to follow," Sean writes.

As I think about my own beginning points of Appalachian recognition, I think about how Sean describes the nature of discovery, about how endings are ultimately unknown but will, in time, reveal themselves:

> In the moments after a journey, after we have taken our final steps in search of whatever elusive thing we have been chasing after, we can never be sure what will become of us. We may never understand how we will be changed because of our long travels, because of the sights seen, because of the knowledge gathered along the way.
>
> At the end of a journey, there is no moment of exact clarity, no moment when we realize that we have finished whatever metamorphosis we will go through. Endings are murky, and it is often months or stretching years before they wrap themselves up, before we understand how our long travels through those many deserts of our lives have reshaped us.

I guess I'm trying to find the false bedrock of my own twisted, resentful identity, about why I am angered by the ways that Tawni O'Dell seems to loathe Indiana County so deeply, and why I loathe her book so deeply for how it characterizes her hatred.

Yet if I'm honest, I also loathe Indiana County, resent being from there, even being Appalachian at all. That's an admission I make with some trepidation because the truth is I couldn't ever figure out who I was until I admitted that I was deeply rooted in Western Pennsylvania. I went away to the desert myself, just like Abbey, and as much as I loved it I couldn't, like him, stay forever. I missed the green, missed my roots, misunderstood the ways of its water, knew there was something back East that I had to uncover.

Also like Abbey, I find myself often aching when I think about my Appalachian home, and I am always at risk of romanticizing it. Abbey is often clear that he found home in the southwestern deserts, that his location in the landscape is self-determined, not natal. Even the mythic name of his Pennsylvania home, that glorious coincidence of being born into a town called Home, is more or less fabricated: after his birth, Abbey was taken home to a relatively nondescript house within the Indiana borough limits, and it was only after several subsequent moves that his family settled on a farm in Home.

As a grown-up, Abbey writes of his Appalachian roots with a longing for an ideal, semi-original relationship to the landscape. He seems always to write about gothic farmhouses on dirt roads or about the beautiful view of Indiana tucked into the hillside. He doesn't write about the close neighborhoods of the town, the university, or the complex reality of a place that wasn't quite Appalachian even when he was a young man. Abbey's connection to Appalachia is real and false, deeply felt and narratively constructed. Abbey moved away to find his real connection. That doesn't exclude him as Appalachian, just indicates that being Appalachian does not preclude the capacity to reinvent, to seek, to discover something previously unknown about place and self. His writing also reveals the way that romantic nostalgia can hum at the edges of our most deeply set senses of where we are from.

"But no person can stop a journey from going forward," Sean writes. "Either a person is searching or a person has given up searching. What we find is what we find. And we must always search for truth."

Back Roads isn't the truth, at least not the whole truth. I recognize it, feel it in ways uncomfortable to my own reckoning of self. But I also have to find the ways it doesn't fit; I need to keep looking for the truth of my home place so I can fully sort the love and resentment. I don't want the dark romance of that novel as my Appalachia, nor do I want the beautiful romance of Abbey's recollections. Neither fits. I feel often that I don't fit either.

In *Back Roads*, Callie is a trapped high-brow, middle-aged woman, someone who tried to get away but winds up stuck. She's written as a tall, lean knockout. She went to a fancy college in the city, worked summers at the local paper, but ends up back on her grandfather's old homestead, married to a man who makes big money working for the bank. She lives in a big, lonely house and is depressed by a life curtailed by the circumstances around her—taking care of the kids, having an often-absent husband, perhaps longing for a lost, wild fantasy girlhood.

On one hand, Callie has achieved beyond the expectations of region, but on the other she's bound forever to this place. From another perspective, her crisis is simply about middle-aged longing with an overlay of dangerous Appalachian landscape. Callie has a placid domestic life, so she finds great release and excitement in the seduction of the semi-dangerous Harley, who comes from a bad family, with an abusive father murdered by a wife now incarcerated. He's bad news, but just sensitive enough that Callie takes his virginity beside the stream at the bottom of her property.

O'Dell writes their first sex scene from Harley's perspective:

> I wasn't afraid at first. I wasn't afraid when I pushed inside her and felt my mind, body, and soul twist themselves into one raw nerve. I wasn't afraid when she gasped and called out to God and I realized there were two people having sex there, not just me. I wasn't even afraid when I realized I wasn't going to last long enough to bring her anything but frustration.
>
> The fear came when I realized my dad had been wrong. It was worth a lifetime of driving a cement truck.
>
> It was worth a lifetime.
>
> The end neared and my hands started trembling so hard I couldn't hold onto her anymore. All my efforts to bring her to me were like grappling for a handhold in crumbling earth. I gave up and let go and let her hold onto me. I came with my fists clenched above her.

Their encounter presages Callie's death, that she will be later felled in a jealous rage by Harley's sister in the decaying mining shack where the young man and middle-aged woman meet for trysts. The passage is as overwrought as it is unsubtle: Appalachian destiny connects destruction and ecstasy.

This is one of the most troubling aspects of the curious verisimilitude of *Back Roads*. I understand that it *isn't* Indiana County, but I also see so much Indiana County appearing within. I am unsettled by how the places I know appear directly in the novel. There's Eat'n Park (a regional diner chain), Lick-N-Putt (an ice cream and mini-golf place near Kittanning, overlooking a massive strip-mining job on a neighboring peak), the Keystone Power Plant (one of three in the county; this one in Shelocta, not far from where my college girlfriend lived), Black Lick Road (near the Homer City generating station where the father of one of my best friends worked), Sharp Pavement (a real paving company, with an owner who once got angry with me for writing a newspaper story about a bad blacktop job they'd done in Shelocta, near the power plant).

O'Dell writes that Harley works at Barclay's Appliance, a nod to the locally famous, old-fashioned Barclay's Hardware, now closed, but where my father would buy nails and I'd roam the creaking floors. Other place names familiar to locals offer minor alterations and therefore carry the tone of reality. Penns Ridge evokes the real Penns Manor school district, while J&P Coal is reminiscent of the old R&P coal company that made a killing in the heyday of mining in the county. O'Dell calls her town Laurel Falls, a portmanteau of the Laurel Highlands adjacent to Indiana County and Bedford Falls, the small town in Jimmy Stewart's *It's a Wonderful Life*, which locals swear is modeled on Indiana. I find these familiar names as disorienting as the dark action of the novel, since they offer a sheen of verifiable reality. This novel is about my home, clearly, and written by someone who knows it, and Oprah labels these descriptions as "dead on."

I'm violating one of the chief dictates of criticism here, applying autobiography and reality to a fantasy world. Fiction exists as a shadow universe to ours, a kind of askew reality, an alternative timeline where Laurel Falls isn't actually Indiana, Callie not a stand-in for Tawni, the despair of entrapment shared by Harley and Callie not precisely what the author herself has felt. Yet that's likely the ground from which this novel was built, the universe populated from the core dirt of Indiana County. The impact of *Back Roads* is that it could be real, is real. That's the same impact of so much realistic Appalachian fiction, the dark and negative world that offers readers a small thrill, useful melodrama that suggests how awful it must be to actually live in such circumstances.

O'Dell's landscape, evoked with skill, becomes an important aspect. Harley admires that Callie inherited fifty acres from her grandfather "with the general rights which meant the old man never sold out to the coal companies while everybody else around him let their land be stripped raw." That means the relic beauty of this property remains intact, a view Harley appreciates as the land "dipped down to a circular pond sitting in the middle of a lawn the color of pool table felt. A twisting section of clear, pebble-shiny creek lay at the foot of their hills; and they were their hills. They owned them. Not like our hills. We just lived on ours."

Possession is a weird curse and aspiration here. Callie is trapped by this ownership, Harley shackled by a lack of ownership, living in a valley carved by the sort of stream that runs at the bottom of the Mercer estate. Understanding the way my own parents have been unable to prevent the drilling of new gas wells on their own property and the scouting of locations for massive Marcellus pads, I also can't help but be jealous of Callie's grandfather, that his wealth allowed for a self-determined fate of her home geology. I'm also struck by Harley's description of the Mercer lawn as like a pool table, a clear echo of the *Back Roads* promo copy that describes her homeland as a place that looks often like "cigarette burns on a green carpet."

Let me describe for a moment the approach to my family farm, what you see when you ride up Twolick Drive. Once you take the left fork a quarter mile in, you let Tawni O'Dell take over, using her words that describe the fictional Black

Lick Road and the approach to Harley's home: "The first half-mile of our road was straight uphill and the trees grew together over the top of it making a tunnel of leaves in the summer, and a tunnel of snow in winter, and a tent of bare branches like charred fingers the rest of the year."

I can't help but be troubled here by how easy it is for me to see Harley's road, since it is the precise view I experience when I return to the family farm, the thrill and settling of my mind when I recognize myself as back home. O'Dell describes the persistent landscape of my youth, where I rode my bike often, where I walked with my family, and where I zoomed my cars, and which contains the hills that, as Scott Russell Sanders writes in *Staying Put* of his own boyhood place, offered the pitch "that became my standard for all hills."

From the top of our family farm, one of the highest hills in the county, you can see the stacks of the Homer City generating station, a strangely calm and beautiful twinkling of safety lights at night, even as it is the vision of a station that has often been cited as one of the most polluting in the country. This, too, is something O'Dell describes almost as if standing atop the farm:

> Across the road was the clearing, stretching out green and smooth, then disappearing over a slope into a rolling sea of hills the color of rust and soot and worn yellow carpet. The power lines and the smoke-belching twin coal stacks of the Keystone Power Plant in the distance were the only signs of humanity. Whenever people asked me how we could stand to stay in the house, I told them I liked the view, and then they thought I was even crazier than before they asked.

Maybe what I find most difficult about O'Dell's writing is how the culmination of words like *rust, soot, worn yellow carpet*, and *charred fingers* accent the negative in a landscape that I want to think of as beautiful or, at least, mixed. Yet I also must acknowledge that her descriptions are accurate. One of the things that bothers me most about *Back Roads* is how I recognize the stain, taint, decay, and ugliness, how I recognize the resenting of ugliness and also the loving of it, decay and affection, a desire to stay forever in this place and leave it behind forever.

Maybe this is another part of the uncomfortable mirror of *Back Roads*: that I actually try to look away from the ugliness even though I know it's there. Or, worse, that often I see only decline and little hope—the rainbow stains of seeping mine water, the cracked and heaving sidewalks of a town where residents often can't afford to fight frost heave, Trump signs and Confederate Battle Flags and coal-rolling diesel pickups. This is another, newer kind of Appalachian problem, particularly for Appalachians who spend their days in colleges and universities and write about the region. We have to argue against the ugliness, even when that's so much of what we see. Optimism must be our position, lest we be cast out, once again, as *against* Appalachia. Ugliness is just another way to mispronounce the region.

I don't know how to reconcile my love of home place with the awful parts of it, to embrace it even as it has been dug out, drilled, and poisoned. Northern Appalachia has fought forward from its cutout past, but the residue of the ugly is never far away. There are some who see art in the presence of decay, maybe even others who fetishize the decline with moody photographs, cover art for alt-bluegrass albums and such things. There are some who see only perpetual despair in boney piles and abandoned mine shafts. And I guess there are people like me, who are trying to figure out how to find the art that layers upon itself like layers of soot, how the decadent misery of the faux-Indiana county in *Back Roads* is overlaid perfectly on the beautiful one I know from my childhood. Each is still there, and I want to find ways to see each, and to understand the combination as another kind of beauty instead of taint.

Maybe Ed Abbey gets it right when he describes Indiana as a mixture of beauty and gauze, one of the few times he describes his hometown:

> There was the town set in the cup of the green hills. In the Alleghenies. A town of trees, two-story houses, red-brick hardware stores, church steeples, the clock tower on the county courthouse, and over all the thin blue haze—partly dust, partly smoke, but mostly moisture—that veils the Appalachian world most of the time. That diaphanous veil that conceals nothing. And beyond the town were the fields, the zigzag rail fences, the old gray barns and gaunt Gothic farmhouses, the webwork of winding roads, the sulfurous creeks, and the black coal mines and—scattered everywhere—the woods.

When I first laid eyes on *Back Roads*, on the moody gold and black cover, on the deckle-edged pages, on those first lines of prose that I read and recognized as being about where I was from, I saw myself and my actual place rendered in print. This is a moment that is both rare and discomfiting for a rural Appalachian. Because when you read a book like *Back Roads*, you suddenly realize that you're from a place that sucks, or is supposed to, even as you're glad to see it portrayed at all. A problem for the literary Appalachian is learning who you are by reading about who you are and where you're from and knowing that not many people would want that legacy.

In *Heat and Light*, Jennifer Haigh describes that phenomenon like this: "Rural Pennsylvania doesn't fascinate the world, not generally. But cyclically, periodically, its innards are of interest. Bore it, strip it, set it on fire, a burnt offering to the collective need." Haigh grew up around a town once called Barnesboro, since renamed *Northern Cambria* when it merged with nearby Spangler, each of those towns having declined enough that they needed to team up to exist. Barnesboro was part of my old *Gazette* beat, a border town in neighboring Cambria County; Spangler was in Indiana County.

Haigh's first novel, *Baker Towers*, was set in a town very much like Barnesboro. *Heat and Light* evokes the Oil City region near where I now live. Each of these novels focuses on the difficult realities of characters living in worlds defined by, respectively, coal and gas exploration. I wonder about these books, why it seems like writing about degradation is the only way to write a book that can be called *Appalachian*. This is another way we function as burnt offerings. We're wrecked, and that's all there is to it. That's the only story we're supposed to tell.

Even attempts to recover are doomed, as Harley describes late in *Back Roads*, when he remembers a moment at the "Carbonville Mine Water Reclamation Plant," a failed experiment in recovery that he calls "a monument to the folly of trying to clean up a region that was poisoned from the inside." He describes a memory with his father, who grew up in a small coal patch that has since been abandoned because of mine contamination:

He stopped when we came within view of a couple dozen small, gray, Insul-brick houses scattered along the outside of the chain-link like the plant had shook and showered its perimeter with tiny replicas of failure. . . .

I couldn't read his expression at first. I expected him to be torn up or pissed. Or he could have been happy: one of those ass-backwards people like Grandpa who only felt fondness for terrible places and bitched like hell if he had to go on a picnic. But I didn't see bitterness or self-pity or some warped nostalgic wistfulness in his face. What I saw was something like pride but pride without ego, something like acceptance but acceptance without ever being allowed to consider any other options. I didn't figure it out until I was back home lying on my sore butt on my new sheets in my new room, feeling the familiar ache spread through my chest and face where Dad had hit me, that what I had seen was a gracious loser.

There's not much untrue about the descriptions, but O'Dell's interpretation offers little hope. Harley isn't a character with much hope. How could he be, abused and surrounded by a shroud of perpetual violence? O'Dell writes of a dark, hopeless Appalachia, unrelenting and ancestral, a past full of miserable fathers and grandfathers, sisters, mothers, towns. The abandoned reclamation plant is a monument to failure, everything so deeply poisoned that there's no way back from the brink. Trying is just another way to lose.

I visited such failed places as a young man, driving my own back roads with my friends. I remember once finding the desolate abandonment of some unknown coal patch town, precisely as Harley's father's hometown is portrayed.

I remember it as a dark clearing, a flat expanse of coal dust and emptiness, not far from where my friend Aaron and I had passed a derelict but inhabited shack we called, uncharitably, the home of The Goat People. I think there was a goat in the yard, which is the only accurate portion of our terminology. Finding such places suggested a lack of hope in coal country, at least in the small places outside of town, where the politics leaned right, the jobless rate climbed, and many people still hoped for the triumphant return of the industry that had literally been killing them for generations. How we described it also designated our self-loathing and sense of superiority, the latter a way to defend ourselves from the former.

Yet there is hope in the Indiana County of my birth, if not in the fiction of *Back Roads*. The Two Lick Creek that shaped my beloved farm valley was a shallow orange waterway when I was a child, fouled by mine acid and incapable of hosting fish. Today the mine leakage has been cleaned enough that trout have returned. In the next valley over, a massive restoration wetland filters the water through natural processes, just like a wetland I once wrote about for the newspaper, located near Ed Abbey's birthplace in Home. These are real-life versions of the failed *reclamation* plant that O'Dell writes about, evidence that the poison can be cleaned, that a new way forward—let's call it hope—is possible. These water projects suggest that we can repair our relationships to the landscape we have wrecked.

Even the old unrestored strip mines of the Two Lick Valley suggest hope. On the slopes beside the Two Lick Reservoir, the trees have grown for fifty years since strip mining carved out the hills beside the now dammed creek. The underbrush is thick enough to almost conceal the remaining highwalls abandoned after the mining was done, and erosion has started to grind away at the awful acuteness of mechanical angles. Leaf matter gathers on the forest floor, slowly degrading into new topsoil. It will take a long time, but the land will restore itself. Among this hope, my father and I recently looked out across the black heap of an old slag pile, the starkest reminder of the strip mining that had devastated this part of the valley. Up the road, someone shot a handgun, target practice aimed into another part of the slag. Maybe this is hopeful too? Fighting back, I suppose, or like to imagine.

That's the Indiana County I've been learning to recognize, even if the origins of my self-recognition as Appalachian first blossomed in the pages of the relentlessly negative vision of *Back Roads*. You can look at either the crumbling infrastructure and say *that's Appalachia* or at the improved water quality and say *that's Appalachia*. Indeed, you can look at both, and you really must, but you need to decide which one is past and which one future, which one inevitable and which aberration, which indicates the foundational Appalachia that we ought to use as reference point.

J. D. Vance uses a flawed reference point, one that cannot separate the substrate from the people and one that fails to engage national conditions as related to regional struggle. He reiterates the old stereotypes in a much less complex way than even O'Dell, who isn't exactly optimistic. This is the fate of reading Appalachia poorly, that you will wind up always engaging the same narratives, bad ones, failed ones, desperate ones. Or, probably just as inaccurately, you wind up reading only positive ones, beautiful ones, nostalgic and simplistic recovery narratives that like to imagine the ground is not wrecked. This might be the chief flaw of an author like my parents' own beloved Wendell Berry, the past a blinding nostalgic hope for a future impossibility.

It is and it isn't forever, that's what I'm trying to say. The mines below my home will continue to pump out their poison for ages, longer than I or my children will be alive, but Appalachia itself isn't those mines. Instead, the restoration wetlands are. We've found the real bedrock, the real substrate that matters most of all. Recognizing it and using it, well, that's how you work against the poison because the poison is us, a fact made clear enough when the hillside directly opposite the worst acid seep in the Two Lick Valley was recently strip mined. How much have we really learned? Economic development encourages us to participate in a perpetual cycle of boom and bust, applied to ourselves. Poison the land. Clean it up. Poison it again, knowing we can clean it.

I'd like to think that Ed Abbey offers a different way through this, as does Sean Prentiss and his desire to journey toward a recognition of what matters in home. Abbey would monkey-wrench the dozers that seek to strip the hills again. Abbey would stick his tongue in his whiskered cheek and declare himself a humanist: "I'd rather kill a *man* than a snake." And he'd then encourage us to think about the beauty of the rocks beneath us in Appalachia, about the timber rattlers chased away and what they deserve, about the stupid industrial degradation that we let wash over us again and again, all of us failing to recognize how we've been written as characters in novels as dark as and even darker than *Back Roads*.

Would that we learned this: we don't have to think of decay as our legacy and fate or that degradation is all we've got. Once we recognize that we come from a land shaped differently, by water and relief, by the dynamics of what has flowed within and around and under, we can start to read our own substrate with an orientation toward the future instead of anchored to the past. We don't have to think coal is all we have. We don't have to look in envy toward the Rockies. We don't have to accept violence, literary or real, as our legacy.

We don't have to believe writers who would rehash the same old narratives and market it as insight. And if we happen to be authors, we can resist writing only degradation, can refuse to locate ourselves as gracious losers not unlike Harley's father. Building a literature based only on darkness is just another way to shackle ourselves to decline. Instead, we are who we are, and that's the sound of red-winged blackbirds chirping in the blowing reeds alongside restoration wetlands, a dark plain bird with a hidden flash of brilliance, the real marker of hope.

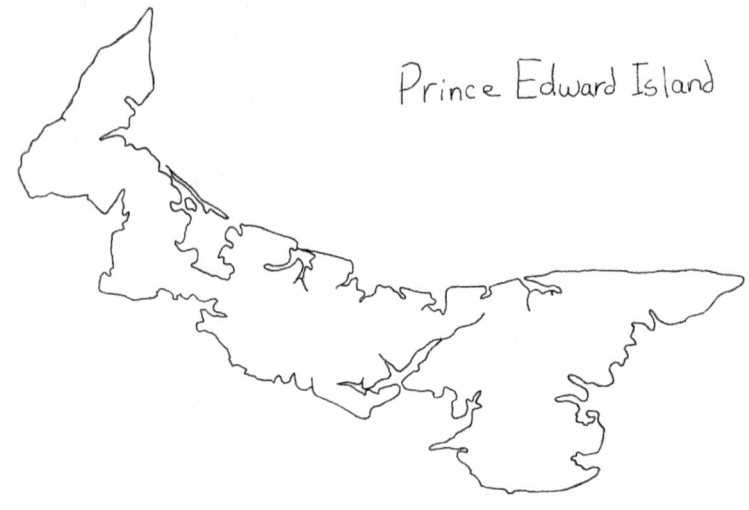

CHAPTER 9

Journey to Canappalachia

When my radiation treatments finally ended in midsummer, my wife and I decided to return to Prince Edward Island. Even a brief trip between treatments and the start of the school year seemed like an important act of recovery, even if I lived in constant exhaustion. Radiation had taken more out of me than I'd expected, leaving me worn out and in bed for nearly as much of the day as I had been when still recovering immediately after brain surgery. Two large patches of hair had fallen out of my head, one the size of a half-dollar behind my left ear and another on top of my skull. These were the sites of my radiation beams, pimples that turned to shed and baldness. I discovered the largest divot one afternoon standing in front of the mirror, first with my fingers then contorting to see the back of my own head. Strangely, I was more relieved than self-conscious about this discovery. The hair loss was at least evidence of *something*. You can't feel radiation, so have to just trust that it's working. Exterior damage implied interior change, a recognition that a path was at least being taken.

Still, I couldn't yet think in terms of recovery. My vision seemed cloudier than when all this began. I was still exhausted, unable to spend more than a couple hours doing anything before I'd have to lie down again. We decided to head to PEI anyway. We needed to, and I needed to, even if we'd spend as many days in the car getting there and back as we would on the Island.

I wish I could wax about the splendid magic of crossing the threshold of New Brunswick, driving off that land and onto the Confederation Bridge, the rolling farm-dotted hills of PEI laid out in front of us, beauty and grace and healing. There's some truth in that, I suppose, or at least it is a story I imagine I might tell someday. Reality proved to be rainier, misty gray, and somewhat disappointing.

So it is when you've been waiting months, lying in bed staring at ceilings, or lying in a Versa proton accelerator while ionized particles blast through your head and kill a tumor that will never shrink, never disappear, just, best-case scenario, stop growing. The damage done to the nerve—reduced vision, a blind spot and a veil, and eye weariness when reading—serve as a permanent reminder of the dead or, worse, dormant seed that will remain tucked in my skull forever. I wanted the Island to heal that, right away. Instead, the landscape felt dimmed, as everything had felt for some time, whether seen through my damaged left eye or the scarred lens of my own imagination. I now think that it is I who was dimmed, and the world I tried to view could not quite break through.

Of course, I also hoped for foxes on the Island, that great false symbol on which I have hung so much. While I knew it would be impossible, I wanted to find the half-blind fox, probably wished I'd find him better, hale and hearty and clear-eyed. For the first several days, I saw no foxes at all. Tourist season had struck, and visitation was up over the summer, good for the Island but bad for fox sightings. Worst of all, the first fox I saw was recent roadkill. I was driving alone, and the fox appeared on the side of the road, a shock of fresh blood streaming from its mouth onto the pavement.

Did you see the fox? I asked my wife a few days later.

Yes, she said, understanding what I really meant, as she always did. If this dead fox was a sign, it was not a good one.

I saw only one other fox before we left the Island at the end of that brief six-day visit, a golden with a clear upper pelt and ragged molt on its lower third. It appeared while I strolled to the tee box of the golf course one afternoon. It seemed healthy, whole or nearly so, poised next to the tall grasses at the golf course margin with one foot in the air, its snout pointed into the thicket. It pounced, a foxy move, flashing its head into the grass and fishing out a large field mouse it soon killed, dropped, and ate. A metaphor, maybe, but if so, meaning what? Am I fox, and if so which one? Or am I a mouse or a man watching or all of these?

I wanted this to mean something. I want it all to mean something, even if I don't yet know how to interpret the symbols I create.

Journeys may have anticipated destinations, but they do not have stable ending points. I think more and more about the journey as the task of life, not in the pat metaphorical way we often hear it offered, *life's a journey,* or rationalizing the heavy suck of terrible life moments as part of the journey we walk. Instead, I think about it in the same way I think about the essayist's impulse to wander around in a vague direction until you recognize where you've gotten.

Narratives seek to stabilize the journey by writing them down. In the worst moments, the narratives we have received through long histories of storytelling presume that a journey will start and end in the known. A medical crisis is a specific kind of journey. A map presumes a certain kind of limit to a journey.

"This journey is about the need to unravel, thread by thread, this mystery—to flow where those threads lead," Sean Prentiss writes, about his own quest for Ed Abbey's grave. "Or maybe we are pulled by mystery like we are pulled by wilderness—that desire to enter self-willed lands."

I have to confront the facts of Appalachian belief, momentum, maybe inertia, even entropy: my desire to reframe the limits of what counts as Appalachia, or to think about the quest for Northern Appalachian identity, is at heart personal and not likely to be widely accepted. I am journeying through Appalachia on the ground and within myself to create a "self-willed" sense of what being Appalachian means. I am journeying through the recognition of what a post-traumatic body becomes as a way to self-will that too.

And is it really that striking or bold to think of Appalachia in terms of journey? After all, don't most people know Appalachia through the Appalachian Trail (AT), a 2,100-mile hiking path of personal transformation, from Georgia's Springer Mountain to Maine's Mount Katahdin? Millions walk the AT each year, nearly 3,000 planning to walk the whole thing in one go, so-called thru hikers who have about a 10 percent chance of succeeding. A bigger chunk of people section-hike the totality, ticking off that task on their outdoorsy list.

I have walked literally zero miles on the AT, and I have no plans to try it. I only know one person who has hiked it, an ex-model who was a fellow graduate student at the University of Arizona during my one semester there. He thru-hiked it after the end of a marriage, redefined himself literally and emotionally, then dropped his first name and in that subtle change became something new. He told me about this while helping me repaint the downstairs of the Arizona house my wife and I had bought shortly after I quit at the university, a place that had a decent view of the tall peaks of a different mountain range, the Huachucas.

The sense of redefinition carries a lot of weight in the culture of hiking lit, as evoked in the large stack of books written about various trails and their hikers. Think about Cheryl Strayed's best-selling memoir, *Wild*, focused on her personal journey of recovery from addiction and self-loathing and, most of all, grief over her mother's death from cancer. She faced these internal aspects while hiking the formidable Pacific Crest Trail.

"I had to change," Strayed writes of her motivations before the hike. "*I had to change* was the thought that drove me in those months of planning. Not into a different person, but back to the person I used to be—strong and responsible, clear-eyed and driven, ethical and good. And the PCT would make me that way. There, I'd walk and think about my entire life. I'd find my strength again, far from everything that had made my life ridiculous."

This is a fine motivation for hiking and self-recognition, just as it is also a familiar sort of goal setting that kicks off the familiar dramatic push of trail books. There are two arcs in such narratives. One is the neatly defined arc of walking, an act with a starting point and an end. You start walking here, and the book ends when you get there. Strayed's other arc, the personal one, is in line with the transformative power of endurance. In focusing on the physical exertion of long-distance hiking, she and others find a meditative exhaustion. Achieving the goal of the trail works as a mechanism for self-discovery, tired feet and backs moving the mind away from itself onto the body, allowing the presence of who you are to become clearer.

Wild is a triumph narrative, as trail books almost always are. They each offer a hero's journey, obstacles overcome and lessons learned. This isn't a bad thing, but it is a thing. There's a particular narrative to trail literature, often focused on gloried exertion leading to ecstatic revelation. Isn't that what *Wild* is all about, why it strikes a chord with so many readers who will never buy a pair of Danners and hit the mountains to learn how they can push through their physical obstacles to succeed? Isn't that really what a lot of travel literature is, the conflict of foreignness leading to writing not so much about the place visited but, instead, the place revealed within the traveler?

Unlike most people I know, I prefer Bill Bryson's *A Walk in the Woods* over other Appalachian Trail books. He whines a lot as he writes of hiking the AT, which other people apparently don't like: his is a transformative experience, so he should be ecstatic. The hike is supposed to be a way to jiggle loose the meaning of life. For Bryson, it's mostly just hard.

L. A. Paul writes:

> Transformative experiences, then, confront you with the basic unknowability of your subjective future in a context where new and dramatic changes are occurring, and transformative decision-making draws out the consequences of that epistemic fact. In an important sense, when facing a transformative choice, you lack the knowledge you need in order to have authority and control over who you will become when you choose how to act.

Maybe this is precisely why trail literature resonates with so many people, and why for Bryson and for me the conclusions are less satisfying. If what Paul suggests is correct, then true transformation is about a lack of control. Trails have ends, and you know where they are. That's a kind of control, the destination known and imaginable. Maybe transformative action requires a recognition of the falsity of the path itself, just as it also denies clear and stable knowledge of destination.

Bryson begins to recognize that the farther he travels, the more things stay the same. For him, the AT is just a tunnel of trees. He writes of his trek: "We spent our days doing precisely what we had done on previous days and would continue to do on future days, over the same sorts of hills, along the same wandering track, through the same endless woods. The trees were so thick that we hardly ever got views, and when we did get views it was of infinite hills covered in more trees."

Bryson's self-willed narrative does not adhere to the conclusions we want in a genre presupposed as triumphant and epiphanic. Trail books are supposed to depict conquests of the external and internal. The end of the walk leads to a narrative release of the tension of the plot—will the hiker make it to the end?—with a simultaneous release of the tension of the intellect. We see the end of the trail coming just as the cresting wave of transformation arrives, each coming as a simultaneous ecstasy of completion. This is false for Bryson, for me, for many. So in the face of the monotonous struggle of hiking the AT, Bryson quits. He and his hiking companion are just done: "So we decided to leave the endless trail and stop pretending we were mountain men because we weren't."

We aren't supposed to quit when we face challenges but should keep searching toward our ecstatic end. We aren't supposed to face the terrifying maw of the beast and turn toward home, giving up on the conclusion that has been predetermined. Trail narratives suggest that journeying functions as a way to pretend and even become something you're not, to discard who you were and take on a new form. Yet most hikers go back to their jobs, gain back their lost weight, show pictures and share stories but, in the end, are who they were before. There's no shame in that, of course. Instead, I think it's what we all need to recognize. Bryson is bluntly calling out the truth most of us don't want to accept: we are who we are. Struggle is sometimes just struggle.

"The question embeds the problem of transformative choice into a context of informed consent," Paul writes. She is here addressing medical treatment, that thorny, messy, terrifying site of change:

> What do we take ourselves to be doing with such consent? The basic idea is that you, as the patient, are supposed to evaluate the different outcomes, determine their values along with the level of risk you can tolerate as a result, and control the decision-making on that basis. But, crucially, then you need to know *how you think you'll respond* to different possible experiential outcomes.
>
> And in this context, you are unable to get the information you'd need.

The narrative trail of medicine requires a trust in the system itself, that each painful step along the way leads us toward the majestic view atop the final mountain. This is as much a feature of the industrial revolution model of medicine and science—problem, rational process, solution—as it is with core Western beliefs in the linearity of story. But struggle is often not about epiphanies, that concept itself a construction of the literary mind. Blame it on Saint Paul, all that light and clarity dropping upon him on the road to Damascus. He sets Western literature as arcing toward those moments when we fall to our knees and see the world afresh. That's why we travel. That's what we gain by moving. That's the payoff for great struggle.

Trail literature satisfies our narrative urge. It offers the payoff that we often don't feel in real life, where pain often leads to nothing at all. Existential crisis is, well, just a crisis without resolution, not because resolution isn't possible but because we lack the narrative framework in our own lives to make the sorts of changes to release ourselves from the conditions of our own journeys. So, yes, my brain might as well be Appalachian, each of these physical locales also an imaginary built of curious existential crises and melodramatic notions of mortality and the way that a brain tumor has the habit of making you think about your life in ways different than you did before. A brain tumor is a rather rough trail, and its struggles deviate from the fantasies of literature.

Let me put it this way: narrative suggests that I am supposed to live in the wake of my personal crisis along a *Wild* sort of arc, where I'm faced with this setback and *do something*. Maybe I hike a trail (nope), maybe I try to reignite my failed professional golf career (well, maybe, but probably nope), maybe I just use the tumor as its own sort of metaphorical journey and come out on the other side transformed and different, certainly better.

But the problem of brain tumors and narrative resolution, or at least the problem of my own brain tumor, is that resolution isn't possible. It's there in my head, will be forever. It's probably dead, so there's a triumph, but it's not gone. And I'm still the same person, just one with new neurological issues that bug the hell out of me. Sometimes my hands tremble. Often my left eye aches when I've been exerting myself or even just reading too much. Some days, I'm just off, dropping shit and unable to make three-foot putts on the golf course. When I look in the mirror, my left eyelid droops noticeably. I do not like what I see.

Maybe I can describe it this way: a year after my recovery ended, summering in Prince Edward Island and walking the golf course with my best Canadian friend, he and I talked about recovery and locale. He suffered testicular cancer when just a young man. At the time, he, his wife, and his young children lived away from Prince Edward Island in Moncton, New Brunswick. I mentioned to him how much the Island means to me now, as a respite from all that I suffered in Pennsylvania. He told me he understood exactly.

I hate even setting foot in Moncton, he said, because that's where he found out about his own mortality.

And maybe this is why the geography of my home Appalachia can sometimes seem too hard to bear. There's too much undermining, literal and figurative, too many foundations at risk because things have been scooped out below. Things subside, but not in a good way, more like the way foundations crumble and buckle as the earth falls into abandoned coal mines. That erosion is unintentional, unnatural.

And for me, my memories of my home are always overlaid with this, a new palimpsest of malady and fear. Worse, my sense of Northwestern Pennsylvania is forever linked to the moment I heard my cell phone ring and I listened to a doctor explain something unreachable, impossible, dire. It is linked to knowing that as I lay etherized for eight hours, my wife sat in a polyester and vinyl waiting room, her phone ringing and a nurse intoning, *everything is going well* and *they're closing now* and *you can see him in the ICU.*

It is linked to a day that began before dawn in a converted convent, now a hotel in a seedy neighborhood of Pittsburgh, when we walked out into the cool March air, first hints of spring in the blooming cherry trees, just a distant hum of traffic, gleaming neon lights atop the US Steel building and the Highmark health insurance building, then on to the washed-out lights of the anxious registration room. I lay all morning in pre-op, watching other patients roll out for their surgeries, seven hours pretending to be hale, healthy, and joking, and somehow apparently happy, dressed in a worn hospital gown, socks with rubber grippers on the soles, watching *Top Gear* on my iPad, eventually with an IV jabbed in each hand. How could I bear to hear over and over again in memory the great cheerfulness of the OR nurse and the anesthesiology intern who came to roll me away, understanding also how leaving meant a gaping emptiness for my wife, marked only by the clunking sound of hospital bed rails being locked into place, the oomph of two women pushing the bed away, and the bed rolling away, gone, my wife left not knowing what or who would return?

I want to be able to quit. Fuck this trail.

There are too many trees, the rocks are a pain in the ass, and I have nothing to prove. So I'm done. No more brain tumor. No more recovery writing. No more comments from family members about God's mercy and compliments about my great attitude and quiet tones of assurance or absent tones from people who just don't want to talk about it or annoying tones from people who say, *you think you have it bad I know a guy who can't eat dairy*, those sorts of diminishing comments that suggest that a brain tumor just needs to be put in perspective, even a bullshit perspective that creates false equations and refuses to acknowledge how much my sense of who I am has shifted.

No, I'm lying. My sense of self hasn't shifted at all. I just find it harder to live the narratives that I've created over forty years, or that have been created for me that I continue to live. The scariest truth is that I hate the life I live in many ways, and I don't know whether this expresses a fundamental truth of myself living contrary to what I desire, or if I'm just playing out a clichéd middle-aged existential crisis with an overtone of medical angst.

I want to quit my job because working with students over and over again each year on the same fundamental aspects of writing gets to be a drag, a conveyor belt of craft lessons with a finite end, graduating students never able to get past a certain point (of course, and this is no fault of theirs, just the fate of teachers of defined parameters, who move students from point C to D, some as far as E, but never further), all of this happening in the context of an America that cares less and less about the importance of deep thinking, let alone the vitality of the arts, therefore making the act of teaching the reality of being part of a declining, financially strapped, hurting-for-respect, unappreciated grind.

I want to quit my godforsaken town in northwestern Pennsylvania that—no matter how often some of my friends say it has potential and is going places and is a good place to live—is really just a dying Rust Belt city that refuses to acknowledge it must let go of what it was if it's ever to be anything better than what it has become, despairing in architecture and meth use and racism and bigotry and a willingness to fall in love with Donald Trump.

Strayed says this:

> *Thank you*, I thought over and over again. *Thank you.* Not just for the long walk, but for everything I could feel finally gathered up inside of me; for everything the trail had taught me and everything I couldn't yet know, though I felt it somehow already contained

within me.... How in fifteen years I'd bring my family to this same white bench and the four of us would eat ice-cream cones while I told them the story of the time I'd been here once before, when I'd finished walking a long way on something called the Pacific Crest Trail. And how it would be only then that the meaning of my hike would unfold inside of me, the secret I'd always told myself finally revealed.

How wild it was, to let it be.

Bryson says this:

I thought for a moment, unsure. I had come to realize that I didn't have any feelings towards the AT that weren't confused and contradictory. I was weary of the trail, but still strangely in its thrall; found the endless slog tedious but irresistible; grew tired of the boundless woods but admired their boundlessness; enjoyed the escape from civilization and ached for its comforts. I wanted to quit and to do this forever, sleep in a bed and in a tent, see what was over the next hill and never see a hill again. All of this all at once, every moment, on the trail or off.

And I say this: I want to quit teaching, but I love my job, love opening students to an understanding of the transformative power of words and the remediating miracle of revision. I want to quit being Appalachian, quit Appalachia, quit having no choice other than exile from self or place or happiness, but I love Pennsylvania and love knowing that I am among the rocks and trees and people who also love Pennsylvania. And I love being Appalachian, with all that such a claim implies.

I live another narrative problem now, more than a year after that quick return to PEI, and more than a year after acute treatments for my brain tumor have finished. I have been treated, restored scientifically and medically, and offered a clean bill of health. I'm supposed to be the man who I was before all of this began, and this is now a problem I share with reclaimed Appalachia.

It has become clear to me that reclamation is a term that binds us to unrecoverable pasts. It supposes, errantly, the same notion as strip mine reclamation: that what was can be again. I have been *returned to contour*, cut open, a hatch of bone laid aside on a table, mined for bone and flesh to clear space for radiation-induced swelling, the hatch placed back with glue and titanium screws. A surgeon sewed my eyelid back together, that location serving as the portal to the shaft of my optic canal. I lay in a hospital, then lay at home, and I recovered.

But things are not the same, even though my surgeons have told me everything has been a rousing success. My vision is still compromised, the blind spot that first signaled my condition unrecoverable. I'll never not have a blind spot in my left eye, never not be color-blind in that eye. And while the vision measures on machines as the same as before the surgery—which is to say it remains medically as poor as it was before we started—it is recognizably worse to me. When I exercise, the vision dims, as if someone is slowly turning a dial. When I drink beer, the vision dims too. When I play my saxophone, the notes on my music rapidly become illegible.

One neurologist thinks this is a vascular issue. She ordered an MR angiogram, which showed a kink in my ophthalmic nerve, a rerouting caused by the tumor, but no impact on blood flow. An ophthalmologist thinks the new blindness is akin to Uhthoff's phenomenon, a condition present in individuals with multiple sclerosis in which damaged nerves become unable to transmit information properly when they heat up. My neurosurgeon has no idea, so he sent me to a stroke neurologist. I waited nine months for that appointment, only for this newest doctor in my collection to say, more or less, *huh*.

There's no sign of stroke, he told me. And that was that.

Yet it really isn't because I live in a constant physical condition of compromise. I suffered a headache every day for a year, pain I knocked back with frequent doses of aspirin and ibuprofen, a recurring reminder of my wounding. My local neurologist administered a spinal tap to check on my cerebral spinal fluid pressures, which she determined were high. But this procedure also caused a leak in my spinal cord that, on the anniversary of my surgery, had me flat in bed again, unable to rise without a debilitating headache and nausea. I lived, once again, in the too familiar walls of the guest room. There was an emergency room visit, IVs, and hours lost before another doctor told me I'd just have to wait it out, because trying to fix a fluid leak meant another spinal tap, which might create another leak. One year post-surgery, I stayed home from work again, neurologically compromised and feeling, deeply, that my life revolved around me flat out and in pain. I began to wonder if I would measure my life forever in exam tables.

So I found myself prescribed Diamox, a drug intended to lower spinal fluid pressures by slowing the body's production of that fluid. Maybe it worked, since the headaches started to diminish. But it also did not work, as my tongue started tingling constantly, and I became dehydrated, so much so that nurses couldn't find veins anymore to draw blood. And my ability to have an MRI for my one-year checkup became questionable, since my dehydrated body wasn't processing fluids enough to allow for the safe administering of necessary contrast dyes for that test. And my hematologist wanted me to start doing therapeutic phlebotomies—again—to lower my elevated red blood count. And I went to do that, and on the first visit, a rather impatient nurse stuck my dried-out veins badly, then wiggled the needle around to get a painful flow going.

I'm losing it, I told her, feeling my head spin, the grayness arrive.

You better not, she scolded.

And I did because how could I help it, the pain, stress, dehydration, and constant flagellation of what personal sense of wholeness still existed. I awakened to smelling salts, and to the now pissed-off nurse complaining that she'd have to wait with me while I recovered, implying that I should bear a heavy dose of blame for having the gall to pass out. Six months later, at a follow-up, she'd flirt with me and tell me I looked like Johnny Depp (which is only true in the sense that I sometimes wear my hair long and have a Van Dyke beard), likely not remembering how much of an inconvenience I had offered before.

My left eyelid droops and will continue to do so unless I have the plastic surgery my eye surgeon keeps recommending, a surgery I liken to planting invasive loosestrife on a former mountain in order to hide the imprecise way it's been *reclaimed*. I suffer concentration problems, something my doctors say has nothing to do with my surgery but which I imagine is a symptom of the exhaustion of dealing with my perpetual recovery. Since radiation, I have suffered recurring bouts of upset stomach and jock itch, as if something's knocked out of whack with the ecosystem of my body. My entire life feels like it needs a reboot.

I do not mean to complain. No one likes a patient who complains. Worse still is someone recovered who complains about the chronic state of being not whole, or suffering pain, or otherwise reminding the world that things are not OK, that recovery is incomplete. Such people call attention to the falsity of narratives, which loosens our grip on the comfort of known or intended destination.

In *Pain Woman Takes Your Keys: Essays from a Nervous System*, Sonya Huber writes, "When the Grim Reaper shuffles in, what we fear most is not the shroud but the sharp scythe he carries, the 'ouch' before the silence. It's hard to confess pain because other people feel it or imagine it. Then they want to solve it. They will tell you the same solutions over and over: have you tried yoga?"

My father asks me repeatedly if I have been tested for Lyme disease. Well-meaning friends mention tai chi and stress management. My mother wants me to go back to church. Yoga has, indeed, been recommended. Certainly, I have felt what Huber references about confessions of chronic pain, how despite only infrequent Facebook postings about the subject, some see her as defined by and constantly declaring her woes, thus she and others who suffer pain learn not to mention it in polite company. We grin and we bear.

"Maybe we learn our carrying capacity as a way to see the cogs of society functioning," she writes. "Maybe we hide the pain to preserve our own pride and autonomy. When a person confesses to being sick, she is seen as less reliable, less capable, and therefore less of a person within the social and production networks of the well."

This is the affront of reclamation, the lies we tell and are told: that we're fine, that we're back to our old selves, that life has become normal again. Life might be normal, but there is no *again*. The old self is gone, and the word *fine* carries different connotations. When I look upon my body, I am looking at the landscape of an undermined region, so I declare about myself the same thing I declare about so many spots in my Pennsylvania birthplace: *this is not a mountain.*

My greatest desire is to transgress borders. Even as I long to leave it, Appalachia matters to me in the complicated, unsettled way that John Lane describes in thinking about his own project of mapping the sphere of his watershed in South Carolina. He writes:

> The world isn't really a map, and it's not made up of circles, and none of us really lives in the center of anything. The Copernican Revolution settled all that, we've been told, no matter what *Black Elk Speaks* claims about Harney Peak being the center of the universe. So why backslide? Why throw everything modern and boundless out of kilter and set about to put some out-of-the-way place like a spot on the east side of Spartanburg, South Carolina, in the center of a circle again?

Lane has his own answer, that of walking the landscape in his watershed to trace the interactions of apparently disconnected places. I seek an answer for myself. However, part of my question is about determining my own center, or even the terms of measurement. Tell me again, how do you pronounce *Appalachian*?

I understand that I'm creating a false, problematic, and maybe offensive equation between blighted landscapes and blighted self, between the Appalachia of cultural history and the Appalachia of geology, and between the Appalachia of my brain tumor and the Appalachia of places that would never consider themselves Appalachian at all. I'm also trying to say something about borders, maps, and blight itself.

We can think many ways about these connections, not always negatively and certainly not nostalgically. For me, for Appalachia, there's no going back. So, no, I am not a strip mine, and, no, I am not Appalachia, and, yes, there's something a bit unsettling about equating the gouging of land with the recovery from a brain tumor, just as there's something unsettling, galling, and wrong about wanting to inscribe my own lines around what counts as Appalachia.

Is it worse to cheapen the environmental and cultural devastation of extractive industry by comparing it to my health? Or is it worse to minimize the grave physical and psychological effects of a serious health scare by likening it to the machinery scraping coal out of the not-mountains? I accept both, and reject them also. At heart I am writing about myself, my relationship to several landscapes—the place I'm from and love and don't quite love and also my body, which I've learned recently to resent, even as I understand it fully as me. Descartes be damned.

Return to the maps and consider their lines: the ones that separate Pennsylvania from West Virginia, the Mason-Dixon line, lines that contain the ARC from the rest of the Northeast, ones that inscribe designations on the land that have nothing to do with geology or life itself. In the end, these lines signal nothing but imaginary separation points, false demarcations as fully felt but ultimately limiting as the line between *App-uh-latch-uh* and *App-uh-lay-sha*. The lines on maps mean nothing to a red-tailed hawk, or to a slow-moving glacier, or to the rumbling birth of a mountain range, or to the long-wearing erosion of time and history, or to wandering foxes. Instead, I choose now to see confluences of the region and mountain range that carry the same Appalachian name, of people across thousands of miles of forgotten, rural, excluded landscapes, geology, and culture.

For a long time, I had to turn south to think about Appalachia, to see my region within the terms defined long ago by writers like Campbell and Kephart or, more recently, by O'Dell and Vance, and to see the various ways that contemporary Appalachia is defined externally, always flawed, broken, and in ruin. I'm done with that, at least from an Appalachian perspective.

Instead, I choose to turn north, not to deny the Appalachia that lies within the ARC but, instead, to think about how my part of the region is its own thing, part of a different whole. In Canada, the residents of the Maritimes are stereotyped in ways similar to the way Appalachians are in the United States, as backward, inbred, lost in time, curiosities. Their economies have struggled, the extraction of fisheries, forests, and salt and coal mines collapsed by the same processes of greed that scoop away the economy of Appalachia. There is such a thing as an Appalachian iceberg, flowing past the coast of Newfoundland, past the end of the Appalachian Mountains, which still carry the same meaning to me despite departures northward.

Or think of the long ribbon of serpentine rock that winds through the entire Appalachian range. This greenish, scaly, metamorphic stone that Kevin Dann calls an "ancient gesture," the only parts of this geology "that have an origin wholly different from the rest of the rocks. . . . the sole representatives of the earth's mantle, a region hidden from our view." Yet if we look, we can see this different rock, even when we can't see it directly. Above the serpentine, trees are shorter and grasses grow poorly, and the land itself carries the marker of difference. These are the "barrens," where the soil chemistry won't support growth. I see this as less a scar than a sign about differences deep within us all. The hair that doesn't grow on my head—well, that's a marker of my own figurative serpentine, a relic of radiation and a response to my tumor. It is me. Always will be. I refuse to define it any longer within the terms of reclamation, or deviance, or a map that suggests I have been broken forever.

It is vital that we see the maps that have been drawn before. We need to know what has been defined before we seek redefinition. Equally as important, we need to do the *ground truthing*, walking the physical spaces on a map to see what the landscape actually is. The poet Will Brewer chatted with me recently about his West Virginia origins, suggesting that being from West Virginia means being surrounded always by death: digging coal is the digging of layered death, emerging from the mines is emerging into a region that has been developed at the expense of its future, that has literally dug death as it careens toward it.

Would that we could think of this differently, seeing the accumulation of decaying organic matter not as death but as transformation. Would that we could think of the value of coal not within the terms of economic value but as metaphorical hope. The ancient seas that were once Appalachia deposited themselves to form our core, and we only destabilize ourselves when we strip that away. Still, as L. A. Paul explains, imagining a future differently oriented places us into an uncomfortable reckoning with the unknown. Mining worked, and at least Appalachia knew what it was getting. Not seeing coal as an economic prospect is scary because what's left to fill the void? And when the nation sees no future for you other than what you always have been made to be, it's even harder to transform into something different, whole and solid.

I am a Northern Appalachian, and I declare the rocks as my delimiter. I am a man with a brain tumor, and I declare life as my unit of measurement. I follow the spine of the mountains to redefine myself and my region as something bigger than I am supposed to allow. We should all think about what that could mean, about the rocks that spread through New York and into Vermont, New Hampshire, and Maine, on across the border into New Brunswick and Quebec, all the way to Newfoundland, a time zone and a half away from the ARC. I want to embrace the spurs of geology and people jutting out through the rest of the Maritimes. My Appalachia, my northernmost sense of self and, in truth, the place where I now feel most at home, is Prince Edward Island, that red rock accumulation of washed out soil, akin in some ways to Edward Abbey's Utah desert, each place built of red sandstone, and no doubt the place I flow toward.

Recognizing that is to ignore the artificiality of the map and inscribe new and better lines on our imaginations, to recognize what has always been. This is Appalachia. Yes, yes, it is. This is me. This is a new vision of both self and place, a turn toward the substrate and a way to refuse to be tethered by the impossible demands of returning to a self that, really, never was.

Back to foxes, and back to before all of this started, back to the accumulation of Appalachian erosion that is Prince Edward Island, the place I felt drawn to as recovery mounted. On the night that I first saw the mottled and half-blind fox in the national park, I also saw a second one, hardly more than a shadow moving across the twilight road. This fox wore a dark black mask, almost as if part raccoon, and the same ragged molting pelt as the first.

The sum of these two foxes equated to a haunting, or so I then felt. I wanted these foxes to portend something I couldn't quite voice but nonetheless desired. Even then, I sought a way to bring order to the disorder of my past few years. I needed a method to assess and read the signs of my life and determine a path. More than anything, I needed these foxes to mean something in a life that seemed to have just accumulated in a pattern unsatisfyingly similar to the one I'd probably always been presumed to live: a good student, good husband, good father, good professor. While there's nothing terrible about such a life, it's also one that has always felt pre-determined, without wildness, simply accruing as a result of my own choices and failures to choose. Nothing I've done has ever worked to twist me off the expected track. Didn't I still wind up where my parents probably always figured I would, living some facsimile of their own pasts? In PEI, among the foxes, I understood exile but not yet how to assemble the collage of my own wanderings. The foxes seemed like a crucial, primal clue.

That summer, I began tallying the foxes I saw, listing each on a piece of paper attached to the cottage refrigerator. I saw a phantom silver fox twice, racing across our lawn on two early mornings. I passed a scratching, mosquito-mad red on the Confederation Trail, way out near O'Leary. I saw foxes galore in the national park, anonymous reds and golden reds who lingered on the road. My tally sheet quickly filled.

One afternoon, while playing outside the cottage with our then two-year-old, I turned to see the phantom silver fox sitting on its haunches in the tall grasses beside the yard. Likely, it had been watching us for some time, curious and silent. As soon as I made eye contact, it darted into the overgrowth and then reappeared a little farther away.

I couldn't help the surge of quick fear, not for me but for my son. I felt embarrassed, a farm boy afraid of a tiny dog-like animal that had always thrilled me, an animal I wanted to think of as my totem. Yet also I couldn't help but wonder about the toddler wobbles of my son, how easily he could be knocked down, how a good-sized fox like this was as big as my boy.

I grabbed my son and whisked him inside. I offered the pretense of getting my camera, but the truth was better described as fear. The fox bolted again when I moved but returned a little farther out, as fearful and curious as I was but not willing to give up.

In my photos, the fox is a dark shadow, a silver fox, rare and formerly valuable to a pelt industry long departed from the Island. One patch of light illuminates the right side of its face, the eyes visible only if I lean in very close to the picture. Both are clear. Of that day, I remember most when the fox disappeared, the longing I felt to see it again though it would never return. I wish I'd never taken its photo, had stayed in the yard with my son and watched it watch us.

Through the rest of that spring, I regularly saw the other fox, the magical blind-eyed creature of the national park. Always he waited and watched me as long as I watched him. But eventually the increased traffic of summer drove him away, as it did the other foxes. Or at least I imagine that's what happened. Maybe I stopped looking as hard. Still, I slowed at the curve where the blind-eyed fox lived, hoping. When I rode my bike past that spot, I could smell the heavy musk of wet dog at the bend where he usually appeared, a sign of his invisible presence. But I never saw him again.

Half a year after I last saw that fox, and after we'd returned to Pennsylvania as my sabbatical ended, and only a few weeks before I learned of the trouble with my brain, the novelist Cathy Chung came to campus as part of our visiting writer series. I taught her novel, *Forgotten Country*, which follows a woman facing her father's cancer-driven death and the ghosts of the family's Korean past. At the reading, she charmed my students with new writing, what she called a ghost story, really her own version of a *kumiho* story, a Korean legend about a shape-shifting fox spirit that seduces young men by appearing as a beautiful woman who holds them in magical thrall while eating their hearts and livers.

After the reading, we headed to dinner, where we talked of France, of swimming in dangerous seas, of Cathy's near drowning while trying to exit the water on sharp rocks. My poet colleague told a story of his own perils at sea, once when he nearly succumbed to a whirlpool in Greece, and another time when heavy California seas forced him to crash into shoals in order to free himself from a dangerous current. In his latter story and in Cathy's, the tellers focused on the people on shore, blithely unaware of the danger and simply waving. This is powerful metaphor as well, that distress is hard to see by the people not in distress.

When I think of that night, however, the cold darkness of February, snow coating our vehicles when we left the restaurant, I think most of all about the *kumiho*. I am spooked by it, and I wonder at the capacity to be deceived, to be consumed from within. Yet isn't this what foxes are supposed to be? Always cunning? Always shape shifting?

The fox is a lesser trickster, not quite coyote, usually driven by ill intent. The fox is deceitful, slippery, deadly to know. The *kumiho* devours the young man. The Japanese *yako kitsune* possesses a human body, revealed only by the sudden onset of illness. The cock Chauntecleer dreams of death arriving in the form of a fox but is assured by one of his wives that it is just a dream, only to be later captured by the fox Don Russel. Aesop's fox can't reach the grapes, then whines that they must be sour. Volpone pretends to be sick so people will bring him gifts.

What, then, are my foxes? Are they apparitions, threats, warnings? Only foxes? I want to think of them as guardians, and though I neither belong to the system of belief nor yet fully understand it, I am comforted by the *zenko* or *Inari kitsune*, good foxes, symbols of benevolence and prosperity. Maybe foxes can be all of these things, as we all can be built of competing parts: Appalachian and not, healthy and broken, fractured for sure but made whole by the ways that joy and despair swirl within. Maybe this is why I cannot stop thinking about foxes. Maybe this is why I think the trickster can never be just evil, shape-shifting too a sort of way of life.

Say you've been going to doctors over and over again, first to have yourself diagnosed with a brain tumor, then to figure out what to do with that brain tumor, then to have that brain tumor not removed in a long surgery, then to have that brain tumor bombarded by milligrays of deadly radiation, then to figure out this symptom and that symptom and this tiredness and that headache and this elevated pressure. Say you feel the thick phlebotomy needle drive into the back of your hand, cringe as the nurse grinds it hard one way and another until, bam, you're unconscious.

Wouldn't you quit that trail? Wouldn't you do what I did that day, go home and post an article on Facebook about "noncompliant patients" who defy doctors' orders because, fuck it, the treatment is no life? Wouldn't you start thinking about how the narrative of recovery, of reclamation, of trying to get back to an unattainable past is a sham treadmill of industrial era metaphors of the body as a machine? Wouldn't you go home, pick up the phone, and cancel every appointment you have, stop taking medications, then flee to Canada to spend a summer thinking not at all about the life that defines you as a patient so you could instead have a life?

A confession: Some nights on Prince Edward Island, in that summer before I found out about my brain tumor, while driving the coast road I thought about steering into the gulf. More than once, I stood on the rocks at the overlook and thought about wading into the cold water or leaping from the eroding cliffs, about the shock of coldness when I entered the sea, how heavy it would be as it soaked into my clothes. Even now, I don't know what this means, whether such impulses are the signs of depression, or that sirens do exist and I heard them on those rocks. Probably, I was tired of feeling tired, of being worn out, tired of hopelessness and the absence of happiness and satisfaction—well, I don't know. Maybe it was the tumor, my body instinctively reacting to the mad growth of cells that had flipped the wrong switch.

I do know that driving home one night, navigating the curve just beyond North Rustico, where the bridge abutments creep in to tighten the road and where the bay would later in the summer be filled with mussel farm buoys and, for one week, a dank blue-green algae bloom, I held the wheel an extra second. I never intended to hold the line long enough to fail, to hurtle off the pavement and into the water. But I held it. A second too long. Then veered back on course and headed home to my wife and children.

I carried then a deep stupor, something I'd prefer to think of as melancholy but that might be less artful than I imagine. Why I hesitate to call it depression, I don't know, but that's probably as good an explanation as any. And this is a cliché of terrible commonality: we too often ignore our hurt psyches because they are invisible and because we count this as weakness. But we are captive to them, even when we remain steadfast in our commitment to denial.

Blindness can be cultivated. It blossoms into a state of being, a fullness of misguided attention, nurtured and abetted by a desire not to see. Moving to PEI for half a year may not have been an act of blindness, but my readiness to see it as some kind of pure escape certainly was. I carried deep wounds, as well as some still unknown, flawed, frantic cell division that was both a propagating blindness and something easy to ignore, until it couldn't be.

Still, even if it was on PEI that I felt the first urge to not be alive, it is simultaneously the place where I feel now most alive. On the last day of our post-treatment return to Prince Edward Island, we decided on a whim to look at a farmhouse up for sale. It rests on a few acres less than a mile from the Gulf of St. Lawrence, among farm fields that roll down toward the Southwest River with a topography nearly identical to the arcs of my parents' Pennsylvania farm, gentle but significant. I know, as well, that this is part of what I love about Prince Edward Island, particularly the central area within which this farm lies. Often, I see the same landscape I know from childhood, but made more vibrant by the brightness of red dirt and made fresher by sea air. I have always loved saltwater, another childhood nostalgia, this one originating in annual trips to the North Carolina coast. PEI is surrounded by saltwater, and after storms the pounding of the gulf whispers just over the breezes that blow past this farm. It's little wonder that with a speed and surety I fear indicates desperation, we offered on that house, eventually agreeing to buy it even though the foundation was shot and would need total replacement. Maybe I'm a sucker for restoration projects, wanting to see the hope that comes with repair. Maybe we just knew we needed a place of refuge, and the Island offered that to us.

Regardless, I returned alone to PEI in October for a final walkthrough before purchase. Hurricane Matthew came with me, heavy rains soaking the province on Thanksgiving, coupled with gale-force winds. When I drove the coast that day, the air was heavy and claustrophobic; tall seas rumbling in, pounding the shore with irregular fury. I looked for the glimpses of beauty, trees in the middle of their autumn blaze, the pastoral landscape, and I couldn't help but wonder if we'd been hasty. Everything was dim and murky and, dare I say, ugly. As with the July visit, I felt cut off.

The storm passed that night, and Tuesday arrived as the kind of brilliant, crisp, high-pressure autumn day that inspires much terrible poetry. I drove from Summerside to the house, running so early for the house inspection appointment that I steered down a side road for a quick exploration. There, I passed an old farmhouse tucked in among linden trees on a high knoll, New London Bay stretching across the background, small waves shimmering in the morning sun above the red layers of so much Appalachian sandstone.

This is me, I said as a dopey smile arrived, meaning something self-deprecating and foolish, mocking myself for the grin: "Ha ha, 'this is me.' Look at the fool driven to joy, agape at the view." But then my emotions welled, and I heard myself in a different way, understood this statement not as mockery but as a declaration: *This is me* meaning *here I am*. It was a declaration of joy, a recognition of my absence. *This is me. This is me.* Hello old friend, thanks for returning here to the Island and to your life, from which you've been absent so long. Thanks for coming back, for revealing yourself as being *here*.

And that, you see, is why Prince Edward Island matters, why my map has led me here, and why you should both distrust and support my new definitions of Appalachia extended north into a new and rocky, beloved *Canappalachia*.

This is how and why I am redrawing lines, because there's something about me that can only be here, and something about me that must always be Appalachian even if my location can't always be where everyone thinks the region has been drawn. Those lines don't work anymore.

CHAPTER 10

Coordinates

N 41°42'53", W 80°30'9"

During the Wisconsin glaciation of the Ice Age, a massive frozen flow crept down from Canada and pushed rock and dirt across what is now Northwestern Pennsylvania. When the ice drew back, scraping the terrain like a mighty grader, it left behind a landscape transformed by the incomprehensible force of slow erosion—newly flat ground, and knobby outcroppings, and weird granite and quartzite boulders that don't fit the underlying substrate, *erratics*, the geologists call these.

A tongue of ice—this is also a term geologists use—licked just west of where I live, excavating the hole that melting ice formed into Conneaut Lake, the largest natural lake in the state. Around its shores, the tongue created a pleasantly rolling terrain of small hills, along with kettles and kames that make the area a remarkable window into the dynamic of the Ice Age. The glacier also makes this corner of the state much flatter than where I grew up, without the deeply eroded mountains that figure prominently elsewhere in the Allegheny Plateau.

US Route 6 cuts through all of this, a back road of Northwestern Pennsylvania called the Grand Highway of the Republic, named in honor of Civil War veterans. The highway takes cars through the rolling moraine, then through flatter ground west of that, past the man-made Pymatuning Reservoir that floods across the border to Ohio and seems, despite the artificiality, like a much more impressive and substantial body of water than the relatively tiny Conneaut Lake. Sometimes the real appears less grand than the built, maybe always.

At times, Route 6's designation seems ironic: Confederate battle flags fly in front of more than a few homes beside the road, a strange conceptual victory the Confederacy has achieved in the century and a half after the Civil War, too many northerners taking to the flag for much the same reasons the slaveholders of the South did, claiming heritage but really meaning something ugly, separate, and evil.

George Stewart, chronicler of US Route 40, describes Route 6 as running "uncertainly from nowhere to nowhere, scarcely to be followed from one end to the other, except by some devoted eccentric." And, truly, there isn't much traffic on Route 6, particularly as the ground beneath the highway grows toward a disembodied flatness, scoured more fully by the ice and far more evocative of the Great Plains than the Appalachian Mountains. The scenery is built by a combination of hanging-in-there farms and Rust Belt collapse, by rusting tractors and faded business signs. A few small grain elevators evoke the round behemoths of the Midwest, their relative tininess an indicator that farms break toward meat and dairy here instead of grain.

At the Ohio border, the highway takes a decidedly non-Appalachian turn, here in the precise location where the ARC separated Appalachia from America until 2008, when the three northeastern counties of Ohio were added into the region, thanks to the work of local representatives who recognized a common economic struggle, if not a common culture, with the rest of Appalachia. There were funds to be had, so the push made sense. Driving across the border now technically means nothing, relative to the position of Appalachia as officially defined. Yet Ohio offers a shocking contrast of form, clearly visible on any map. The curved, chaotic wandering of Route 6 becomes immediately straight.

At the Ohio border, Route 6 straightens like someone has pulled a piece of yarn tight. There it goes, pavement all the way to the horizon. Beneath a car, the terrain still undulates some, but suddenly Ohio appears as a land of right angles. Intersections become square, ninety degrees to the right after a few miles, then ninety degrees left. You don't feel that landscape, or maybe you do: a nothingness, a blandness, something un-Appalachian about it all.

Breece D'J Pancake has written about the Appalachian instinct of straight highway, about how growing up among the ubiquity of hard-curving roads leads a person to philosophical requirement. "I have heard it said that Georgians are unable to drive in snow, and that Arizonans go bonkers behind the wheel in the rain," he writes, "but no true-blooded West Virginia boy would ever do less than 120 mph on a straight stretch, because those runs are hard won in a land where road maps resemble a barrel of worms with Saint Vitus' dance." I have driven in the heavy disorienting rains of Arizona monsoons, and I have felt the urge he suggests comes innately in Appalachia when the pavement straightens. I feel called to drive such roads fast because they are strange, to be gobbled up in search of the next view around the next curve, which in fact will not be coming. The speed might also feel like a substitute for escape, the experience of quickness implying the gathering of exit velocity.

I grew up on a country road, one that wound uphill slowly, more or less an echo of the meandering drainage stream that cut the valley of the family farm. The last hill was the steepest, one I challenged myself as a kid to ride up without stopping on a bicycle. Doing so became an accomplishment of age, strength gathered. Once I began driving, I took this relatively straight portion of road, just past the last neighbor and before the curve at the farmhouse, as five hundred feet of opportunity. I used to stomp the gas pedal on the car I inherited from my grandmother, a 1969 Chevy Bel Air stacked with a powerful 327 motor that gearheads frequently inquired about purchasing. I enjoyed the snap of the acceleration, the thrill of topping seventy on a country road, then hitting the brake fast enough to be going a respectable twenty by the time my mother could see.

N 40°27'26", W 80°0'12"

First, we arrived in a room full of other early morning waiters, patients checking in and families offering the kindness of presence. It was early, half past five by the time the paperwork was done and my wife and I were ushered into pre-op. I stripped down to boxers, the thin, oft-washed hospital gown tied in the way it can never quite be secure. A nurse had me put on two pairs of socks, first a special kind without toes and heels, the open skin available for pricking during surgery, to make sure my brain still worked; the second, a pair with bottoms coated in rubber grippers, to make sure I didn't slip and fall and break open my skull before the surgeons planned to do it.

A steady stream of patients passed through beside us. There had been an emergency case, and we'd been bumped back for a seven-hour delay. Jen and I talked some. I watched videos on my iPad. We grew anxious, but also maybe a little hopeful that my turn would never come.

Aziz arrived, flipped through my chart, greeting me as *professor*, a rare doctor who recognizes how the powerful honor of titles goes in both directions. He used a black magic marker to scribble on my forehead, just above my right eye. I imagined it as an X, or a *cut here*, or just a dotted line for the scalpel to follow, even though I knew the incision would be in the fold of my eyelid.

It's the other eye, I said.

What? he said. Paused.

I mentioned the tumor, its location, the impacted vision on my left side, all things he knew. It didn't really matter, he told me, since the tumor lay nestled close to the chiasma where the optic nerves crossed. He could go in either way, but he agreed it made sense to work around the damaged eye.

He scratched out the ink on my forehead with more magic marker, put a new sign on my left side. He scribbled on my charts also, confirming the change. Then he walked away, and I would not see him until the day after surgery, even though he would soon spend eight hours inside my skull, following digital coordinates provided by a navigational MRI I'd had the afternoon before.

Soon enough, a nurse and an anesthesiologist intern arrived to wheel me away through several sets of double doors, then into the operating room awash in revealing light, arrays of bulbs above and around me, the scope of everything shades of clinical white in my memory. There was chatting, me joking to hide how terrified I felt, then the flip of a switch, and a drop of fluid into my veins, whatever first blend of the cocktail of barbiturates and other sedatives that would take me and keep me under.

I know this only because I have been told: Happ cut a line in my eyelid, just below the second black X Aziz wrote on my forehead. The skin was stretched wide to reveal my skull, which I would later see in a startling iPhone image, presented to me in the ICU by an ophthalmology fellow. *I don't want to gross you out*, he would say, then show my drug-addled self images of a surprisingly dark skull, the bone stained for some reason, maybe because I took tetracycline for acne when I was a teenager, maybe for some other medical reason he didn't know but would suggest I have checked out.

The surgeons cut into that darkened skull with a bone drill, then opened a hatch with a saw, maybe a power one, maybe a wire Gigli. Now exposed, the dura around my brain could be pierced and gauze could be used to retract my brain and allow access into the eye socket, where Aziz began removing bone and tissue.

At some point, Aziz called Happ back, having found the tumor encased within the dura surrounding my optic nerve. The two agreed it was too risky for biopsy, let alone removal, so Aziz finished scooping out material to create a hollow space into which the tumor could later swell during radiation. The dura was stitched back together, the brain settled back into place, the hatch of my own skull refitted, secured with titanium screws and bone putty spackle, the skin released and the eyelid stitched.

Orderlies wheeled me to the ICU, where I remember only voices, and the pain of a young nurse grabbing my penis and withdrawing the catheter she told me hadn't been put in well, *sorry to do this to you*. She probably knew what I would learn, that pissing would feel like passing molten cottage cheese for several days, my whole body uneasy and looping from oxy painkillers and occasional bursts of fentanyl when the pain spiked, my body at risk of another, newer, sinister Appalachian affliction, addiction to instant release and disembodiment. I would hold off pissing as long as I could, because of the unmaskable pain I knew would arrive with the urine, then call a nurse to clutch my elbow while I held a canister over my dick and looked out uneasily at the Pittsburgh skyline in my window.

At night, I lay in bed, frequently in a generalized agony, pain without location beyond me. Doped on heavy opioids, I listened to strange recorded voices outside my window, snippets of movie clips, it seemed, sounds I imagine must have been intended to ward away roosting pigeons but felt like atmospheric grief and surreal disconnection. Sometimes I saw ghosts, apparitions of unrecognizable children and adults moving through my room. Some looked at me, some just walked past. I wondered about my grandmother, who learned of her own pending death in this very hospital. I remember the terror in her eyes, when I visited, when a doctor had her inhale drugs through a vapor tube. It was the first time I saw mortality, or rather the first time I saw someone recognize her own nearing end. After my surgery, I wondered whether the psychedelic sounds outside the hospital were her, or simple hallucinations, or radio signals from local stations, or growing madness. Even during daylight, shapes and figures, evil sinister things, closed in on me when I shut my eyes, rushing demons from every direction driving me to embarrassed tears, my parents sitting at the foot of my bed while Jen tried to console me.

Lying awake at night, I listened also to the apparitional roll of medical carts, moving nurses, moaning patients, footsteps that never seemed to bring me medicine. When I dozed, I dreamed of violence, murder, fear and pain, a haunting that persisted for months. And when I awoke in the darkened room, I listened to the ethereal noises outside my window, wished for an end to this suffering also.

N 41°51'12", W 81°0'8"

At the border between the counties of Ashtabula and Lake, at the line that moved Appalachia westward just a decade ago, I found two pieces of litter, one on each side of the border. A bottle of premixed Kahlua White Russian lay in Lake County, and a crushed can of Budweiser in Ashtabula, these two items separated by less than three feet, equidistant from the county line marker showing the first to be trash and the second to be Appalachian trash.

Other than these two items, the line that appears on the ARC as a clearly designated separator of region offers little difference. Nearby, weathered concrete pipe lay in the tall grass, perhaps flotsam from a large concrete plant a quarter mile farther west. To my right was a Lake County sewage treatment plant, and next to it the Arcola Creek wetlands, where effluent from the plant filters through the natural dynamic of water, sediment, and reeds into Lake Erie.

Cleveland is not that far away, at the western edge of Lake County, where the richness of suburban convenience makes the prosperous bedroom community of Madison. Here at the ARC line, however, there's a trailer park in Lake County that closely mirrors one on the other side of County Line Road, in Ashtabula County. Farther east, the city of Ashtabula has an attractively old downtown strip made up of a few upscale looking shops, coffee and chocolate and flowers, the sorts of rehabbed spots that are meant to draw tourists. There's a massive drawbridge, an industrial waterfront, a huge rail yard. Still, it's a tough town facing tough times, with a departed steel industry that had once fueled labor migration from West Virginia fifty years before Ashtabula would decline enough to actually join Appalachia. Just outside of the city, a lakeside coal-fired power plant was decommissioned in 2015, too expensive to retrofit in compliance with air-quality standards, a massive art-deco-industrial-brick monolith that appears as part decaying past and part nostalgic relic.

Closer to the ARC border, Geneva-On-the-Lake presents, at least on a cold March day, an eerie, abandoned amusement park vibe, it too a relic of a past hey-day, when motorists drove along the lake from Erie or Cleveland to frolic on the beaches and take in a boardwalk experience. Now, despite upgrades to a tourist and convention center, the main drag stretches for three blocks as a honky-tonk of garish seaside colors painted thick over particle board. There's a hybrid pawnshop and antique store. There's a tattoo shop with a sign announcing that customers under eighteen need to be accompanied by a parent. There's a Chronic Smoke Shop, for everyone's summer "tobacco" needs. There's a Goblin Custom cycle shop catering to the Harley drivers who rumble through each summer during Thunder on the Strip, one of many mini-Sturgis events small towns in the region put on. Erie has a Roar by the Shore. The town where I live, Thunder in the City. The town where my wife was born, Thunder in the Valley.

Back by the sewage treatment plant, straight up County Line Road, the newest, most northwesterly corner of Appalachia lies at the end of a crumbling asphalt ramp that dives into Lake Erie. Battered concrete riddles the shoreline, remnants of a breakwater or dock. A rusting metal pipe juts into the air, affixed to the shoreline in a massive gob of concrete. It could be an old fence post, or it might literally be a county line marker, certainly is now where the water of Lake Erie separates between Appalachia and the rest of Ohio, a recent designation that doesn't seem to mean much, even if it means everything.

N 40°49'20", W 80°6'16"

A week after surgery, maybe because I could now piss without calling a nurse in to hold me up, or maybe because I dropped the bottle one afternoon and poured the accumulated filth on the floor, or maybe because six nights of no sleep and missed meds and overflow trauma patients in the neuro-ward—drunk and disorderlies from the Pirates reaching Opening Day and the Penguins charging for the playoffs on the same weekend—or probably because the bed is expensive and I seemed to be getting better and the hospital is no place to recover, I was sent home.

The drainage tube was withdrawn from my skull, the other one from my back. Those tiny holes were then closed by a staple pressed into my head with a lever and another shot into my back by, more or less, an office stapler. The nurses wanted me to walk, to prove I was OK, so I dragged my still-connected IV tower down the hallway, stumbling dizzy while my wife walked beside me.

This was good enough, I got my papers, and Jen went for the car. A volunteer showed up with a wheelchair, which I slumped into, somehow the exertion of walking driving a headache the likes of which I had never known. I closed my eyes and felt the pain of motion, the bump into the elevator, the lurch over the threshold to sit beside the underground pickup lane breathing in car exhaust. My wife helped me into the passenger's side of our car, and we steered out of the city onto I-79, headed north.

I felt good, at first, giddy at my release. My head hurt. My back hurt. But I was out. Soon I began to feel the highway beneath me, every granule of the concrete amplified into a searing radiance of pain, unknown neural pathways lighting up with the basest animal instinct: do not move the injured. I felt knives. Barbed wire. Toothed attack.

I think, now, of my crushed childhood dog, caught beneath the wheels of my Bel Air one night, her aged arthritic joints seeking the warmth of the engine, then feeling the wheels roll over her when I hustled toward a weekend gathering. I fetched a sled from the barn, pushed her whimpering mass on board. I remember how much she trusted me, her caretaker and best love, who first ran her over then, no doubt, caused more pain tending to her, the catching whimper as I moved her, she who would linger for two days on that sled, the smell of gathered piss rising in her fur, the broken hips that meant, finally, I would dig her grave before—a father's mercy—being sent inside. My father retrieved his rifle and, himself broken in despair, ended it.

Eventually, I could bear it no longer. I opened eyes crushed together in pain, lifted my head from my huddle. Our city lay at mile marker 147, and the sign we passed had not yet reached one hundred. I retreated into myself again, my wife beginning to carry a guilt I can only imagine. Some days, even now, she breaks down in tears, apologizes for putting me in so much pain, knowing but not feeling that there was nothing to be done. I was at her mercy, but there was no way to offer mercy. Roads are roads, pain is pain.

At home, my wife took one arm, and my sister rushed outside to take the other, stumbling me forward. My boys were there, and my notes tell me I saw them, described them as flat-faced and concerned. I remember only the face of my visiting nine-year-old niece, a frozen confusion that, later, I would learn was a breaking heart. She was terrified of what had happened to me, could not bear to see someone unable to carry himself even the few steps from car to home. Maybe she saw in my eyes what I remember seeing in my grandmother's so many years before.

I would lie in the guest room of our house for several months, at first unable to shower without sitting on a stool, my wife angry when I would try to pee without telling her. The trip across the hall to the bathroom would leave me exhausted, heart aflutter and winded. I did not leave the house until the third week, when my seven-year-old walked outside with me. I leaned against a cane and stumbled beside him, all the way to the stop sign at the end of the block, two houses away, then returned to fall into an hour of exhausted sleep.

N 39°55'43", W 82°27'40"

Buckeye Lake itself is relatively unremarkable, one of countless flood control projects around the country that seek to mitigate the natural flow of water and preserve property that could otherwise be caught up in the natural cycles of flood. On the southern shore, there's a fairly ratty kind of lakeside resort community called Snug Harbor, just a few streets of shabby cottages and a few trailers alongside builder-grade renovations. Nearby earthen flood-control embankments, a small outcropping of McMansions has sprung up, peripheral to a planned enterprise called Snug Harbor Village, envisioned as condos and boathouses and cottages designed for "a lifestyle you didn't think was possible in Central Ohio." The website for the development advertises low property taxes, and half-hour proximity to Columbus, and Buckeye Lake, and a master plan that calls for an eclectic vision with "architectural standards [that] encompass coastal architecture from around the world."

Beyond that, Buckeye Lake also happens to contain the southwestern corner of Northern Appalachia, where the corner of Perry County lies submerged and invisible. As far as designating lines go, I acknowledge it as my own invention: by extending through Ohio the Mason-Dixon line that terminates along the southern border of Pennsylvania, you get more or less to the northern limit of Perry County. The ARC itself also happens to terminate at the northern limit of Perry County, Appalachia taking a little J here around the curve of Perry, Muskingum, Coshocton, and Holmes counties, then running roughly east-west above Tuscarawas and Carroll and Columbiana; the three counties along the state line—Mahoning, Trumbull, and Ashtabula—are the newcomers to Appalachia.

That means that the southern shore of Buckeye Lake, or at least the eastern half of it, lies within Appalachia, and the northern shore does not. It also means that driving through the lush, rolling hills of Licking and Knox counties means driving a stretch of Appalachian border country. I find that drive disorienting, though, because the landscape of the *not*-Appalachian Ohio counties is reminiscent of my birthplace in southwestern Pennsylvania, the glaciers having flattened the counties actually *in* Appalachia more than here. The Ohio of Northern Appalachia lies in what geologists call the end moraine, and not-Appalachia lies less affected by the ice.

Driving the non-Appalachian Killbuck Valley might as well be driving Appalachia, and is in fact driving through the same dissected plateau that makes my home. In the Killbuck, you see pumpjacks out in the fields pushing gas, and some of the hillsides carry the aspect of strip-mine recovery. There are handwritten signs that echo ones I've seen well within the ARC, like the one hastily scrawled on white wooden boards, on a gleaming April afternoon in 2017: "God, Guns, Coal, Trump." Not much farther up the road, a pickup truck roared out of a small rural gas station, a giant Confederate Battle Flag half the size of the vehicle flying out of the bed.

N 40°38'10", W 80°6'16"

Five weeks after surgery, I drove myself back down I-79, across the threshold of my own recent despair and pain. I had recovered enough to enter the cancer center, bite into a paper towel to form a quick impression of my teeth, have technicians select a properly-sized tray filled with a dark blue caulk, bite into that for a gagging, drooling five minutes, wait for the new mouthguard to set, then lay down on a table with the new device inserted between my teeth. I was well enough to allow the technicians to attach my new mouthguard to an arm attached to a giant machine, everything clipped tight by wrenching jarring levers that shot the force of connection through my teeth as a shockwave that reverberated in my skull. I was strong enough to be locked down by my teeth to a table, to wait while the techs stretched a warm piece of fiberglass over my eyes, it too locked tightly to the machine.

I allowed all of this in order to create the apparatus that would secure my body five days a week for six weeks, this new brank of mine and this new blind superhero mask dotted with target marks intended to make sure I couldn't move and that the radiation hit where it was supposed to. I was thus calibrated and triangulated, the borders of my tumor known through MRIs and translated corporeally by a series of numbers that, for each of thirty sessions, the technicians I got to know would shout out as they adjusted the pitch and aspect of the table on which I lay, setting the beam.

In the future that was then yet to come, I will drive each day, usually accompanied by one of many generous friends who will chat with me about various topics while we travel down I-79: Huck Finn; *Go Set a Watchman*; ECLA vs. Missouri Synod Lutheranism; Piatigorsky; the ecstatic resting of Yo Yo Ma; *Fallout 4* particularly Far Harbor, Maine; Farmington; hipster hairdos; first-gen college students; Super Nintendo; PEI Camping; coffee; house foundation repair; tenure processes; Pierre Bourdieu; literary theorists; bad teaching; baseball, particularly the Tigers and the Pirates; fathers; hitting a baseball; hitting a golf ball; the conservative politics of golf; public schooling; gifted programs; strip mall architecture; search committees; the future of English studies.

These conversations will stop at the edge of the waiting room, where my friends will seem always slightly uncomfortable, surrounded by people everyone knows are here for the same reason I am, to have a tumor irradiated. My friends will listen to conversations about prostates and the vague but unabashed penis-talk of suffering old men, and they will blanch upon walking into the cancer center and tell me they haven't set foot in one since their father died of brain cancer, and they will check Facebook and grade papers and be surprised at how fast my sessions are.

A Versa HD Proton Accelerator will hit me with radiation from seven angles, six around the latitude of my head, and one straight down through the top of my skull. Each location will develop a pimple, and each will develop a bald spot, but all in all a nurse will tell me, *I've never seen someone tolerate brain radiation so well.*

I will lay in the room among hanging racks of body pillows, each custom fit to a person, each representing a life in flux, each is someone's life, the array hanging as silent sentinel to treatment, brown raw fabric almost like burlap molded tight to a body. These objects create a strange clinical intimacy in this room, each seems like a cradle around a precise, unique form, a reminder that this is all so custom, each treatment carrying different coordinates on the machine, different dreams and fears and prognoses. Each is also a customized garment of restraint, an object intended to immobilize and force each of us to wait, still, maybe silent, and be treated.

My treatment: I'm blind, alone, clamped to the machine by face and teeth. I listen to the machine whir around me. I smell it when it radiates, heated plastic and ionized air. Radiation, of course, has no smell. But there is an odor when it fires, and I will count one through seven, missing only one of the two hundred and ten shots in my aggregate personal count. Each day, certain blasts will light up my optic nerve, a flash of white light, sometimes an intense blue in the middle of my vision.

I will listen to the Bee Gees sing "Stayin' Alive" during more than one of my sessions, a song in the official treatment room mix that strikes me as both hilarious and terrifying. I will realize that I have no evidence for the success of these treatments, beyond light and smell, each of which signifies nothing in particular. I am helpless in treatment, will wait only for side effects as a peculiar, welcome sign of effect. I will decide to trust the flashes of light in my eye, reversals of the blindness that led me to diagnosis, will consider all of this a kind of faith or, at least, trust.

Should I raise my voice in song, offer a canticle to ozone and protons and the company that built the machine, the technicians as acolytes, doctor as priest?

I will await the release of my mask and mouthguard, leap from the table and wish goodbye to my technicians. I will return to my waiting friend, perhaps have lunch together, then drive home. Again.

N 39°43'19", W 78°6'6"

In Pennsylvania, the ARC sweeps into the southern part of the state more or less in the center, at the border between Fulton and Franklin counties. This dividing line follows the sweeping arc of the ridges that make up the Allegheny Front, that notable, famous, beautiful sweep of geology visible from space and that separates western and eastern Pennsylvania from one another.

Finding this precise border isn't easy, though, as the terrain is quite steep, the roads properly indirect. Looking for the triangulation of Mason-Dixon, ARC, and Pennsylvania means inadvertently winding up, again and again, in Maryland, understanding this only because of a tiny line in the road pavement separating maintenance districts and, most reliably, which license plates are on the cars in the driveways.

I'd hoped to find a Mason-Dixon marker, one of the relic stones that lie within the woods along this border. I hoped, most of all, for a romantic and beautiful marker that would serendipitously appear as an Appalachian corner post. Instead, I wound up finding a box turtle on the road beside Dickey Mountain. The woods beside the road were peppered with No Trespassing signs, some orange, some yellow, all of them clear in their intent to keep people like me out. When I climbed out of my car to lift the turtle from the pavement to the roadside, the air smelled like lilac and mountain laurel, April spring in the mountains here, almost precisely a year since I'd been released from the hospital. All around me, mountains bloomed from the bottom, trees budding in neon green at the base while the tops still awaited the signal to turn from winter gray to life.

The mountains in this corner feel Appalachian. This is the edge of Pennsylvania's Ridge and Valley, tall parallel swaths of mountains separated by the fertile glaciated valleys of Amish country and Penn State. Towns generally lie in the valleys, long ridges forming tall horizons in two directions, long ones in the other two. Despite this beauty, I am not quite home. The flats remind me too much of Northwestern Pennsylvania, where there's nothing that pretends to be a mountain. Here in the southeastern corner of Appalachia, there's too much space between the mountains. Perhaps that's too fine a distinction, but it's what I carry within me.

All around, Trump signs lingered in yards, that administration nearly one hundred days old at the time, each of these signs left out intentionally, no doubt, as aggressive middle fingers. Still other signs warned against the economic disaster of factory hog farms, the farmers of the region concerned by this imposition of smell and threat to the traditional livelihood of small pig farmers who have been working the land for generations, and about defending against pig shit, and about losing control over these rural valleys. Maybe these are confluences of signs as Appalachian as I can imagine, a combo defense of local farming and the political apex of neoliberal big business amorality.

Eventually I found the corner I sought, just a rusted culvert and small stream separating Fulton County, PA, from Washington County, MD. On the Pennsylvania side, there's a junkyard or, really, someone's house with a yard full of old cars, an old bus, lots of metal. On one side, a Pennsylvania junkyard marked Northern Appalachia. On the other, an extraordinarily narrow road, still separated by a double yellow centerline, signaled Appalachia.

N 42°47'46", W 74°15'51"

How, then, do we triangulate ourselves? How do we find the coordinates of ourselves, our regions, our sense of who and what and where we come from? Margins are in flux, coordinates rendered easily in the form of degrees, seconds, minutes, these terms also carrying the weight of multiplicity and, in the end, agreed-upon measurements that signify nothing beyond what we make of them.

"Borders are set up to define the places that are safe and unsafe, to distinguish us from them. A border is a dividing line, a narrow strip along a steep edge," Gloria Anzaldua writes, in considering the fruitful cultural mixture, oft denied and misunderstood, of the border between the United States and Mexico.

I am moved to find the corners of Northern Appalachia, just as I am moved to contain my sense of recovery within the framework of moments. These desires are driven by falsity, clear enough on the ground of Northern Appalachia. There is no difference between here and there, no stability to the line itself, only surfaces that have been worn, shaped, and wrought by the scraping away of so many glacial elements, real and imagined. What does not change is the rock, the substrate. No, it changes too, as rock is a process also, the compressed dust of a galactic Big Bang, folded, cut, morphed, spewed, and laid.

To another edge, then, the northeastern-most portion of the ARC, riding Route 20 through the Finger Lakes along the top edge of the Southern Tier, this highway a rough divide between Appalachian and not. Here, the Finger Lakes are beautiful, offering a combination of once glorious towns and others still so: graceful Empire-style farmhouses, some in need of restoration, others having had it; tidy downtowns in Seneca Falls and Skaneateles; worn-out shells of houses and businesses in Otsego; more Confederate battle flags; a Wal-Mart distribution center; "Dump the Dump" signs in protest of a landfill project; and Trump signs in support of a vision of America as false as it is built on nostalgic hatred. Appalachia is always a great sacrificial zone, a constant merge of outside prosperity and internal despair.

Finally, at that edge, I pulled into Esperance, New York, drove uphill and parked at the Landis Arboretum, a 548-acre preserve at the border between Schoharie and Schenectady Counties. An improbably sweltering May afternoon had struck, the heat overstrong when I let the dog out of the car to take a whiz. Bees mobbed us, and she tried to catch them in her mouth: *sentinels from a new hive*, a volunteer explained. We gathered instructions from other volunteers assembled for spring planting and set off uphill to gain a view of the deep Schoharie Creek valley, the end of Appalachia but just the beginning of the mountains that stretch northward though New England.

Tracing geology lets me consider the constructions of borders between regions, sub-regions, nations, and concepts of identity, all of which roughen up the edges of what we think of when we say *Appalachia*. How far north can you go and still be in the region? How far east and west? How far inside myself am I still Appalachian?

Scott Russell Sanders encourages deep embeddedness: "We can lie to ourselves about many things; but if we lie about our relationship to the land, the land will suffer, and soon we and all other creatures that share the land will suffer."

We can lie, also, about our own coordinates, both in failing to see how our sense of who we are can be determined only in relation to things outside of ourselves and in failing to understand how the things we think of as stable are nothing more real than the margin of the ARC beneath Buckeye Lake, are no easier found than the invisible boundary between Maryland and Pennsylvania, are no more tangible than the demarcation between Rust Belt and Appalachia, are no more artificial than the line separating the United States from Canada. We are, perhaps, all erratics, tiny shards who wind up in both unexpected and inevitable places.

I think of this also, that a brain tumor is not external. It is a part of me, grew from me, is made up of the same substances as I am. Yet the outcome of having had a brain tumor—that difficult reckoning of how you move through life after finding one—is to feel a deep and profound separation of yourself from yourself.

"Like all people, we perceive the version of reality that our culture communicates," Anzaldua writes. "Like others having or living in more than one culture, we get multiple, often opposing messages. The coming together of two self-consistent but habitually incomparable frames of reference causes *un choque*, a cultural collision."

Healthy and not. Appalachian and Northern. Dead and alive. Asleep and awake. Dreaming and awake. App-uh-latch-un and App-uh-lay-shun. The recognition of particular places near other particular places, each alike and dissimilar, real and imagined. Flat and steep. Eroded and uplifted. The *choque* of considering a life defined by pre- and post-. Staying and going. Both, somehow.

"Only by understanding where I live can I learn how to live," Sanders writes.

At the Landis Arboretum, the dog and I stood on the deck of the meeting house and looked across the wide view, the river valley, the border, all of this really part of the Appalachians. Nearby, modern iron sculptures made from welded gears and bicycle parts dotted this landscape devoted to the reintroduction of native flora. From here, you can easily see how you might as well not divide such things, art and nature, regions, how you should just keep following the rocks. It's gorgeous, of course, a high view, rusty sculptures, and devotion to the restoration of native plants.

"A deep past intimate to thinking the future's advent, a perspectivism that at once speeds and slows time, geophilia names a reciprocal and intimate bond, signaling attractions, affiliations, and movements toward connection often recognized retroactively, a proliferation of relation most evident over long distance. Lithic intimacy runs slow and deep," writes Jeffrey Jerome Cohen, in devotion to literature, rocks, and the literariness of rocks.

Instead of redrawing the same old lines, thinking about how the ARC must always be a virulent circle around the worst of poverty, containing that horror within the mountains, we can start thinking about better, more useful, more accurate ways to start to delineate. No. Let me correct myself. We can't delineate, because lines are the root of the problem. Lines say here and there, yours and mine, one way and different. That's just it, the lines aren't really clear at all.

Yes, the corner counties of Appalachia appear to be in dire straits, are as poor as you can get. And, yes, there's the curious phenomena of Appalachian corners having neighbor counties that are suburban buffer zones between recovering cities and the imagined horrors of hillbilly hell. Cleveland, Columbus, Poughkeepsie, these cities seem like and, I would wager, see themselves as a world apart from Appalachia. The lines of the ARC, whether the cities know it or not, function as insulators, warding off the degradation, the stereotypes, the economic woes. *We're not Appalachia*, the cities can say, most of America can say. *And here's the map that proves it.*

Let's think about the ARC as a map of containment, as one of the many ways America looks away from its poverty, treating zones like Appalachia, inner cities, and the Mexican border the same way. Don't cross that line, don't pass that street, because then you're *there*.

"A border is a vague and undetermined place created by the emotional residue of an unnatural boundary. It is in a constant state of transition. The prohibited and forbidden are its inhabitants," Anzaldua writes.

Lines on maps are false when they create a sense of absolute and inevitable differentiation. At each corner of Appalachia, I made the effort of stepping across the county lines. In Appalachia, not in Appalachia. In, out, in out. Nothing was different. This is no great epiphany, something we all can easily understand. On paper Lake County ranks No. 7 among Ohio median household incomes ($55,000) and Ashtabula ranks No. 68 ($42,000). But there's hardly a difference when you cross the border. You can see the sewage treatment plant from both sides.

Border zones are contact zones, artificial measuring points along a continuum. Borders are drawn on a map with stark lines that offer division based on an unspoken but very real and full-force epistemology. Appalachian maps were drawn more than a hundred years ago, reinforced by the "reporting" of Kephart and Campbell, drawn again in exactly the same ink by J. D. Vance, that Appalachian insider who just wants to say, yup, Appalachia is what you thought it was.

The Landis Arboretum offers a different map though, just as tangible on paper, but built on a philosophy with implications I prefer. Take a hike, away from the easiest spots, all the way to the northeastern edge of the preserve, and you're in an old-growth oak forest, trees spared the fate of timber, which have grown in a way we might fully recognize as natural. Ancient trees are a different kind of marker, a better way to think about the map. I hesitate to call this a reclamation, and instead I'll use the term *recognition*.

Walking through old-growth oaks offers a reminder of what has been here, what *really* has been here, what persisted and grew and is literally rooted in the ground. A tree cannot do anything other than relate directly to its geology and is affected by the pH of soil, annual rainfall, and the presence of topsoil and the components of rock. So too are we, even if we draw maps that pretend otherwise. And I think it wise that we walk among such trees, to remind ourselves of what this landscape is and was and can be. Remember the borders of the Seneca warriors, who knew they were home when they recognized the trees.

There's no reclamation. I return to that because reclamation is as philosophically problematic as cartography. Someone has to decide what to reclaim to, and the risk is that grading a mountain to make way for development could be, indeed, a reclamation, a claim renewed, the surrounding principles of exploitative culture carving rocks as it sees value. That's reclamation at heart, the building of pixelated mountains, or fresh flats ready for shopping malls.

Real recovery is a more fundamental recognition, longer to establish and commit to, harder to do, and it requires that you decide what you really *are* at core. In Appalachia, the nation has decided that the core is extractive industry, that the relationship to geology—to our actual substrate—is one of profit and removal. That's a bad relationship, one always fraught and ready to collapse. That's a relationship defined only by its very end. There can be no reclamation when you destroy your substance. Thus I discard that core, recognizing instead that the not-mountains of Appalachia are my bedrock, that erosion is just another way to shape stone into sculpture. My geology matters, makes me who I am, and I commit myself to reconciling with a relationship delivered to me already broken. The rocks forgive. The rocks remain. My way of looking at them and at myself may be unsettled but is at the very least ready.

So for me, this is the most beautiful corner of official Northern Appalachia, this Landis Arboretum in the Southern Tier of New York. It offers hope, conceptual orientation toward recovery of the self. Here, I have to admit that nothing is pure. Just one ridge over, there's a big divot in the hillside, a flat cut space filled with a junkyard. That's an evocation of the regrettably consistent Appalachian conflict, the junking of land and cars, the orientation toward decay. So I turn willfully toward the old growth, toward a desire to think about what these mountains are and to restore, preserve, and renew.

The dog and I hiked back to the car, where I filled a pan with water. She drank at length, then hopped into the shotgun seat. The sun churned out its heat, and we settled back into the air conditioning and hit the road again. We left the ARC, but we followed the mountains relentlessly, first through the Catskills to the Taconic Mountains, then up through New England across the bottom of the White Mountains, within spitting distance of Maine's Cadillac Mountain, eventually across the border into coastal New Brunswick, along the massive tides and rift valley of the Bay of Fundy, heading toward new and beloved coordinates, forever among the Appalachians: N 46°32'30", W 63°47'35".

Bibliography

Abbey, Edward. *Desert Solitaire*. Ballantine, 1968.

———. *Fool's Progress*. Holt, 1988.

———. *Jonathan Troy*. Dodd, Mead & Company, 1954.

Anzaldua, Gloria. *Borderlands/La Frontera*. Aunt Lute Books, 1987.

Appalachia Then and Now: Examining Changes to the Appalachian Region since 1965. Executive Summary. Center for Regional Economic Competitiveness and West Virginia University, for the Appalachian Regional Commission. 2015.

Appalachia Then and Now: Examining Changes to the Appalachian Region since 1965. State Meetings Report. Center for Regional Economic Competitiveness and West Virginia University, for the Appalachian Regional Commission. 2015.

Batteau, Allen. *The Invention of Appalachia*. U Arizona Press, 1990.

Berry, Wendell. "The Making of a Marginal Farm." *Recollected Essays, 1965–1980*. North Point Press, 1981: 329–40.

Birkerts, Sven. *The Gutenberg Elegies*. Faber & Faber, 1994.

Brewer, William. *I Know Your Kind*. Milkweed Editions, 2017.

Bryson, Bill. *A Walk in the Woods*. Random House, 1997.

Buckland, Adeline. *Novel Science: Fiction and the Invention of Nineteenth-Century Geology*. U Chicago Press, 2013.

Cahalan, James. *Edward Abbey: A Life*. U Arizona Press, 2001.

Campbell, John C. *The Southern Highlander and His Homeland*. Russell Sage Foundation, 1921.

Caudill, Harry M. *Night Came to the Cumberlands*. Little, Brown, 1962.

Chung, Catherine. *Forgotten Country*. Riverhead, 2012.

Cohen, Jeffrey Jerome. *Stone: An Ecology of the Inhuman*. U Minnesota Press, 2015.

Dann, Kevin T. *Traces on the Appalachians: A Natural History of Serpentine in Eastern North America*. Rutgers U Press, 1988.

Danson, Edwin. *Drawing the Line: How Mason and Dixon Surveyed the Most Famous Border in America*. Wiley, 2001.

Dillard, Annie. *Pilgrim at Tinker Creek*. Harper, 1974.

Gould, Stephen Jay. *Time's Arrow, Time's Cycle: Myth and Metaphor in the Discovery of Geological Time*. Harvard U Press, 1987.

Haigh, Jennifer. *Baker Towers*. William Morrow, 2005.

———. *Heat and Light*. Ecco, 2016.

The History of Cartography: Cartography in Prehistoric, Ancient, and Medieval Europe and the Mediterranean, Vol. 2, Book 1. Eds. Dave Woodward and G. Malcolm Lewis. U Chicago Press, 1998.

Huber, Sonya. *Pain Woman Takes Your Keys: Essays from a Nervous System*. U Nebraska Press, 2017.

Isserman, Andrew M. "Appalachia Then and Now: Update of 'The Realities of Deprivation' Reported to the President in 1964." *Journal of Appalachian Studies*, 3.1 (Spring 1997): 43–69.

Kephart, Horace. *Our Southern Highlanders*. MacMillan, 1913.

Lane, John. *Circling Home*. U Georgia Press, 2007.

Lenfestey, James P. *Seeking the Cave: A Pilgrimage to Cold Mountain*. Milkweed Editions, 2014.

Leopold, Aldo. *A Sand County Almanac*. Oxford U Press, 1949.

Malinowski, Bronisław. *Magic, Science, and Religion and Other Essays*. Free Press, 1948.

Marshall, Ian. *Border Crossings: Walking the Haiku Path on the International Appalachian Trail*. Hiraeth Press, 2012.

McCrumb, Sharyn. " 'Appalachia': A Guide to Pronunciation." *YouTube*, uploaded by Ross Sauce, April 28, 2010, www.youtube.com/watch?v=eGCqWrsAZ_o.

Michener, James. *Chesapeake*. Random House, 1978.

O'Dell, Tawni. *Back Roads*. Viking, 2000.

O'Neill, Brian. "Yes, We and Yinz Are Part of Appalachia." *Pittsburgh Post-Gazette*, December 8, 2011.

Paul, L. A. *Transformative Experience*. Oxford U Press, 2014.

Porter, Eliot, and Edward Abbey. *Appalachian Wilderness: The Great Smoky Mountains*. Dutton, 1970.

Prentiss, Sean. *Finding Abbey: The Search for Edward Abbey and His Hidden Desert Grave*. U New Mexico Press, 2015.

Raitz, Karl B., and Richard Ulack. *Appalachia: A Regional Geography*. Westview Press, 1984.

Ray, Janisse. *Ecology of a Cracker Childhood*. Milkweed Editions, 1999.

Sanders, Scott Russell. "The Singular First Person." *Earth Works: Selected Essays*. Indiana U Press, 2012: 1–11.

———. *Staying Put*. Beacon Press, 2003.

Sebald, W. G. *The Rings of Saturn*. The Harvill Press, 1998.

Stewart, George R. *U.S. 40: Cross Section of the United States of America*. Houghton-Mifflin, 1953.

Strayed, Cheryl. *Wild*. Knopf, 2012.

Thornbury, William D. *Regional Geomorphology of the United States*. John Wiley & Sons, 1965.

Trumbull, Robert. "Sun Shines and River Flows, But Senecas Must Leave Land." *The New York Times*, March 1, 1964.

United States, Congress. *Appalachia: A Report by the President's Appalachian Regional Commission*, 1964.

United States, Congress. *Surface Mining Control and Reclamation Act*, 1977.

United States Code Title 40 Subtitle IV—Appalachian Regional Development.

Vance, J. D. *Hillbilly Elegy.* HarperCollins, 2016.
Weidensaul, Scott. *Mountains of the Heart: A Natural History of the Appalachians.* Fulcrum, 1994.
Weller, Jack E. *Yesterday's People: Life in Contemporary Appalachia.* U Kentucky Press, 1965.

www.ingramcontent.com/pod-product-compliance
Lightning Source LLC
Chambersburg PA
CBHW031423150426
43191CB00006B/369